Instructed Second Language Acquisition of Arabic

Instructed Second Language Acquisition of Arabic examines the acquisition of agreement asymmetries in the grammatical system of Arabic as a second/foreign language through the lens of instructed second language acquisition. The book explores how to improve the processes of L2 learning of Arabic using evidence-based classroom research. Before it does this, it characterizes the variable challenges that English L2 learners of Arabic face when they acquire four structural cases in Arabic grammar that entail agreement asymmetries. Using the pretest–posttest design, it examines the effects of four classroom interventions using quantitative and qualitative measures. In these interventions, form-based and meaning-based measures were used to reveal to what degree learners have developed explicit and implicit knowledge of these aspects of asymmetry. In the concluding chapter, the book provides focused and specific implications based on the results of the four studies. It provides theoretical implications that enrich the discussions of instructed second language Acquisition in Arabic and other languages more broadly. It also provides implications for teachers, curriculum designers, and textbook writers of Arabic.

This book will be informative for Arabic applied linguists, researchers of Arabic SLA, Arabic instructors (at the K–12 and the college level), and Arabic program directors and coordinators. The book will also appeal to all SLA and ISLA researchers.

Mahmoud Azaz is Associate Professor of Arabic Language, Linguistics and Pedagogy and Second Language Acquisition and Teaching, and Distinguished Fellow at the University of Arizona. He is the Director of Graduate Studies at the School of Middle Eastern and North African Studies and the chair of the instructional dimension in the PhD program in Second Language Acquisition and Teaching.

Instructed Second Language Acquisition of Arabic

Contextualized Input, Output, and Conversational Form-Focused Instruction of Agreement Asymmetries

Mahmoud Azaz

Routledge
Taylor & Francis Group
LONDON AND NEW YORK

Designed cover image: Gert-Jan van Vliet via Getty Images

First published 2024
by Routledge
4 Park Square, Milton Park, Abingdon, Oxon OX14 4RN

and by Routledge
605 Third Avenue, New York, NY 10158

Routledge is an imprint of the Taylor & Francis Group, an informa business

British Library Cataloguing-in-Publication Data
A catalogue record for this book is available from the British Library

ISBN: 978-0-367-51887-5 (hbk)
ISBN: 978-0-367-51885-1 (pbk)
ISBN: 978-1-003-05560-0 (ebk)

DOI: 10.4324/9781003055600

Typeset in Times New Roman
by Apex CoVantage, LLC

Contents

Acknowledgments *vi*
List of Abbreviations *vii*
Transliteration Symbols *viii*
About the Author *x*

Introduction: What Is This Book About? 1

1 Agreement Symmetries and Asymmetries in Standard Arabic 7

2 The Academic Discipline of Instructed Second Language Acquisition 30

3 Instructed Second Language Acquisition of Noun–Adjective Agreement Asymmetry: Input-Based Exposure and Output-Based Present-Produce-Practice 54

4 Instructed Second Language Acquisition of Referential Agreement Asymmetries: Incidental Focus on Form and Planned Focus on Form 75

5 Instructed Second Language Acquisition of Subject–Verb Agreement Asymmetries: Structured Input-Based and Structured Output-Based Activities 95

6 Instructed Second Language Acquisition of Numeral Agreement Asymmetries: Enriched Input-Based and Enhanced Input-Based Instruction 112

7 Theoretical and Pedagogical Implications 131

References *143*
Appendix 1 *156*
Appendix 2 *170*
Index *171*

Acknowledgments

This research would not have been possible without the support of the research participants, instructors, and colleagues at the University of Arizona. Also, I am very grateful to Dr. Ayman Mohamed at Michigan State University for sharing his insights as an expert in SLA about the book. I am also grateful to Andrea Hartill and Iola Ashby at Routledge for their insightful comments and guidance. All remaining errors are mine. The genesis for this book started in 2015 with a Faculty Seed Research Grant from the Office for Research, Discovery and Innovation (RII) at the University of Arizona. Generously, the RII funded the project with another Faculty Seed Research Grant in 2020 that was pivotal to the completion of the project. I am very grateful to this tremendous support for research that advances the scholarship of Arabic SLA and pedagogy. Also, I am grateful to my wife and children. This book would not have been possible without their tremendous support and enthusiasm. I appreciate their tremendous patience during the five years it took to plan for and complete. This book is dedicated to the memory of my father who understood and appreciated the value of higher education.

Abbreviations

1	first person
2	second person
3	third person
nom	nominative
acc	accusative
gen	genitive
s	singular
d	dual
p	plural
m	first person
f	second person
perf	perfective
imperf	imperfective
L1	first language
L2	second language
def	definite
indef	indefinite
Sub	subject
V	verb
O	object
VSO	verb–subject–object
SVO	subject–verb–object
MSA	Modern Standard Arabic
PT	processability theory
SI	structured input
SO	structured output
MOI	meaningful output instruction
EI	explicit information/instruction
FoFs	focus on forms
FoF	focus on form

Transliteration Symbols

The transcription of all Arabic texts in the body of the book follows mostly the system of the *Middle Eastern Studies* journal by Cambridge University Press. Two changes have been made based on standard usage in Arabic and *Middle Eastern Studies* journals. The symbol "ʔ" represents the hamza (glottal stop) and "ʕ" represents the ‘ayn (voiced pharyngeal fricative consonant). Also, following standard practice, the definite article {*ʔal-*} is fully stated (without assimilating any part) in all of the Arabic examples. For the long vowels (*ā, ū, ī*), the vowel was typed twice for reader convenience (*aa, uu, ii*). In case of gemination, the consonants were represented twice to show doubling. This is a list with all the symbols used.

Consonants

Arabic consonant	*English symbol*	*Arabic consonant*	*English symbol*
ب	b	ط	ṭ
ت	t	ظ	ẓ
ث	th	ع	ʕ
ج	j	غ	gh
ح	ḥ	ف	f
خ	kh	ق	q
د	d	ك	k
ذ	dh	ل	l
ر	r	م	m
ز	z	ن	n
س	s	ه	h
ش	sh	و	w
ص	ṣ	ء	ʔ
ض	ḍ		

Vowels

Arabic vowel	*English symbol*
◌َ	a
◌ُ	u
◌ِ	i
ا	aa
و	uu
ي	ii

About the Author

Mahmoud Azaz is Associate Professor of Arabic Language, Linguistics and Pedagogy, and Second Language Acquisition and Teaching, and Distinguished Fellow at the University of Arizona (UA). He is the director of graduate studies at the School of Middle Eastern and North African Studies and the chair of the instructional dimension in the PhD program in second language acquisition and teaching. He holds a PhD with distinction in Arabic SLA and pedagogy from the UA's SLAT program. His research focuses on Arabic SLA from linguistic and sociocultural perspectives, and his work has appeared in multiple journals in SLA and applied linguistics. He edited the 34th volume of *Perspectives on Arabic Linguistics* (John Benjamins Publishing) and co-authored a textbook on Egyptian Arabic that is scheduled to appear in 2023 (Georgetown University Press). Also, he is currently co-editing a special issue on multilingual perspectives in L2 Arabic (*Journal of Critical Multilingual Studies*) and co-authoring a textbook on Arabic SLA. His recent work focuses on the development of socio-pragmatic competence, translingual and multidialectal practices, and linguistic complexity in L2 Arabic.

December 31, 2022
Mahmoud Azaz
University of Arizona

Introduction

What Is This Book About?

Arabic is exceptionally challenging to learn and teach. The Foreign Service Institute (FSI) at the School of Language Studies at the U.S. Department of State has officially classified Arabic as Category V (highest level) in terms of difficulty for English natives (Foreign Service Institute, 2018). This is in part due to its complex grammatical system that is very different from English and other European languages. Agreement asymmetries or irregularities between two linguistic units or more in terms of linguistic features (particularly gender and number) in this system represent some of its puzzling aspects that have driven some to include Arabic among these languages with "rogue" or "wild" grammar (Lardiere, 2008). These asymmetries have been the focus of extensive theoretical linguistic analysis for decades (Alqassas, 2017; Aoun et al., 2010; Bahloul & Harbert, 1993; Benmamoun, 2000; Belnap & Shabaneh, 1992; Fassi Fehri, 1993; Ferguson, 1989; Mohammad, 1990, 2000; Soltan, 2007).

However, agreement asymmetries have not been explored in Arabic second language (L2) acquisition and pedagogical research, despite increasing interest in Arabic as a critical language. Basic exploratory research on these asymmetries does not exist in Arabic second language acquisition (SLA) books (Alhawary, 2009, 2019; Husseinali, 2016) or edited volumes (Alhawary, 2018) or Arabic linguistics (Azaz, 2023). Instead, these books tend to focus on common agreement facts. Additionally, the framework used in books with an SLA focus cannot be characterized as instructed SLA (ISLA). For example, they do not examine the differential effects of certain instructional interventions, but rather test the adequacy of certain theoretical hypotheses in SLA, particularly the processability theory (Pienemann, 1998), full-transfer (Schwartz & Sprouse, 1994, 1996; White, 2003, 2009), and feature-(re)assembly (Lardiere, 2008) accounts. With this status quo, research on the acquisition of Arabic morphosyntactic (ir)regularities is still parsimonious and sporadic, with very few systematic longitudinal and cross-sectional studies having been completed (Alhawary, 2019; Azaz, 2016, 2019). Thus, a data-driven understanding of how Arabic morphosyntax is acquired and how it should be taught is not well established yet in current research. This unfortunate state presents major challenges for applied linguists and instructors of Arabic.

This book examines the acquisition of agreement asymmetries in the grammatical system of Arabic as a second/foreign language through the lens of ISLA. This subfield of SLA generally explores how to improve the processes of L2

DOI: 10.4324/9781003055600-1

learning using evidence-based classroom research. It has held a narrower definition as a "field of academic inquiry that aims to understand how the systematic manipulation of the mechanisms of learning or the conditions under which they occur enable or facilitate the development and acquisition of an additional language" (Loewen, 2015, p. 2). With its wide appeal in SLA research, ISLA is often conceptualized in terms of the conditions that affect the development of implicit and explicit knowledge of target linguistic features in some macro-options. These include input-based or output-based options, implicit or explicit options, meaning-focused or form-focused options, along with corrective-feedback options (R. Ellis et al., 2009, p. 237). This field has theoretical implications that support or refute certain hypotheses or positions in language-learning theories based on the results of classroom investigations. It also has direct implications that guide instructional and material selection and design in second/foreign-language programs.

The initial assumption in this book is that not all aspects of Arabic grammar are equally difficult or complex. Symmetrical and asymmetrical patterns of agreement face learners of comparable proficiency with challenges that vary according to the structural case at hand. More importantly, certain cases of asymmetry may vary in difficulty or complexity. This is in part due to the inherent characteristics in each case. For example, certain asymmetries are more salient than others (see chapter on referential asymmetries). Therefore, some morphosyntactic phenomena that entail agreement asymmetries need to be taught with *careful* planning. Another assumption in this book is that instruction with good design matters in the development of implicit and explicit knowledge of these complex aspects, but this instruction does not necessarily yield identical results in each case of asymmetry. Different pedagogical techniques engage learners differently and yield variable empirical findings based on the cognitive engagement they entail. A last assumption is that although there are *dominant* patterns of linguistic performance that are noticeable as a result of careful design and intervention, sometimes there is learner performance variability and differences that run against the dominant patterns.

Aims and Questions This Book Addresses

Guided by these needs and assumptions and remaining within the boundaries and scope of ISLA, this book achieves three main goals:

- First, it characterizes the variable challenges that English L2 learners of Arabic face when they acquire four structural cases in Arabic grammar that entail agreement asymmetries.
- Second, using the pretest–posttest design, it examines the effects of four classroom interventions that address these four common cases of agreement asymmetries. In-depth accounts of two contrasting instructional techniques are provided in each, and findings using quantitative and qualitative measures are

presented. In these interventions, form-based (forced choice, grammaticality judgment, and metalinguistic tests) and meaning-based measures (written sentence completion and oral narrative tests) were used to reveal to what degree learners have developed explicit and implicit knowledge of these aspects of asymmetry. The latter measures faced the learners with tasks that were appropriate to their proficiency levels (novice or intermediate) and challenged them to produce the target agreement asymmetries. With these features, this underlying design allows for testing the development of explicit and implicit knowledge as a result of the techniques utilized.

- Last, in the concluding chapter the book provides focused and specific implications based on the results of the four studies. It provides theoretical implications that enrich the discussions of ISLA in Arabic and other languages more broadly. It also provides implications for teachers, curriculum designers, and textbook writers of Arabic.

With these assumptions and goals, this book offers answers to these specific six questions:

- What are the acquisition trajectories of four common cases of agreement asymmetries in the grammatical system of Arabic?
- Can certain cases of agreement asymmetries that vary in salience (being prominent or easily noticed) be acquired incidentally in Arabic?
- What are the differential gains of input enrichment or flooding in incidental exposure and pushed output in the present–practice–produce technique in the development of explicit and implicit knowledge of noun–adjective agreement asymmetries?
- What are the differential gains of incidental and planned focus on form in the development of explicit and implicit knowledge of two cases of referential asymmetries that vary in perceptual salience: demonstratives and clitics?
- What are the differential gains of structured input-based and output-based instruction in the development of implicit and explicit knowledge of subject–verb agreement asymmetries?
- What are the differential gains of incidental instruction via input enrichment and explicit instruction via input enhancement in the development of explicit and implicit knowledge of numeric asymmetries?

In providing answers to these questions, the book presents data collected from two Arabic programs in large public institutions in the United States. The project was supported with two seed grants from the Office for Research Innovation and Impact at the University of Arizona. This greatly helped with participants' pay and course buyouts for the author. The book analyzes data collected from a total of 207 students at the novice and intermediate levels of proficiency over ten semesters (2017–2022). The participants' first language was exclusively English to minimize the effect of previous language backgrounds and to uniformly control for feature instantiation in their first language. The book presents the performance patterns that emerge in the learner interlanguage, and best explains these patterns in relation to the complexity entailed in each case of asymmetry. Also, the pretest data of the four studies, when put together, answer important questions about the hierarchy of difficulty and order of acquisition of asymmetries in Arabic. Although part of the data reported in this book have been presented at national conferences that focus on Middle East Studies, applied linguistics, and Arabic linguistics, the results of the four studies have not been published before.

Target Instructional Techniques and Agreement Asymmetries

Types of instruction tested in this book along with the paired cases of asymmetry are listed here:

Asymmetrical case	*Instructional techniques*
Noun–adjective agreement asymmetries	Input flooding/enrichment (Leow, 2001; Reinders & R. Ellis, 2009) Present–practice–produce (Nassaji & Fotos, 2011)
Referential agreement asymmetries (demonstratives and clitics)	Incidental/implicit focus on form (R. Ellis, 2001) Planned/explicit focus on form (Long, 1991, 2000; R. Ellis et al., 2002)
Subject–verb agreement asymmetries	Structured input (VanPatten, 2004) Strucuted output (Swain, 1995, 2005)
Numeric-noun agreement asymmetries	Input enrichment (Leow, 2001; Reinders & R. Ellis, 2009) Input enhancement (Leow, 2001; Reinders & R. Ellis, 2009)

The Structure of This Book

This book is organized as follows:

Chapter 1 overviews symmetrical and asymmetrical agreement patterns in Arabic grammar and the articulation of linguistic features (number, gender, person, case, and definiteness) in them. Major works on Arabic grammar that analyze these symmetries and asymmetries are reviewed and summarized in descriptive terms (e.g., Benmamoun, 2000; Aoun et al., 2010; Mohammad, 1990, 2000; Soltan, 2007).

Chapter 2 overviews the field of ISLA as a subfield of SLA. It describes its aims and scope. Given the focus of the book, this chapter overviews recent research in ISLA of grammar and morphosyntax in particular. It reviews and discusses previous research that has examined the effectiveness of certain types of instruction including input-based, output-based, incidental focus on form, and planned focus on form in relevant second/foreign-language contexts. Also, it overviews extant research in Arabic I/SLA. The chapter concludes with the overall gaps that the book addresses.

Chapter 3 presents the design and results of a classroom intervention that examined the differential gains of input enrichment or flooding (Leow, 2001; Reinders & R. Ellis, 2009) and the present–practice–produce technique (Nassaji & Fotos, 2011) in the acquisition of noun–adjective agreement asymmetries. Using a pretest–posttest design, the chapter presents the effects of each type of instruction in the development of explicit and implicit knowledge of the target asymmetries. It discusses the results in terms of the debates on incidental and intentional learning in the acquisition of grammar.

Chapter 4 presents the design and results of a classroom intervention that explored the differential gains of incidental focus on form (R. Ellis, 2001; Loewen, 2005) and planned focus on form (Long, 1991, 2000; R. Ellis et al., 2002) in the development of explicit and implicit knowledge of two cases of referential asymmetries that vary in salience: demonstratives (of high salience) and clitics (of low salience). Using a pretest–posttest design, the chapter presents the effects of each type of instruction and discusses how the inherent characteristics of each case affect the gains in these interventions.

Chapter 5 presents the design and results of an intervention that compared the differential gains of structured input activities following the tenets of processing instruction (VanPatten, 2004) and output-based activities following the tenets of the output hypothesis (Swain, 1995, 2005) in the acquisition of subject–verb agreement asymmetry. Using a pretest–posttest design, the chapter presents the effects of each intervention on the interpretation and production of the target asymmetries. It discusses the results in terms of the roles of these two activity types in restructuring learner interlanguage.

Chapter 6 presents the design and results of a classroom intervention that compares the effects of implicit instruction via input enrichment (Leow, 2001; Reinders & Ellis, 2009) and explicit instruction via input enhancement (Leow, 2001; Reinders & R. Ellis, 2009) in the development of explicit and implicit knowledge of numeric asymmetries. Using a pretest–posttest design, the chapter presents the effects of each input type. The discussion section couches the results within a broader discussion of the role of input types in L2 development of grammar.

Chapter 7 presents the theoretical and pedagogical implications of the four studies. The theoretical part presents implications to ISLA as a subfield of SLA. Special focus is given to the positions taken on the role of these manipulated learning conditions in developing explicit and implicit knowledge of grammar. The pedagogical section translates the findings into the Arabic classroom. It makes recommendations that guide the teachers, textbook writers, and material designers when they teach and present the target agreement asymmetries.

With this scope, the book has important implications for how agreement asymmetries should be taught and presented in current textbooks of Arabic as a foreign/

second language. Importantly, work in ISLA has guided teachers to understand the nature and effect of certain pedagogical approaches and techniques in SLA processes. This book, accordingly, is directed to teachers of Arabic as a foreign/second language. Sample testing materials and tasks developed for the book (provided in the appendices) are good sources for teachers when they teach these asymmetries. Also, learners will find them useful sources in independent study and self-learning.

1 Agreement Symmetries and Asymmetries in Standard Arabic

Introduction

Agreement is a prominent morphosyntactic phenomenon in many languages of the world. It is defined in the established literature (Corbett, 2006; Preminger, 2019) as the covariation between the formal features of one grammatical element (agreement target) and the formal or semantic features of another (agreement controller). For example, in the sentence in (1) in Standard Arabic, the form of the imperfective *ya-mshii* "3.m-walk" is conditioned by features of the subject, *ʔal-walad-(u)* "the boy," which is singular masculine. This can be seen by substituting "the boy" with an element whose inherent features are different, as in (2). In this example, the alteration to *ʔal-bint-(u)* "the girl" results in a change in the form of the verb from *ya-mshii* to *ta-mshii* (or alternatively, a change of the inflection that marks gender from {*ya-*} to {*ta-*}):

(1)	*ʔal-walad-(u)*[1]	*ya-mshii*	*ʔila*	*ʔal-jaamiʕa.*
	the-boy.s.m-(nom)	3.s.m-walk.imperf	to	the university.
	The boy walks every morning to the university.			
(2)	*ʔal-bint-(u)*	*ta-mshii*	*ʔila*	*ʔal-jaamiʕa.*
	the-girl.s.f-(nom)	3.s.f-walk.imperf	to	the university.
	The girl walks every morning.			

This demonstration of how the subject agrees with the verb elucidates how agreement works in the linguistic system of Standard Arabic. As it is commonly known, as a heavily inflected language, linguistic elements in Arabic (at phrasal, clausal, and sentential levels) show agreement (or disagreement) in some form. To understand the underpinnings of this agreement system, the formal features of number, gender, case, and definiteness are introduced first.

DOI: 10.4324/9781003055600-2

Formal Features in Standard Arabic

Number

Grammatical number has various manifestations in terms of form or function. It is often stated in descriptive literature that Arabic nouns fall into three categories in terms of nominal number (Wright, 1964; Hassan, 1981): singular (if they refer to one countable entity), dual (if they refer to two), and plural (if they refer to three or more). This ternary classification is exemplified by the following patterns in (3):

(3) a. *mudarris-(u)-(n)*
teacher.s.m-(nom)-(indef)
a (male) teacher
b. *mudarris-aa-n*
teacher.s.m-d.nom-indef
two (male) teachers
c. *mudarris-uu-n*
teacher.s.m-p.nom-indef
(some male) teachers

But observe that only the dual is systematically "sound," in the sense that it is formed from the singular by the concatenative vowel lengthening [aa]. A singular noun can be dualized by adding a suffix {-*aan*} for nominative case or {-*iin*} for accusative and genitive cases (as determined by its position in word order) to the singular noun. The plural noun provided in (3) is sound, and there are plural nouns that are rather "broken," as illustrated in (4) and (5):

(4) a. *ṭaalib-(u)-(n)*
student.s.m.-(nom)-(indef)
a (male) student
b. *ṭullaab-(u)-(n)*
student.p.m-(nom)-(indef)
(some male) students

(5) a. *kaatib-(u)-(n)*
writer.s.m-(nom)-(indef)
a writer
b. *kuttaab-(u)-(n)*
writers.p.m-(nom)-(indef)
(some) writers

The sound–broken terminology is standard in Arabic linguistics studies, compared to the more technical concatenative/non-concatenative distinction. "Broken" means that the vocalic pattern of the singular is lost (or not carried over) in a derivation of a plural, although the latter form can be related to the former through a morphological process of a more abstract sort (McCarthy, 1981; McCarthy & Prince, 1990).[2] For example, the plural *ṭullaab* "male students" in (4b), being broken, does not preserve the vowels of the singular *ṭaalib* "a male student" in (4a), whereas the dual in (3b), being sound, does.

With this sound–broken distinction, pluralization in Arabic is accomplished by applying two morphological procedures. The first is linear suffixation: adding a suffix to the end of a singular noun (as in (3)). The second is the nonlinear superimposition of templatic consonant–vowel patterns onto the singular-noun roots (as in (4) and (5)). It is more common and productive in Arabic in general, yet very complex. It involves making changes in the form of the singular noun through morpho-phonological processes such as vowel insertion, consonant gemination, and the affixation (prefixation and infixation) of consonants besides those of the root (Holes, 2004; Ryding, 2005). Selecting between these two processes in Arabic is determined *in part* by the morphological pattern of its singular form coupled with its inherent features such as humanness (human or nonhuman) and gender (masculine or feminine). For example, the sound plural is rendered by applying the suffixes {*uu-n*} (for nominative case) or {*ii-n*} (accusative and genitive cases) with singular masculine human nouns, as in (5).

Gender

The second linguistic feature of importance to understand the underpinnings of agreement is gender. Standard Arabic (also Arabic dialects) distinguishes two genders: masculine and feminine. Three important things determine the gender of singular nouns: the first is form. Certain singular masculine nouns become feminine by suffixing {*-a*}, as in (6), in which *ṭaalib* is "a male student" and *ṭaalib-a* is "a female student":

(6) a. *ṭaalib-(u)-(n)*
student.s.m-(nom)-(indef)
a (male) student
b. *ṭaalib-a{t}-(u)-(n)*
student.m.f.-(nom)-(indef)
a female student

The second factor is sex or biological gender. For example, in (7) the word *walad-(u)-(n)* "a boy" is masculine and the word *bint-(u)-(n)* "girl" is feminine regardless of the word form. The same applies to (8).

(7) a. *walad-(u)-(n)*
boy.s.m-(nom)-(indef)
a boy
b. *bint-(u)-(n)*
girl.s.f-(nom)-(indef)
a girl

(8) a. *ʔukht-(u)-(n)*
sister.s.f-(nom)-(indef)
a sister

b. *ʔakh-(u)-(n)*
brother.s.m-(nom)-(indef)
a brother

Typically, feminine nouns are marked with {*-a*} if they are singular and with {*-aat*} if plural, as in (9):

(9) a. *ṭaalib-a{t}-(u)-(n)*
student-s.f-(nom)-(indef)
a female student
b. *ṭaalib-aat-(u)-(n)*
student-p.f-(nom)-(indef)
female students

For the rest of the common nouns that are nonhuman, gender continues to be largely determined by form; feminine nouns are marked with {*-a*} if they are singular and with {*-aat*} if they are plural, as in (10):

(10) a. *jamiʕ-a{t}-(u)-(n)*
university-s.f-(nom)-(indef)
a university
b. *jamiʕ-aat-(u)-(n)*
university-.p.f-(nom)-(indef)
(some) universities

The third factor that determines the gender of nouns is convention. As it is known, some nouns are lexicalized as feminine although they do not end in {*-a*}. For example, the word *ḥarb* "war" in (11) is feminine in Arabic, although it lacks the feminine marker {*-a*}.

(11) *ḥarb-(u)-(n)*
war.s.f-(nom)-(indef)
a war

This explanation of the factors that determine gender means that its assignment is not entirely arbitrary. It is also rule-based. Arabic gender assignment is a mixed system involving semantic and formal gender-assignment properties (see Alhawary, 2011; Holes, 2004; Ryding, 2005, for an overview of Arabic nouns). It can be described as a morpho-semantic system in which, for example, certain nouns would receive a gender value with clear semantic reasons (i.e., sex). However, Arabic nouns can also receive a gender value without a clear semantic reason but for a formal reason. Here, the rule would be: nouns ending in {*-a*}; coda would commonly be feminine while nouns ending in {–ϕ} would be masculine.[3]

Gender in Demonstratives and Clitics

So far, gender in Standard Arabic has been shown to surface in nouns. Standard Arabic is also known for gender distinctions or articulations in other ways. One common way is the distribution of pronominals (pronouns) in which pronouns vary from masculine to feminine, as illustrated in Table 1.1:

Table 1.1 Distribution of Pronominals in Standard Arabic

Person	*Singular*		*Dual*		*Plural*	
	Masculine	*Feminine*	*Masculine*	*Feminine*	*Masculine*	*Feminine*
First person	*ʔana* I	*ʔana* I	*naḥnu* we	*naḥnu* we	*naḥnu* we	*naḥnu* we
Second person	*ʔanta* you	*ʔantii* you	*ʔantuma* you	*ʔantuma* you	*ʔantum* you	*ʔantum* you
Third person	*huwa* he	*hiya* she	*huma* they	*hunna* they	*hum* they	*hunna* they

As shown in this table, Arabic distinguishes between masculine and feminine in second person (singular) and in third person (singular, dual, and plural).

Another way in which Standard Arabic distinguishes between masculine and feminine is in demonstratives: a different demonstrative is used for masculine and feminine singular, dual, and plural human nouns. This is illustrated in Table 1.2:

Table 1.2 Gender Distinction in Demonstratives

	Masculine		*Feminine*	
Singular	*haadha* this this boy	*ʔal-walad* def-boy	*haadhihi* this this girl	*ʔal-bint* def-girl
Dual	*haadhaan* these these two boys	*ʔal-waladaa-n* def-boy-dual	*haatayyin* these these two girls	*ʔal-bintayyin* def-girl-dual
Plural	*haaʔulaaʔ-u* these these boys	*ʔal-ʔulaad-u* def-boys-nom	*haaʔulaaʔ-u* these these girls	*ʔal-banaat-i* def-girls-nom

Gender is also known in Arabic to occur on verbs, nouns, prepositions, and other particles such as complementizers in the form of clitics. In verbs, subject clitics can be prefixal only or both prefixal and suffixal according to the subject pronoun and whether the tense is perfective or imperfective. Object clitics are exclusively suffixal, that is, on the right of the verb stem, which is exactly the canonical position of the object. This is demonstrated in Table 1.3.

Table 1.3 Gender Distinction in Object Clitics in Perfective and Imperfective

Perfective

Person	*Singular*	*Dual*	*Plural*
1	*shakara-nii* he thanked-me	*shakara-naa* he thanked-us	*shakara-naa* he thanked-us
2m	*shakara-k(a)* he thanked-you	*shakara-kumaa* he thanked-you	*shakara-kum* he thanked-you
2f	*shakara-k(ii)* he thanked-you	*shakara-kumaa* he thanked-you	*shakara-kunna* he thanked-you
3m	*shakara-hu* he thanked-him	*shakara-humaa* he thanked-them	*shakara-hum* he thanked-them
3f	*shakara-haa* he thanked-her	*shakara-humaa* he thanked-them	*shakara-hunaa* he thanked-them

Imperfective

Person	*Singular*	*Dual*	*Plural*
1	*ya-shkurun-ii* he thanks-me	*ya-shkuru-naa* he thanks-us	*ya-shkuru-naa* he thanks-us
2m	*ya-shkuru-k(a)* he thanks-you	*ya-shkuru-kumaa* he thanks-you	*ya-shkuru-kum* he thanks-you
2f	*ya-shkuru-k(ii)* he thanks- you	*ya-shkuru-kumaa* he thanks-you	*ya-shkuru-kunna* he thanks-you
3m	*ya-shkuru-hu* he thanks-him	*ya-shkuru-humaa* he thanks-them	*ya-shkuru-hum* he thanks-them
3f	*ya-shkuru-haa* he thanks-her	*ya-shkuru-humaa* he thanks-them	*ya-shkuru-hunaa* he thanks-them

Also, gender occurs on genitive/possessive clitics and oblique/prepositional clitics, as in Tables 1.4 and 1.5:

Table 1.4 Gender Distinction in Genitive/Possessive Clitics

Person	*Singular*	*Dual*	*Plural*
1	*kitaab-ii* book-my	*kitaabu-naa* book-our	*kitaabu-naa* book-our
2m	*kitaabu-k(a)* book-your	*kitaabu-kumaa* book-your	*kitaabu-kum* book-your
2f	*kitaabu-k(ii)* book-your	*kitaabu-kumaa* book-your	*kitaabu-kunna* book-your
3m	*kitaabu-hu* book-his	*kitaabu-humaa* book-their	*kitaabu-kum* book-their
3f	*kitaabu-haa* book-her	*kitaabu-humaa* book-their	*kitaabu-hunaa* book-their

Table 1.5 Gender Distinction in Oblique/Prepositional Clitics

Person	*Singular*	*Dual*	*Plural*
1	*maʕ-ii* with-me	*maʕa-naa* with-us	*maʕa-naa* with-us
2m	*maʕa-k(a)* with-you	*maʕa-kumaa* with-you	*maʕa-kum* with-you
2f	*maʕa-k(ii)* with-you	*maʕa-humaa* with-you	*maʕa-kunna* with-you
3m	*maʕa-hu* with-you	*maʕa-humaa* with-them	*maʕa-hum* with-them
3f	*maʕa-haa* with-you	*maʕa-humaa* with-them	*maʕa-hunaa* with-them

Definiteness

Another linguistic feature in Arabic that is of significance is definiteness. Nouns and adjectives are inflected for these two features. In Standard Arabic (and the dialects), the definite article {-ʔal} is a proclitic. In the written modality, it is attached to the nouns it defines. In the oral modality, the second sound {*-l*} of the definite article is absorbed as a result of assimilation in certain phonological contexts. It is highly controversial whether Arabic has an indefinite article. Several studies have arguably claimed that nunation {*-n*} that is suffixed to nouns in Standard Arabic and certain Arabic dialects (such as Haili Arabic) acts as a marker of indefiniteness (e.g., Fassi Fehri, 1993, 2004; Jarrah & Zibin, 2016). Consider (12) for examples of the definite and indefinite articles in Arabic:

(12) a. *jaamiʕ-a{t}-(u)-(n)*
university-s.f-(nom)-(indef)
a university

b. *ʔal-jaamiʕ-a{t}-(u)*
def-university-s.f-(nom)
the university

Case

As the previous examples illustrate, Arabic nouns (definite or indefinite) are inflected for one of three cases: nominative *ʔal-rafʕ*, in the subject position; accusative *ʔal-naṣb*, in object position; and genitive *ʔal-jarr*, after a preposition and time and place adverbials. Table 1.6 provides example articulations of case marking in definite and indefinite forms:

Table 1.6 Gender Distinction in Case-Marking in Singulars and Duals

Nominative

	Definite	*Indefinite*
s.m.	*ʔal-ṭaalib-(u)* def-student.s.m-(nom) the (male) student	*ṭaalib-(u)-(n)* student.s.m-(nom)-(indef) a (male) student
s.f.	*ʔal-ṭaalib-a{t}-u* def-student-s.f-(nom) the (female) student	*ṭaalib-a{t}-u-n* student-s.m-(nom)-(indef) a (female) student
d.m.	*ʔal-ṭaalib-aan-(i)* def-student-d.m-(nom) two (male) students	*ṭaalib-aan-(i)* student-d.m-(nom) two (male) students
d.f.	*ʔal-ṭaalib-at-aan-(i)* def-student-f-d-(nom) the two (female) students	*ṭaalib-a{t}-aan-(i)* student-f-d-(nom) two (female) students
p.m.	*ʔal-ṭulaab-(u)* def-students.p.m-(nom) the (male) students	*ṭulaab-(u)-(n)* students.p.m-(nom)-(indef) some (male) students
p.f.	*ʔal-ṭaalib-aat-(u)* def-student-p.f-(nom) the (female) students	*ṭaalib-aat-(u)-(n)* student-p.m-(nom)-(indef) some (female) students

Accusative

	Definite	*Indefinite*
s.m.	*ʔal-ṭaalib-(a)* def-student.s.m-(acc) the (male) student	*ṭaalib-a-n* student.s.m.-acc-indef a (male) student
s.f.	*ʔal-ṭaalib-a{t}-(a)* def-student-s.f-(acc) the (female) student	*ṭaalib-a-ta-n* student-.s.m.-acc-indef a (female) student
d.m.	*ʔal-ṭaalib-ayyn-(i)* def-student-d.m.-(acc) two (male) students	*ṭaalib-ayyn-i* student-d.m.-acc two (male) students
d.f.	*ʔal-ṭaalib-at-ayyn-(i)* def-student-f-d-acc the two (female) students	*ṭaalib-at-ayyn-i* student-f-d-acc two (female) students
p.m.	*ʔal-ṭulaab-(a)* def-students.p.m-(acc) the (male) students	*ṭulaab-a-n* students.m.p.-acc-indef some (male) students
p.f.	*ʔal-ṭaalib-aat-(i)* def-student-p.f-(acc) the (female) students	*ṭaalib-aat-i-n* student-f.p.-acc-indef some (female) students

Genitive

	Definite	*Indefinite*
s.m.	*ʔal-ṭaalib-(i)* def-student.s.m-(gen) the (male) student	*ṭaalib-(i)-(n)* student.s.m-(gen)-(indef) a (male) student

Genitive		
	Definite	*Indefinite*
s.f.	*ʔal-ṭaalib-a{t}-(i)* def-student-s.f-(gen) the(female) student	*ṭaalib-a{t}-(i)-(n)* student-m.f-(gen)-(indef) a (female) student
d.m.	*ʔal-ṭaalib-ayyn-(i)* def-student-d.m-(gen) two (male) students	*ṭaalib-ayyn-(i)* student-d.m-(gen) two (male) students
d.f.	*ʔal-ṭaalib-at-ayyn-(i)* def-student-d.f-(gen) the two (female) students	*ṭaalib-a{t}-ayyn-(i)* student-f.d-gen-(indef) two (female) students
p.m.	*ʔal-ṭulaab-(i)* def-students.p.m-(gen) the (male) students	*ṭulaab-(i)-(n)* students.p.m-(gen)-(indef) some (male) students
p.f.	*ʔal-ṭaalib-aat-(i)* def-student-p.f-(gen) the (female) students	*ṭaalib-aat-(i)-(n)* student-f.p-(gen)-(indef) some (female) students

As illustrated in these tables, indefinite singulars (human and nonhuman) are marked for case with a short vowel combined with nunation {*-n*} ({*-un*} in the nominative, {*-an*} in the accusative, and {*-in*} in the genitive). Indefinite duals (human and nonhuman) are marked for case with a short vowel combined with nunation {*-n*} ({*-an*} in the nominative and {*-in*} for accusative and genitive cases). Definite singulars (human and nonhuman) are inflected for case with a short vowel only ({*-u*} in the nominative, {*-a*} in the accusative, and {*-i*} in the genitive). Definite duals (human and nonhuman) are marked for case with a short vowel combined with nunation {*-n*} ({*-an*} in the nominative and {*-in*} for accusative and genitive cases).

In plural nouns, case marking is more complex since it is determined by the category of the noun as illustrated in Table 1.7:

Table 1.7 Gender Distinction with Case-Marking in Plural Nouns

Nominative		
Masculine	*Definite*	*Indefinite*
Human sound	*ʔal-muhandis-uun-(a)* def-engineer-p.m-nom the (male) engineers	*muhandis-uun-(a)* engineer-m.p.-nom-indef some (male) engineers
Human broken	*ʔal-ṭulaab-(u)* def-students.p.m-(nom) the (male) students	*ṭulaab-(u)-(n)* students.p.m-(nom)-(indef) some (male) students
Nonhuman sound	Not attested	Not attested
Nonhuman broken	*ʔal-kutub-(u)* def-books-p.m-(nom) the books"	*kutub-(u)-(n)* books-p.m-(nom)-(indef) some books

(Continued)

Table 1.7 (Continued)

Feminine	*Definite*	*Indefinite*
Human sound	*ʔal-ṭaalib-aat-(u)* def-student-p.f-(nom) the (female) students	*ṭaalib-aat-(u)-(n)* student-p.f-(nom)-(indef) some (female) students
Nonhuman sound	*ʔal-jaamiʕ-aat-u* def-university-p.f-(nom) the universities	*jaamiʕ-aat-(u)-(n)* university-p.f-(nom)-(indef) (some) universities
Human broken	Not attested	Not attested
Nonhuman broken	*ʔal-mudun-(u)* def-cities.pf.-(nom) the cities	*mudun-(u)-(n)* cities.p.f-(nom)-(indef) (some) cities

For example, masculine human and nonhuman broken plurals (definite and indefinite) take the same case marks of singular nouns. That is, for indefinite configurations, they are marked for case with a short vowel combined with nunation {*-n*} ({*-un*} in the nominative, {*-an*} in the accusative, and {*-in*} in the genitive). For definite forms, they are inflected for case with a short vowel only ({*-u*} in the nominative, {*-a*} in the accusative, and {*-i*} in the genitive). Masculine human sound plurals (definite and indefinite) behave differently; they are marked with {*-uuna*} for the nominative case and with {*-iina*} for the accusative and genitive cases. For feminine plurals, feminine human broken plurals are not attested in Standard Arabic. Feminine nonhuman broken plurals (definite and indefinite) take the same case marks of their singular counterparts. Feminine human sound plurals behave differently. For indefinite forms, they are marked for case with a short vowel combined with nunation {*-n*} ({*-un*} in the nominative, {*-an*} in the accusative, and {*-in*} in the genitive). For the definite forms, definite feminine human sound plurals are inflected for case with a short vowel only ({*-u*} in the nominative, {*-a*} in the accusative, and {*-i*} in the genitive).

Symmetrical and Asymmetrical Agreement Patterns

The linguistic system of Standard Arabic shows symmetrical and asymmetrical agreement patterns between these linguistic features in a good number of structural phenomena at the phrasal and clausal levels. For convenience of presentation, this section offers these patterns in the context of the phenomena under consideration in this book.

Noun–Adjective Agreement

Symmetrical Pattern

It is uniformly agreed that, in Arabic, attributive and predicative adjectives agree fully with the head noun in terms of the four features: gender, number, case, and definiteness. This is exemplified in (13) and (14) for human and nonhuman singular nouns, respectively:

(13)	a.	*muhandis-(u)-(n)* engineer.s.m-(nom)-(indef) an Egyptian male teacher	*miṣṣriyy-u-n* Egyptian.s.m-(nom)-(indef)
	b.	*muhandis-a{t}-u-n* engineer.s.f-(nom)-(indef) an Egyptian female teacher	*miṣṣriyy-a{t}-(u)-(n)* Egyptian.s.f-(nom)-(indef)
(14)	a.	*kitaab-(u)-(n)* book.s.m-(nom)-(indef) a new book	*jadiid-(u)-(n)* new.m.s.-(nom)-(indef)
	b.	*qiṣaa{t}-(u)-(n)* story.m.f-(nom)-(indef) a new story	*jadiid-a{t}-(u)-(n)* new-s.f-(nom)-(indef)

This example shows the working definition of agreement as a process in which one element (controller) controls another (target). In (13a) and (13b), an indefinite singular masculine noun with the nominative case takes an indefinite singular masculine with the nominative case. In a similar vein, an indefinite singular feminine noun takes a singular feminine adjective, with the same case. This also applies to duals as in (15) and (16):

(15)	a.	muhandis-aan-(i) engineer-d.m-(nom) two Egyptian male engineers	miṣṣriyy-aan-(i) Egyptian-.d.m-(nom)
	b.	muhandisa-taan-(i) engineer-d.f-(nom) two Egyptian female engineers	miṣṣriyya-taan-(i) engineer-d.f-(nom)
(16)	a.	*kitab-aan-(i)* book-d.m-(nom) two new books	*jadiid-aan-(i)* new-d.m-(nom)
	b.	*qiṣat-aan-(i)* story-d.f-(nom) two new stories	*jadiida-taan-(i)* new-d.f-(nom)

Asymmetrical Pattern

Although the previous explanations show multiple cases of symmetries, a common phenomenon in Standard Arabic is when the *controller* is nonhuman plural and the *target* is singular feminine. That is, plural nonhuman nouns (masculine and feminine) are treated as singular feminine nouns (see Belnap & Shabaneh, 1992).

This phenomenon is traditionally referred to as feminine singular agreement with nonhuman plurals. In the context of noun–adjective agreement, adjectives show masculine and feminine grammatical gender distinction when agreeing with singular, nonhuman head nouns as in (17). However, adjective agreement with plural nonhuman head nouns shows no corresponding differentiation; the same type of adjective agreement occurs with all nonhuman plurals, regardless of the gender of the corresponding singular of the head noun as illustrated in (18).

(17)	a.	kitaab-(u)-(n) *book.s.m-(nom)-(indef)* a new book	jadiid-(u)-(n) *new.s.m-(nom)-(indef)*
	b.	qiṣṣat-u-n *story.s.f-(nom)-(indef)* a new story	jadiida{t}-(u)-(n) *new.s.f-(nom)-(indef)*
(18)	a.	kutub-(u)-(n) *book.p.m-(nom)-(indef)* new books	jadiida{t}-(u)-(n) *new.s.f-(nom)-(indef)*
	b.	*qiṣaṣ-(u)-(n)* story.p.f-(nom)-(indef) new stories	*jadiida{t}-(u)-(n)* new.s.f-(nom)-(indef)

In (18a), the head noun is nonhuman *plural* feminine (books), but the adjective is *singular* feminine. The same rule applies to (18b) in which the feminine plural noun takes a singular feminine adjective. This shows disagreement between the noun and the adjective in terms of number *and* gender in (18a) and number *only* in (18b). So, it seems that what determines whether the agreement pattern is symmetrical or asymmetrical in plural nouns is the semantic feature of nonhuman. This pattern of agreement has been referred to as "deflected," as opposed to "strict," agreement (Ferguson, 1989). Strict agreement here means plural form targets occurring with plural controllers. However, grammatical gender of target and controller are not the same in the case of feminine plurals, and hence they are "deflected."

Referential Agreement

What determines whether the noun–pronoun agreement pattern is symmetrical or asymmetrical is whether the plural noun is human or nonhuman. This pertains to different types of pronouns. The focus here is on demonstratives, pronominals, and clitics.

Symmetrical Pattern

For human nouns (singular, dual, and plural), there is symmetrical agreement between the head nouns and the demonstratives. This is demonstrated in Table 1.8:

Table 1.8 Gender Distinction in Demonstratives with Human Nouns

	Masculine		*Feminine*	
Singular	*haadha* this this boy	*ʔal-walad* def-boy	*haadhihi* this this girl	*ʔal-bint* def-girl
Dual	*haadhaan* these these two boys	*ʔal-walad-aan* def-boy-dual	*haatayyin* these these two girls	*ʔal-bint-ayyin* def-girl-dual
Plural	*haaʔulaaʔ* these these boys	*ʔal-ʔulaad* def-boys	*haaʔulaaʔ* these these girls	*ʔal-banaat* def-girls

Asymmetrical Pattern

The rule that nonhuman plural head nouns are treated as singular feminine nouns manifests itself also in demonstrative-noun asymmetrical pattern of agreement. That is, a nonhuman plural takes a singular feminine demonstrative as illustrated in the last part of Table 1.9:

Table 1.9 Gender Distinction in Demonstratives with Nonhumans

	Masculine		*Feminine*	
Singular	*haadha* this this book	*ʔal-kitaab* def-book	*haadhihi* this this story	*ʔal-qiṣṣaa* def-story
Dual	*haadha-aan* these these two books	*ʔal-kitaab-aan* def-book-dual	*haataan* these these two stories	*ʔal-qiṣṣa-taan* def-story-dual
Plural	*haadhihi* these these books	*ʔal-kutuub* def-books	*haadhihi* these these stories	*ʔal-qiṣṣaṣ* def-stories

As shown in the last part of the table, there is disagreement between the demonstrative (*haadhihi*) and the nonhuman masculine plural noun (*ʔal-kutuub*) in terms of both number (a plural took a singular demonstrative) and gender (a masculine noun took a feminine demonstrative).

Also, the underlying rule in Arabic that plural nonhuman nouns are treated as singular feminine nouns manifests itself also in pronominals and object clitics, as illustrated earlier. When referring to a third-person nonhuman plural (masculine or feminine), a third-person feminine pronominal (*hiya*) is used:

Table 1.10 Distribution of Pronominals in Standard Arabic

Person	*Plural*	
	Masculine	*Feminine*
3rd	*hiya* she	*hiya* she

(19) *hiya* *jaamiʕ-aat-u-n* *mumtaaz-at-u-n.*
they universities-p.f-nom-indef excellent-f.s.-nom-indef
They are excellent universities.

In (19), there is disagreement between the anaphoric singular pronoun (*hiya*, she) and the plural antecedent (*jaamiʕ-aat-(u)-(n)*, universities). The same rule manifests in object clitics in perfective and imperfective contexts as illustrated in Table 1.11 and in (20):

Table 1.11 Gender Distinction in Object Clitics in the Perfective and Imperfective

Person	*Perfective*	*Imperfective*
	Plural	
3m	*qaraʔa-haa* he reads-them	*ya-qaraʔu-haa* he reads-them
3f	*kataba-haa* he wrote-them	*ya-ktubu-haa* he wrote-them

(20) *Ahmad ʕindahu qiṣaṣ jadiid-a. hwa qaraʔa-haa kathiiran ʔams.*
Ahmad has stories new. he read-them a lot yesterday.
Ahmad has new stories. He read them a lot yesterday.

In (20), there is disagreement between the anaphoric object pronoun (*haa*, her) and its plural nonhuman antecedent (*qissas*, stories). The same disagreement pattern extends to oblique/prepositional clitics as illustrated in Table 1.12 and in (21):

Table 1.12 Gender Distinction in Oblique/ Prepositional Clitics

Person	*Plural*
3m	fii-haa in-them
3f	fii-haa in-them

(21) *jaamiʕ-aat busṭun mumtaaza. ʔuriid-u ʔan ʔadrus fii-haa.*
universities-p.f. Boston excellent.s.f I want to study in-her (p.f.)
The Universities of Boston are excellent. I want to study in them.

In (21), there is disagreement between the anaphoric oblique ({*-haa*}, third-person feminine singular) attached to the pronoun, and its plural nonhuman feminine antecedent (*jaamiʕ-aat*, universities).

Subject–Verb Agreement

Standard Arabic has a rich subject–verb agreement paradigm. Arabic verbs are inflected for tense (perfective/past or imperfective/present) and mood (indicative, subjunctive, jussive, and imperative). They generally agree with their subjects (whether nouns or pronouns) in terms of number, gender, and person (Ryding, 2005; Alhawary, 2011). In the perfective verb, the subject agreement is realized as a suffix to the verb. This is illustrated in Table 1.13 from Aoun et al. (2010):

Table 1.13 Agreement System of Standard Arabic (Perfective)

Person	*Number*	*Gender*	*Affix*	*Verb + affix*
1	Singular	F/M	*-tu*	*daras-t-(u)*
2	S	M	*-ta*	*daras-t-(a)*
2	S	F	*-ti*	*daras-t-(i)*
3	S	M	*-a*	*daras-(a)*
3	S	F	*-at*	*daras-at*
2	Dual	M/F	*-tumaa*	*daras-tumaa*
3	D	M	*-aa*	*daras-aa*
3	D	F	*-ataa*	*daras-ataa*
1	Plural	M/F	*-naa*	*daras-naa*
2	P	M	*-tum*	*daras-tum*
2	P	F	*-tunna*	*daras-tunna*
3	P	M	*-uu*	*daras-uu*
3	P	F	*-na*	*daras-na*

In the imperfective, by contrast, the realization of agreement is radically different. It is realized by both prefixes and suffixes, as illustrated in Table 1.14:

Table 1.14 Agreement System of Standard Arabic (Imperfective)

Person	*Number*	*Gender*	*Affix*	*Verb + affix*
1	Singular	F/M	*ʔa-*	*ʔa-drus(u)*
2	S	M	*ta-*	*ta-drus(u)*
2	S	F	*ta—iin(a)*	*ta-drus-iin(a)*
3	S	M	*ya-*	*ya-drus(u)*
3	S	F	*ta-*	*ta-drus(u)*
2	Dual	M/F	*ta—aan(i)*	*ta-drus-aan(i)*
3	D	M	*ya—aan(i)*	*ya-drus-aan(i)*
3	D	F	*ta—aa*	*ta-drus-aan(i)*
1	Plural	M/F	*na-*	*na-drus(a)*

(Continued)

Table 1.14 (Continued)

Person	*Number*	*Gender*	*Affix*	*Verb + affix*
2	P	M	*ta—uun(a)*	*ta-drus-uun(a)*
2	P	F	*ta—na*	*ta-drus-n(a)*
3	P	M	*ya—uun(a)*	*ya-drus-uun(a)*
3	P	F	*ya—na*	*ta-drus-n(a)*

This agreement paradigm is attested in the two main types of Arabic sentence: the nominal sentence (*ʔal-jumla ʔal-ʔismiyya,* literally "nominal sentence") and the verbal sentence (*ʔal-jumla ʔal-fiʕliyya,* literally "verbal sentence") (for an overview see Alhawary, 2011; Ryding, 2005). As the name suggests, a nominal sentence starts with the subject (S) that could be a noun or a pronoun, and it may or may not contain a verb (V) (for an extensive discussion of the subtypes of the nominal sentence, see Alhawary (2011, pp. 90–102)). When a nominal sentence contains a verb and the subject is a lexical noun, the subject surfaces first, followed by the verb to form the SV word order.

A verbal sentence, on the other hand, must start with a verb. When the subject is a noun, it could surface after the verb to form the VS word order. The choice between these two-word orders (in addition to other word orders that are permissible in Arabic) is determined by certain pragmatic and discourse conditions. Descriptive linguistic studies showed that the VS word order is the most common, basic, and unmarked (i.e., frequent) word order (Soltan, 2007, p. 34; Holes, 2004; Ryding, 2005, p. 65).

Symmetrical Pattern

In subject-initial sentences, the subject and the verb in the SV word order exhibit a rich symmetrical pattern of agreement in terms of person (first, second, or third), number (singular, dual, or plural), and gender (masculine or feminine). This is illustrated in the examples (22)–(26):

(22) *ʔal-ṭaalib-(u)* *yu-ḥibb-(u)* *ʔal-ʔustaadh-(a)* *kathirann.*
def-student.s.m-(nom) 3.s.m-like.imperf-indic def-teacher.s.m-(acc) a lot.
The (male) student likes the (male) teacher a lot.

(23) *ʔal-ṭaalibat-(u)* *tu-ḥibb-(u)* *al-ʔustaadha{t}-(a)* *kathirann.*
def-student.sf-(nom) 3.s.f-like.imperf-(indic) def-teacher.s.f-(acc) a lot.
The (female) student likes the (female) teacher a lot.

(24) *ʔal-jaamiʕa{t}-(u)* *fataḥ-at* *ʔabwaabaha* *ʔams.*
def-university.s.f-(nom) open-perfect-3.s.f doors yesterday.
The university opened its door yesterday.

(25) *ʔal-ṭulaab-(u)* *yu-ḥibb-uu-na* *ʔal-ʔustaadh-(a)* *kathirann.*
def-student.p.m-(nom) 3.p.m-like.imperf-indic def-teacher.s.m-(acc) a lot.
The (male) students like the (male) teacher a lot.

(26)	*ʔal-ṭaalibaat-(u)*	*yu-ḥibb-na*	*al-ʔustaadha{t}-(a)*	*kathirann.*
	def-student.p.f-(nom)	3.p.f-like.imperf-indic	def-teacher.s.f-(acc)	a lot.

The (female) students like the (female) teacher a lot.

These examples all show a symmetrical pattern of agreement: a singular masculine subject takes a singular masculine verb and a singular feminine subject takes a singular feminine verb. In the same vein, a plural masculine noun takes a plural masculine verb, and a plural feminine noun takes a plural feminine verb.

This symmetrical pattern of agreement is still maintained in VS word orders when the subject is a singular lexical noun, human or nonhuman. It continues to show a symmetrical pattern of agreement with the verb; they agree in person (first, second, or third), number (singular, dual, or plural), and gender (masculine or feminine). Consider (27) and (29):

(27)	*yu-ḥibb-(u)*	*ʔal-ṭaalib-(u)*	*ʔal-ʔustaadh-(a)*	*kathirann.*
	3.s.m-like.imperf-indic	def-student.s.m-(nom)	def-teacher.s.m-(acc)	a lot.

The (male) student likes the (male) teacher a lot.

(28)	*tu-ḥibb-(u)*	*ʔal-ṭaalibat-(u)*	*al-ʔustaadha{t}-(a)*	*kathirann.*
	3.s.f-like.imperf-(indic)	def-student.sf-(nom)	def-teacher.s.f-(acc)	a lot.

The (female) student likes the (female) teacher a lot.

(29)	*fataḥ-at*	*ʔal-jaamiʕa{t}-(u)*	*ʔabwaabaha*	*ʔams.*
	open-perfect-3.s.f	def-university.s.f-(nom)	doors	yesterday.

The university opened its door yesterday.

Asymmetrical Pattern

The asymmetrical pattern in subject–verb agreement manifests in both types of sentences. The underlying rule in Arabic that plural nonhuman nouns are treated as singular feminine nouns manifests itself in subject–verb agreement in both types of sentences. That is, if the subject is nonhuman plural lexical noun, the verb remains in the singular feminine, regardless of the word order, whether subject-first as in (30) or verb-first as in (31):

(30)	*ʔal-jaamiʕaat-(u)*	*fataḥ-at*	*ʔabwaabaha*	*ʔams.*
	def-university.p.f-(nom)	open-perfect-3.s.f	doors	yesterday.

The university opened their doors yesterday.

(31)	*fataḥ-at*	*ʔal-jaamiʕaat-(u)*	*ʔabwaabaha*	*ʔams.*
	open-perfect-3.s.f	def-university.p.f-(nom)	doors	yesterday.

The universities opened their doors yesterday.

In the verb-initial sentence, when the subject is a dual or plural lexical noun, it shows an asymmetrical pattern of agreement with the verb; they agree in person (first, second, or third), gender (masculine or feminine), but they disagree in number. That is, a dual or plural subject will take a singular verb. This asymmetrical pattern of agreement is illustrated in (33) for a plural masculine subject, and in (36) for a plural feminine subject. Maintaining the symmetrical pattern of agreement renders the structure ungrammatical as illustrated in the examples:

(32)	*ʔal-ṭulaab-(u)*	*yu-ḥibb-uu-na*	*ʔal-ʔustaadh-(a)*	*kathirann.*
	def-student.p.m-(nom)	3.p.m-like. imperf-indic	def-teacher.s.m-(acc)	a lot.
	The (male) students like the (male) teacher a lot.			
(33)	*yu-ḥibb-(u)*	*ʔal-ṭulaab-(u)*	*al-ʔustaadha{t}-(a)*	*kathirann.*
	3.s.m-like. imperf-indic	def-student.p.m-(nom)	def-teacher.s.f-(acc)	a lot.
	The (male) students like the (female) teacher a lot.			
(34)	**yu-ḥibb-uu-na*	*ʔal-ṭulaab-(u)*	*al-ʔustaadha{t}-(a)*	*kathirann.*
	3.p.m-like. imperf-indic	def-student.p.m-(nom)	def-teacher.s.f-(acc)	a lot.
	The (male) students like the (female) teacher a lot.			
(35)	*ʔal-ṭaalibaat-(u)*	*yu-ḥibb-na*	*al-ʔustaadha{t}-(a)*	*kathirann.*
	def-student.p.f-(nom)	3.p.f-like.imperf-indic	def-teacher.s.f-(acc)	a lot.
	The (female) students like the (female) teacher a lot.			
(36)	*tu-ḥibb-(u)*	*yu-ḥibb-na*	*al-ʔustaadha{t}-(a)*	*kathirann.*
	3.s.f-like.imperf-indic	3.p.f-like.imperf-indic	def-teacher.s.f-(acc)	a lot.
	The (female) students like the (female) teacher a lot.			
(37)	**yu-ḥibb-na*	*ʔal-ṭaalibaat-(u)*	*al-ʔustaadha{t}-(a)*	*kathirann.*
	3.p.f-like.imperf-indic	def-student.p.f-(nom)	def-teacher.s.f-(acc)	a lot.
	The (female) students like the (female) teacher a lot.			

The agreement pattern exemplified in the previous examples is characterized as "asymmetrical, non-canonical, or partial" in Arabic syntactic studies (Bahloul & Harbert, 1993; Mohammad, 1990; Soltan, 2007). It is "asymmetrical" and "non-canonical" because the verb and the subject disagree in the linguistic feature of number. It is "partial" because the verb and the subject agree in two linguistic features, which are "person" and "gender." In this case, "partial" agreement is contrasted to "full" agreement in which the subject and the verb agree in terms of person, gender, and number in the subject-initial word order, as demonstrated in the previous examples.

Work in Arabic syntax has proposed four controversial accounts to explain the derivation of this asymmetrical or partial pattern. These explanations are abstract in nature. For space limitations, the key aspects of each explanation are presented (for an overview, see Soltan, 2007). The first explanation is the *null expletive explanation* (Mohammad, 1990). According to this explanation, the symmetrical agreement in subject-initial sentences is the result of a relation between the head of the verb phrase (the subject) and its specifier. The asymmetrical agreement, on the other hand, is the result of a relation between the inflection (INFL) and an embedded null expletive (*there* or *seem*). These two types of relations are discussed in detail in Soltan (2007, p. 37).

Although the fact that Standard Arabic is a null-subject language gives credibility to this explanation, there are two critiques against it. First, this explanation does not account for why null expletives have to be third-person singular (Soltan, 2007). Second, assuming that null expletives are third-person singulars does not adequately reflect the properties of overt expletives in the system of standard Arabic (see Fassi Fehri, 1993, for more details). The second explanation is known as the *agreement loss analysis* (Aoun et al., 1994). According to this explanation, agreement is assumed to appear in the subject-initial and verb-initial word orders, but agreement in verb-initial sentences was lost when the head was moved to the head position. Under this explanation, the motivation for agreement loss in the derivation is not clear.

The third explanation, which dates back to early and Medieval Arabic grammarians, is known as the *incorporation analysis* (see Bolotin, 1995, for an overview). According to this explanation, the asymmetrical pattern is understood in light of the symmetrical one. It assumes that there is a pronoun that serves as a placeholder for the topicalized subject in the subject-initial word order. This pronoun has been incorporated (pronominally cliticized) onto the verb, and the subject is assumed to be uniformly *pro*. The incorporation analysis continues to assume that the lexical subject and the cliticized pro are in complementary distribution in the postverbal position. Benmamoun (2000) points out that this incorporation analysis faces empirical problems once other agreement phenomena in Arabic are considered, such as compound-tense constructions.

Benmamoun proposes an alternative explanation that he terms the *merger analysis*. According to this theory, the verb and the subject in verb-initial sentences merge. In that merging operation, the number feature is spelled out on the verb, and this can explain its absence in the verb morphology. This explanation also faces an empirical problem: it requires the verb and the subject to be adjacent in the verb-initial sentences, which is not always the case in Arabic syntax. The agreement asymmetry is also attested when the verb and the subject are separated by another word.

Numeric Agreement

Generally, numeric agreement in Standard Arabic is known for its remarkable complexity (Al-Bataineh & Branigan, 2020; Kouloughli, 1994: Ryding, 2005). Number–noun constructions in cardinals in particular have been subject to considerable attention from both classical grammarians (e.g., Al-Ansari, 1991; Al-Mubarrad, 1994; Aqeel, 1980; Sibawayh, 1988; Ya'īsh, 2001) and generative linguists (Alqarni, 2015; Alqassas, 2017; Danon, 2009; Marcin, 2016) due to the symmetrical and asymmetrical realities they manifest.

Symmetrical Pattern

Simplex numerals are classified into two groups in Standard Arabic according to their agreement behavior: 1–2 and 3–10. For simplex 1 and 2, they are shown in the literature to occur only post-nominally and to agree with the numerated noun in gender, definiteness, and case. This means if the noun is masculine, the number is masculine as well, and if the noun is feminine, the number should be feminine as well, as exemplified in (38) and (39):

(38)	*qaraʔtu*	*kitaab-a-n*	*waaḥid-a-n*
	I read	book.s.m-acc-indef	one.s.m-acc-indef
	I read one book.		
(39)	*qaraʔtu*	*qiṣṣat-a-n*	*waaḥida-ta-n*
	I read	story.s.f- acc-indef	one.f.s.- acc-indef
	I read one story.		

This agreement pattern also applies to these two numbers when they are part of compound numbers as in these examples:

(40)	*qaraʔtu*	*ʔaḥaha*	*ʕashr-a*	*kitaab-a-n*
	I read	one.s.m-acc	ten.s.m-acc	book.s.m-acc-indef
	I read eleven books.			
(41)	*qaraʔtu*	*ʔiḥdaa*	*ʕashra-ta*	*qiṣṣa-a-n*
	I read	story.s.f-indef	ten.s.f-acc	story.s.f-acc-indef
	I read eleven stories.			
(42)	*qaraʔtu*	*ʔaḥaha*	*wa-ʕishriin-a*	*kitaab-a-n*
	I read	one.m.s-acc-indef	and-twenty-acc	book.s.m-acc-indef
	I read twenty-one books.			
(43)	*qaraʔtu*	*ʔiḥdaa*	*wa-ʕishriin*	*qiṣṣa-a-n*
	I read	one.s.f-nom-indef	and-twenty.acc	one.f.s.- acc-indef
	I read twenty-one stories.			

However, when these two numbers are part of a compound construction or coupled with tens, they surface before the nouns. They are not therefore treated as adjectives. In this configuration, they precede the nouns that must be consistently in indefinite accusative singular form (*tamyiiz*, or disambiguation). In ordinal configurations of these two numbers (first and second), an agreement pattern is also discernible. As adjectives, they agree with their corresponding nouns in gender, case, and definiteness, as in the examples:

(44)	*qaraʔtu*	*ʔal-kitaab-a*	*ʔal-ʔawwal-a*	*wa-ʔal-thaanii-a.*
	I read	def-book.s.m-acc	def-first.s.m-acc.	and-def-second.s.m-acc.
	I read the first and second book.			
(45)	*qaraʔtu*	*ʔal-qiṣṣa-ta*	*ʔal-ʔuula-a*	*wa-ʔal-thaaniiyat-a.*
	I read	def-story.s.f-acc	def-first.s.f-acc.	def-second.s.f-acc.
	I read the first story.			

Asymmetrical Pattern

In contrast to the symmetrical agreement pattern noticed in simplex number 1 and 2, simplex numbers 3–10 show a disagreement pattern with the nouns they combine with in terms of gender. This gender reversal means that if the noun is masculine, the number is set in the feminine form, and if the noun is feminine, the number should be masculine. This is illustrated in these examples:

(46)	*qaraʔtu*	*thalaath-at-(a)*	*kutuub-(i)-(n).*
	I read	three-s.f-acc	book.p.m-gen-indef.
	I read three books.		
(47)	*qaraʔtu*	*thalaath-(a)*	*qiṣaṣ-(i)-(n).*
	I read	three.s.m-acc	stories.s.f-gen-indef.
	I read three stories.		

There are four important observations about these two examples. First, the number precedes the noun. Second, they show reverse gender agreement, that is, the numeral takes the masculine marker when defining a feminine noun, and vice versa. The inverted gender agreement is determined by the gender of the singular form of the enumerated noun rather than by the gender of the plural form as in cases involving broken plurals of inanimate objects; notice that in *kitaab* "book" is masculine, but *kutub* "books" is feminine. Third, the plural noun is consistently in the genitive case because the number and the noun form a construct state or annexation phrase in which the second noun has to be in the genitive case. Fourth, whereas the counted noun can be definite or indefinite, the numerals can have neither the definite article {*-ʔal*} nor the indefinite article {*-n*}.

This asymmetrical pattern (gender reversal in the number) is attested in other number types in which numbers 3–10 are part of compound numbers (11–19) and tens (numbers). Compound numerals, as the name denotes (11–19), are formed of two parts: the first digit and "ten." They show three main things. First, except for 12, compound numerals are invariable in case, that is, they are always marked accusative; regardless of their role in the sentence, the noun that is counted is assigned the accusative case. Second, all compound numerals require the following counted noun to be singular and accusative. Third, regarding gender agreement, the two digits in the compound numeral show two opposite patterns; the first digit shows gender reversal, whereas the second digit "ten" agrees with the counted noun. This is illustrated in these examples:

(48)	*qaraʔtu*	*thalaath-at-a*	*ʕashr-a*	*kitaab-a-n.*
	I read	three-s.f-acc	ten.s.m-acc	book.s.f-acc-indef
	I read thirteen books.			
(49)	*qaraʔtu*	*thalaath-a*	*ʕashr-a-ta*	*qiṣṣat-a-n.*
	I read	three.s.m-acc	ten-s.f-acc	story.s.f-acc-indef
	I read thirteen stories.			

However, there is an agreement pattern between the tens and the numbers. In this configuration, they precede the nouns that must be consistently in indefinite accusative singular form (*tamyiiz*, or disambiguation). In the ordinal configurations (third-tenth) of these numbers, the disagreement pattern is not noticed. As adjectives, they agree with their corresponding nouns in gender, case, and definiteness as in these examples:

(50)	*qaraʔtu*	*ʔal-kitaab-a*	*ʔalthaalith-a.*
	I read	def-book.s.m-acc	def-third.s.m-acc.
	I read the third book.		
(51)	*qaraʔtu*	*ʔal-qiṣṣa-ta*	*ʔal-thaalithata-ta.*
	I read	def-story.s.f-acc	def-third.f.s-acc.
	I read the first story.		

Gender reversal in numerals 3–10 has been the focus of syntactic studies. Alqassas (2017) argues that gender anti-agreement is caused by a morphological deletion process that is triggered by the feminine morpheme of the enumerated noun, that is, the feminine morpheme of the numeral is deleted only if the enumerated noun is feminine. This process affects only the numerals 3–10, since they are underlyingly feminine, in contrast with other cardinals that do not have a default [*fem*] feature. Contra Alqassas (2017), Al-Bataineh and Branigan (2020) argue that gender polarity is a morphological process that applies to all simple nominal cardinals unless other lexical or morphological processes block it. 1 and 2 show agreement with the counted noun because they are selected from the lexicon with a gender value already determined, and which cannot, therefore, disagree with the associated noun.

Summary

In this chapter, the symmetrical and asymmetrical agreement realities were overviewed in descriptive terms. The symmetrical pattern shows congruence between the target and the controller in terms of the two linguistic features of gender and number. On the other hand, the asymmetrical pattern shows incongruence in differential degrees. In some cases, the asymmetrical pattern entails disagreement in terms of the two linguistic features of gender and number as in masculine nonhuman plural nouns that are assigned singular feminine adjectives, demonstratives, and other types of pronouns. In other cases, the asymmetrical pattern entails disagreement in terms of one linguistic feature of gender as in feminine nonhuman plurals that are assigned singular feminine adjectives, demonstratives, and anaphoric expressions.

This differentiation between disagreement, in terms of one or two features, is attested also in nominal and verbal sentences with nonhuman plural nouns. In both types of sentences, masculine nonhuman plural nouns are assigned singular feminine verbs (disagree in the two features of number and gender) and feminine nonhuman plural nouns are assigned singular feminine verbs (difference in the feature of gender). With human plurals, disagreement is noted only in the linguistic feature of number: masculine human plurals are assigned masculine singular verbs, and feminine human plurals are assigned feminine singular verbs. Numeric constructions in the simplex numbers (3–10) also show disagreement in the linguistic feature of gender (presented as gender reversal).

As mentioned in the introduction, these agreement asymmetries pose learnability issues to learners of Arabic at a variety proficiency levels. It is assumed that agreement symmetries are easier to acquire than agreement asymmetries. Also, asymmetries that entail disagreement in two features (tentatively) are assumed to be harder to acquire than asymmetries that entail disagreement in one feature. Also, the difficulty of learning certain cases of asymmetries may be heightened due to their inherent complexity. Some features vary in their perceptual salience to the learners. Referential asymmetries in demonstratives, for example, could be easier to notice than referential asymmetries in clitics.

In terms of instruction, the intricate aspects of Arabic morphosyntax that entail agreement asymmetries need to be taught with careful planning. Instruction with good design matters in learning these complex aspects, but this instruction does not necessarily yield identical results in each case of asymmetry. These issues are systematically addressed in this book from an instructed second language acquisition (ISLA) perspective. They are provided fully in the next chapter.

Notes

1 In the transliteration, (-) is going to be used to refer to optional case marks in Standard Arabic. As it is known, some case marks are not represented in Arabic script. This is the situation in most Arabic textbooks.

2 According to established classical and grammatical literature (McCarthy, 1981; Yaquub, 2001), the ultimate form of a word is the result of three tiers. First, the consonantal roots are represented on a separate tier that supplies the basic meaning. Second, this root is mapped into a templatic form tier, in which the constants and vowels are slotted. Third, there is the vocalic melody tier that supplies the actual vowels. For example, the ultimate outcome in the formation of the plural of the singular noun *kushk* "booth" is two variants that fall into two different morphological forms: *ʔakshaak*, a broken plural falling under the form of *ʔafʕaal* and *kushkaat*, a sound plural falling under the form of *fuʕlaat*. In the same vein, the ultimate outcome in the formation of the plural of the singular noun *biṭaaqa* "card" is two variants that fall into two different morphological forms: *biṭaaqaat*, a sound plural falling under the form of *fiʕalaat* and *baṭaaʔiq*, a broken plural falling under the form of *faʕaaʔil*.

3 For extensive discussion of gender in Arabic, see Fassi Fehri (2017), who adopts a multilayered approach exhibits a variety of distinct controllers and properties of agreement based on Distributed Morphology.

2 The Academic Discipline of Instructed Second Language Acquisition

Instructed Second Language Acquisition as a Subfield of SLA

Second language acquisition (SLA) is a complex phenomenon of study. Historically, it has been viewed as a field that examines how cognitive processes are used to learn the linguistic system of a *second* language (Firth & Wagner, 2007). With the rise of the social turn in applied linguistics (Block, 2003), the field has taken a new direction to also examine the social and contextual factors that shape the process of SLA in multiple social settings. Nowadays, three distinct perspectives are well defined in researching the processes of SLA: linguistic, cognitive (psychological), and sociocultural (interactional). Under these three perspectives, multiple theories and approaches have been proposed, reaching their own conclusions with no single theory or approach fully accounting for the complexity of SLA. VanPatten (2004, p. 5) attributes this complexity to two reasons. First, SLA involves the acquisition of a complex implicit linguistic system consisting of lexical entries and their features and forms, an abstract syntactic system, a phonological system, and rules of the pragmatic use of language. Also, SLA is best thought of as involving multiple processes that in turn may contain sub-processes that work at every stage of acquisition. The parable of a group of blind men trying to describe the elephant in the room with each identifying one part of it is an amusing and apt analogy for the attempt to characterize the complexity of the SLA phenomenon (Saville-Troike & Barto, 2006).

With these three main approaches to SLA becoming more distinct over time, the role of instruction has never been lost. Instructed second language acquisition (ISLA) has emerged as an established academic subdiscipline of SLA and applied linguistics that systemically examines the processes and the outcomes of instruction. It has gained a significant position in SLA from the growing proliferation of theoretical and empirical studies in language teaching mostly in the classroom (for example, R. Ellis, 1990; Long, 2015, 2017; Loewen, 2015; Loewen & Sato, 2017; Nassaji, 2016). As a subfield, it has benefitted tremendously from the fields of cognitive science, educational psychology, and linguistics. With its theoretical and empirical focus, Loewen (2020, p. 3) defines it as a "field of academic inquiry that aims to understand how the systemic manipulation of the mechanisms of learning and/or conditions under which they occur enable or facilitate the development of

DOI: 10.4324/9781003055600-3

acquisition of an additional language." Earlier, Loewen (2015) defines it as a "theoretically and empirically based field of academic inquiry that aims to understand how the systematic manipulation of the mechanisms of learning and/or the conditions under which they occur enable or facilitate the development and acquisition of an additional language" (p. 2).

Using this conceptualization, ISLA is also viewed by Nassaji (2016) as

> as an area of SLA that investigates any processes and mechanisms (social and cognitive) involved in any form-focused intervention (explicit or implicit). In this area of research, instruction is loosely construed as staged not just by human participants (e.g., the teacher and the student) but also by the social context.
>
> (p. 13)

Emphasizing this "intervention" aspect of ISLA, Loewen and Sato (2017) state that "ISLA research is concerned with L2 learning processes that are hypothesized to be or have been found to be amenable to intervention" (p. 3). Han and Nassaji (2018) highlight important observations about these definitions: first, they confine ISLA to scholarly ("academic"), experimental ("manipulation"), and circumscribed ("conditions [that] . . . enable or facilitate . . . acquisition") endeavors. Also, they underscore the cognitive perspective in ISLA, emphasizing mental processes such as information processing and internalization, storage of knowledge, and production of language as correlates of some form of pedagogical intervention.

With these definitions that put pedagogical interventions in the center, ISLA answers two questions: the first is whether and to what extent instruction is beneficial for second/foreign-language learning and, *second*, if so, how can the effectiveness be optimized (Loewen, 2020). By using the term "instructed" to "modify" second language acquisition, there is a presupposition there is a difference between *instructed* and *uninstructed* second language acquisition with practical validity of this difference (R. Ellis, 1990; Klein, 1986; Larsen-Freeman & Long, 1991).

The distinction between instructed and uninstructed L2 acquisition is often thought of as the difference between learners being inside or outside of the classroom, although the classroom is still construed to be providing more formal opportunities for learning (R. Ellis, 1990). In other settings, such as in study-abroad and self-instructed/independent or individual-study programs, learning happens in environments that are less structured with minimal intervention. That means that under certain pedagogical interventions, the process of SLA can be improved and facilitated (Housen & Pierrard, 2005). However, how this process compares to uninstructed or naturalistic environments that differ widely is not always clear. Therefore, the exploration of the instructed nature of ISLA also entails comparisons to learning that occurs in these settings.

Some SLA researchers would contend, in fact, that L2 learners acquire very little in the classroom that enables them to use the L2 for spontaneous communicative purposes. For example, Krashen (1982, 2003) rules out the possibility of instruction intervening in the acquisition process as it proceeds along some fixed natural order. Relating his view to ISLA, Housen and Pierrard (2005) concludes that the implication here is that the only "real" SLA—or at least the only kind of SLA that merits the researcher's attention—is uninstructed SLA—that is, SLA uncontaminated by the intervention and control exerted by the classroom, instructor, or textbook. Researchers such as Krashen and others (e.g., Lichtman & VanPatten, 2021; VanPatten, 2017) argue that learners acquire a second language in a similar way to their first language, by being exposed to large amounts of input from speakers and from other sources such as books, movies, and music. This view is made explicit in the following quote by Wong-Fillmore (1989): "What happens in school has very little to do with language learning. Language can't be taught. It can only be learned" (p. 315). Even though such views about the overall ineffectiveness of L2 instruction are in the minority in the field of SLA, it is nevertheless important to ask, and investigate, if instruction really makes a difference and under which circumstances.

But the common view about ISLA is that it examines the effect of instruction in the context of the classroom (Leow, 2018). R. Ellis (2005) further states that "instruction can be viewed as an attempt to intervene in the process of language learning" (p. 9). Later, Loewen (2013) states that ISLA investigates L2 learning or acquisition that occurs as a result of teaching and that "the defining feature of L2 instruction is that there is an attempt by teachers, or instructional materials, to guide and facilitate the process of L2 acquisition" (p. 2716). An even more detailed definition is provided by Housen and Pierrard (2005), who defined ISLA as "any systematic attempt to enable or facilitate language learning by manipulating the mechanisms of learning and/or the conditions under which these occur" (p. 2). However, this manipulation should be coupled with the desire to learn the language.

Loewen (2020) lists two prerequisites for ISLA: instruction and the intention to acquire the L2. Without these two conditions, ISLA does not exist. A main assumption here is that the learners make some effort to learn the L2, and if acquisition is not a goal of an encounter with the L2, then such a situation would fall outside of the realm of ISLA. With this role of effort, Loewen presents the relationship between these two prerequisites in terms of scenarios or quadrants (p. 5). In this representation, ISLA is located in scenario or quadrant 2, in which there is systematic manipulation of the learning conditions coupled with intention and effort of the learners to acquire the second language. Scenario 1 represents the uninstructed learning settings in which learners have the intention to acquire the second language, but the learning conditions around them are not manipulated, as in study-abroad programs where they are fully immersed in the L2 environment. Scenario 3 represents situations in which the individuals (expatriates such as workers and diplomats) are surrounded with the L2 but they interact with other L1 speakers. Scenario 4 represents the very unlikely situation in which learners do not have the intention to acquire the second language, but the learning conditions are manipulated.

With the previously discussed definitions of instruction and acquisition in mind, it is feasible to draw the following foundational premises about ISLA. When considering acquisition, it is true that it does not always occur even though there is effort on the part of learners and teachers. This begs the question about the specific factors that may explain this. Second, the fundamental difference between instructed and uninstructed SLA remains in the systematic attempt to manipulate the conditions for learning, mostly in the classroom. The main question in this regard is the variable degrees of learning that occur as a result of this manipulation under different circumstances. Also, assuming that not all aspects of the linguistic system of the second language are on equal degrees of complexity or difficulty, this provokes the question of whether ISLA is more effective than uninstructed SLA in learning these aspects. Although individuals may be immersed in an L2 environment, and they may *generally* acquire the language incidentally when they do not have the time or make the effort to engage in any type of more formal or systematic study, it is not clear whether this incidental acquisition would be the same with more complex aspects of the linguistic system of the language they are immersed in. In the end, there are also a myriad of individual differences among the learners that certainly result in variability in instructed and uninstructed settings.

The Cognitive Process of Input Processing in ISLA

The definitions overviewed so far emphasize how the ISLA research agenda seeks to form a better understanding of the many variables that contribute to (robust) language learning and teaching in the classroom, which is a relatively impoverished setting when compared to the naturalistic setting in which acquisition occurs (Leow, 2018). In this research agenda, the focus is on how to manipulate the cognitive process(es) of input processing through instructional interventions. These processes are elaborated in the representation in Table 2.1 from work by Leow (2015):

Table 2.1 Stages of Learning Processes in ISLA (Leow, 2015, p. 17)

Input	{>	Intake	>	Internal system	>}	Output
	Stage I	Stage 2	Stage 3	Stage 4	Stage 5	
(Product)	process	(product)	(process)	(product)	(process)	(product)
(input)	(input)	(intake)	(intake)	(L2 knowledge)	(L2 knowledge/ output)	(Representative L2 knowledge)
	Input-processing stage		Intake-processing stage		Knowledge-processing stage	

Broadly defined, input processing refers to the process of how the learners make sense of the linguistic data they are exposed to. In this regard, two concepts are important to differentiate: input and intake. To Corder (1967, p. 165),

> the simple fact of presenting a certain linguistic form to a learner . . . does not necessarily qualify it for the status of input. For that reason, input is *what goes in*, not what is available for going in, and we may reasonably suppose that it is the learner who controls this input or more properly his intake.

In a similar vein, Hatch (1983, p. 81) thinks that "input" is what the learner hears and attempts to process. The part that learners process only *partially* is still input, though traces of it may remain and help in building the internal representation of the language. The part the learner successfully and completely processes is a subset called "intake." Chaudron (1985) defines it as "the mediating process between the target language available to learners and the learners' internalized set of L2 rules" (p. 5).

The input–intake distinction in ISLA has been expanded in the seminal work by VanPatten (1996), who defines intake as "the subset of filtered input that serves as the data for accommodation by developing system" (p. 10). VanPatten (2000) later provides three main characteristics of intake: (a) intake as incorporated data into the linguistic system of the learner; (b) intake as process—intake is not a product, but rather the process of successively incorporating grammatical features into the linguistic system. This process includes sub-processes such as "initial intake" and "final intake"; and (c) intake as a filtered subset of input before incorporation—this is the product of input processing. These filtered data are stored in working memory and are available for subsequent processing.

Gass (1997) equates "intake" with selective processing, which mediates between input and production. It is what is incorporated into the L2 learner's grammar, and it is envisioned as a process and not a product. The following quote from Gass and Selinker (1994) provides more elaboration:

> It is the process of assimilating linguistic material . . . it is the mental activity that mediates between input and grammar, and it is different from apperception or comprehension, as the latter do not necessarily lead to grammar formation. This, of course, suggests that intake is not merely a subset of input. Rather, input and intake refer to two fundamentally different phenomena.
>
> (p. 485)

Sharwood Smith (1986) outline five stages of input processing. In the first, the learner begins to compare the knowledge they already have to the new knowledge they notice in the input they are exposed to. It is the *comparison* between the preexisting semantic representations and new ones offered in the input. The second stage is a process of *adjustment*, in which the learner makes modifications to their semantic representations as they begin to compare these two types of knowledge. The third stage is the process of *generating* a surface structure from the adjusted semantic representations. At this stage, language learners still make use of their current grammar. The fourth is the process of *comparing* the generated surface structure and the original surface structure, and this is followed by the process of noticing a discrepancy, if any. The last stage is the process of restructuring the current competence system of the learners (Sun, 2008).

This conceptualization of input processing adduces two main reasons why processing would fail: the first is the absence of "a noticeable gap" between the two representations or when there is a gap between them, but the learner has not been able to attend to it. Second, processing might break if learners form incorrect representations based on extra-linguistic information. The result of this misrepresentation, as Sun (2008) indicates, is incorrect mapping into the learner's linguistic system. This conceptualization of input processing considers the process of adjusting the mental representations that are in contrast with the data in the input.

Schmidt (1990, 1994, 1995, 2001) advanced this notion of noticing to what has become known as the "noticing hypothesis." According to this hypothesis, for acquisition to take place, learners must consciously notice forms (and the meanings these forms realize) in the input. Noticing, however, does not guarantee acquisition. It is only "the necessary and sufficient condition for the conversion of input to intake for learning" (Schmidt, 1994, p. 17). That is, noticing enables learners to process forms in short-term memory but does not assure incorporation into their developing interlanguage. The "noticing hypothesis" contradicts Krashen's (1981) claim that the process of acquisition is unconscious. It is compatible with certain positions in explicit instruction that drawing learners' attention to forms in the input supports acquisition. Schmidt's hypothesis, while widely accepted by SLA researchers, remains controversial (see Tomlin & Villa, 1994; Truscott, 1998, for a different view of the role of attention in language acquisition).

Despite the differences in defining and interpreting the notions of input and intake, there is consensus that "input" is the surrounding linguistic data that the learner reads or hears, and "intake" constitutes the data, which is ultimately available to the learner's developing system. Thus, it necessarily serves as the mediating process between input exposure and actual acquisition. Researchers disagree on how intake is processed and how it interacts with the existing linguistic system in the learner's mind. They also disagree about whether intake is a product or a process or even a combination of both. However, in the development of the ISLA theory, there is a strong disagreement regarding the conditions under which L2 input is presented. The central question in this regard is what type of learning (explicit/intentional vs. implicit/incidental) is important for subsequent learning or internalization of the L2 input (for a further review, see Hulstijn, 2013; N. Ellis, 2015; Leow, 2015; Nassaji, 2017). I turn to this point in the next section, which provides an overview of the scope of ISLA.

Scope of ISLA

Although the definitions of ISLA presented so far focus on the manipulation of the L2 learning process with focus on input, the use of the term in this book refers to the manipulation of L2 learning in the classroom under certain conditions that are modulated in measured ways that go beyond input presentation. This manipulation is interchangeably used to refer to the intervention that accelerates or improves learning. These include the materials that the learners are exposed to, the teaching techniques used, and the sequence of procedures learners followed. The definition adopted in this book is aligned with Nassaji's view of ISLA as "an area of SLA that investigates. . . [any] processes and mechanisms [social and cognitive] involved in any form-focused intervention (explicit or implicit)" (Nassaji, 2016, p. 13). In the sections that follow, three main areas of interest that fall within the scope of

ISLA are presented: (1) the nature of L2 knowledge; (2) the nature and forms of L2 instruction; and (3) L2 performance or use in instructed settings under certain conditions of instruction.

The Nature and Measures of L2 Knowledge

As a subfield of SLA, ISLA focuses on the nature of L2 knowledge that L2 learners develop as a result of instruction. DeKeyser (2007b) lists common dichotomies that sometimes result in confusion for researchers: implicit/explicit knowledge, declarative/procedural knowledge, incidental/intentional learning, instructed/naturalistic learning, inductive/deductive learning, and item/rule learning, to name the most common ones. To DeKeyser, it is even more intriguing when we ask about the subtle differences between three of them: implicit versus explicit knowledge, declarative versus procedural knowledge, and incidental versus intentional teaching.

It is commonly held that for practical purposes, the declarative/procedural and the explicit/implicit tend to be equivalent, but from the perspective of cognitive neuroscience, they are not. Explicit knowledge is knowledge that one is aware of, and implicit knowledge is knowledge without awareness (see A. Rebuschat, 2013; Williams, 2005). Declarative knowledge is mostly explicit but it can be implicit (as in the Chomskyan concept of grammatical competence). Explicit knowledge, however, is considered by many to be necessarily declarative (Paradis, 1994; Ullman, 2001).

In L2 learning theories, the term "explicit knowledge" is used to refer to learners' conscious knowledge of the linguistic rules of a particular language (e.g., DeKeyser, 2003; R. Ellis, 2004; Hu, 2002). This construct is often distinguished from implicit knowledge that cannot be brought to awareness and verbalized (see Rebuschat, 2013; R. Ellis, 2005). Implicit knowledge, on the other hand, refers to learner knowledge *of* the language that is distinguished from knowledge *about* the language. It is often taken to mean knowledge that is unconscious or tacit, but learners cannot verbalize it (Loewen, 2020). However, they utilize this knowledge in the communication of their messages. It always manifests in the form of a feeling or a gut or an intuition that certain linguistic forms or structures are just "ungrammatical" and the learners cannot offer a reason or a justification for it (Ur, 2011). According to R. Ellis (2004, further elaborated in 2005), an adequate operationalization that captures the intricacies of explicit knowledge should include primarily analyzed knowledge (i.e., structural knowledge that learners are aware of) and secondary metalanguage (i.e., the use of technical and semi-technical linguistic terms) that explain these rules. In the context of L2 instruction in the classroom, there are important questions that arise about these dichotomies: what is the nature of the L2 knowledge that instructed L2 learners develop? How does it differ from the L2 knowledge that develops in naturalistic, uninstructed SLA? And most importantly, what are some common measures for these two types of knowledge?

An important question that follows the characterization of both types of knowledge is how to better measure them using reliable and valid tests. Traditionally, explicit knowledge is thought as easier to assess than implicit knowledge that is often verbalized in terms of intuition. Common tests include asking the learners to verbalize the rules in consideration. They can also be asked to provide grammaticality judgments in terms of categorical or gradient acceptability. A third test may ask the learners to choose the correct linguistic form in the context of some sentences. A fourth would require them to fill in the blanks providing the correct linguistic form. On the other hand, measuring implicit knowledge, given its nature, is harder. In the established literature (Suzuki & DeKeyser, 2017), the learners are given a narration task that requires spontaneous production with focus on the target linguistic item or structure. They can also be given comprehension questions that would require understanding of the details before they answer these questions after the listening task. Patterns of provision and omission of the target items are analyzed in real-time production as a manifestation of this type of linguistic knowledge.

In instructed L2 learning, it is generally assumed that learners develop a higher level of explicit knowledge because of adopting techniques that highlight this kind of knowledge (Alderson & Hudson, 2013). To make sure that the learners utilized their explicit knowledge in completing the task, retrospective think-aloud interviews are often conducted with the learners to capture the manifestations of their linguistic knowledge and whether it drove their performance on the L2 tasks (Ericsson & Simon, 1984; Gass & Mackey, 2000; Leow, 2001; Wrembel, 2015). They are usually asked to comment on the (un)grammaticality of the target items. Another aim of its use is to determine whether the learners are able to use the technical terms that shape their grammatical knowledge.

The importance of explicit knowledge in L2 communicative use has been controversial. Results of a large body of experimental research are divided among three positions. First is the dismissive view that posits that there is no role for this knowledge in L2 use (e.g., Alderson et al., 1997; Elder et al., 1999; Krashen, 1987; Paradis, 1994). According to this view, L2 performance, particularly communicative use, is not affected by explicit knowledge of grammar, but rather by implicit unconscious knowledge. This view has been very influential in L2 pedagogy, and for decades many language instructors and methodologists recognized no role for explicit knowledge of L2 grammar, marking a pendulum swing from the grammar-translation method. The second view, on the other hand, establishes strong links between explicit knowledge and L2 performance (e.g., Hu, 2011; Roehr, 2006, 2007). Proponents of this view posit that L2 learners' performance on various tasks is associated with their reported use of explicit linguistic knowledge.

The third view, a compromise between these two conflicting orientations, establishes indirect links between explicit knowledge and L2 use. According to this view, linguistic knowledge plays a role only when it is proceduralized and automatized through practice (DeKeyser, 1998, 2009; R. Ellis, 1994). DeKeyser (2020, 2007a, 2007b), in his skill-acquisition theory, posits that practice is precisely what is needed to turn declarative/explicit knowledge into procedural/implicit knowledge. Declarative knowledge becomes proceduralized through slow and deliberate practice, while declarative knowledge is acquired through the judicious use of rules and examples (DeKeyser, 2020). For example, DeKeyser (2007b) expressly states that explicit instruction needs to be integrated with input and output practice in theoretically supported ways, following the stages proposed by skill-acquisition theory. The ability to use knowledge automatically is the goal of skill-acquisition theory, and DeKeyser argues that automatization requires procedural knowledge, which in turn is dependent upon declarative knowledge.

L2 Learning and Forms of Instruction in ISLA

Various types of instruction are often associated with the development of explicit and implicit knowledge in ISLA. These include three macro-options: input-based instruction, output-based instruction, and form-focused instruction. Each type of these options includes other sub-types. For example, input-based instruction includes input flooding (also input enrichment), input enhancement, instruction that provides comprehensible input with ample positive and negative evidence, and instruction that provides strategies for input processing. Also, output-based instruction may include instruction that runs in the present–practice–produce technique and instruction that pushes learners to produce the target features (pushed output) in meaningful communication in interactive episodes. Form-focused instruction includes focus-on-form instruction (incidental and planned), focus-on-form*s* instruction, and instruction that offers corrective feedback.

Understanding what these different forms of instruction have in common and how they differ is one of the main lines of inquiry in ISLA. Also, an important question in these types is whether L2 learners are *aware* of the target linguistic features. In the parts that follow, I discuss the concepts of implicit and explicit learning and outline the basic characteristics of each type of instruction with particular focus on the ones investigated in this book.

Implicit versus Explicit Learning

The notion of implicit/incidental learning is typically taken to mean learning without awareness (Leow, 2000; Rebuschat & Williams, 2012; Williams, 2005). Reber (1967b) defines it as a "process whereby a subject becomes sensitive to the structure inherent in a complex array by developing (implicitly) a conceptual model which reflects the structure to some degree" (p. 88). As this definition shows, implicit learning is characterized by the absence of any deliberate intention before exposure to the L2 data to learn target L2 information in such input (Leow, 2019). The early empirical beginnings of this area were in experimental psychology studies (see Reber, 1967a, 1989). These studies employ artificial or finite-state grammars that generate meaningless letter strings with the assumption that learners are able to absorb statistical regularities in the input they are exposed to (Bybee & Hopper, 2001; N. Ellis, 2002).

Implicit learning has made its way to the field of (I)SLA, with beginnings in Krashen's studies (1982) that distinguished between "learning" as a conscious process and "acquisition" as an unconscious process. Acquisition is described by Krashen as "*implicit* learning, informal learning, and natural learning. In non-technical language, acquisition is picking up a language" (p. 10). With this characterization, acquisition, incidental learning, and implicit learning all share two important features: an absence of awareness and a low depth of metalinguistic processing during the learning process (Leow & Zamora, 2017). With this characterization, there is direct association between the acquisition process and incidental learning (Leow & Zamora, 2017). In the words of R. Ellis (1994), "Thus, the acquisition process is identical to what was termed 'incidental learning'" (p. 212).

Explicit learning, on the other hand, refers to learning in which learners are made *aware* of the regularities of the linguistic data they are exposed to. The role of learner (un)awareness of the input has motivated a good number of theoretical discussions (see next section on output-based instruction). For example, the construct "awareness" is taken to be quite distinct from noticing, which is defined as "a particular state of mind in which an individual has undergone a specific subjective experience of some cognitive content or external stimulus" (Tomlin & Villa, 1994, p. 193), or "refers to a state of mind in which one has become cognizant of the regularities underlying the data" (Schacter, 1989, p. 577).

Forms of Instruction in ISLA

Input-Based Instruction

The effect of input-based instruction remains a central topic in ISLA research. Krashen's (1982) input hypothesis postulated that for second language acquisition to progress, second language (L2) learners should be exposed to input that is (a) comprehensible and (b) beyond their current linguistic knowledge. This comprehensible input may lead to rich intake (Chaudron, 1985; Corder, 1967; Hatch, 1983; VanPatten, 1996, 1999). There are multiple subtypes of instruction that go under input-based instruction. Some of these are discussed next.

Input Enrichment and Input Enhancement

Input enrichment (also known as input flooding or enriched input) constitutes a form of implicit instruction designed in a way in which a specific L2 feature occurs with high frequency. It is often contrasted with input enhancement, which refers to enriched input combined with an explicit explanation of the target structure (Reinders & R. Ellis, 2009). As defined by Leow (2001), enhanced input is used for input (mostly written) that has been manipulated to enhance the saliency of target forms. Such typological means may include italicization, bold print, underlining, shading, the use of different font types and sizes, and capitalization. Although both types fall under input options, they are often considered *unobtrusive* techniques that focus on certain language forms. In this respect, they contrast with obtrusive techniques such as input-processing instruction (VanPatten, 1996) and consciousness-raising tasks (Fotos & R. Ellis, 1991).

As an implicit instructional technique, input *enrichment* is often used in the context of a meaning-focused activity in which L2 learners are provided with rich L2 input, without telling them that they will be tested afterwards (Hulstijn, 2003). In the testing phase, the L2 learners are faced with tasks that show whether they have developed implicit or explicit knowledge of the target feature. According to R. Ellis (2009), implicit instruction, including input enrichment, provides learners with conditions under which they can infer the rules without awareness. The result will be internalizing the pattern without having their attention focused on it. Most of the studies of incidental acquisition using input enrichment have focused on vocabulary learning, while very few have examined its effects in grammar (Hulstijn, 2003).

Instruction with input *enhancement* is differentiated from instruction with input *enrichment* in two respects. First, the target feature or form is often manipulated in certain ways, such as underlining, bolding, or simply reading it with high intonation to draw the learner's attention. This manipulation depends primarily on the premise that in order for learners to acquire from input, they must first pay conscious attention to exemplars of particular forms. By artificially increasing the saliency of the target structure, it is thought that learners will notice and thus acquire the structure more easily. L2 learners often do not learn forms that are abundant in the input (such as tense markers: Cadierno, 1995; Overstreet, 1998; or morphology that carries little meaning: VanPatten, 1989) because the forms are, for various reasons, not salient to the learners (Sharwood Smith, 1993). According to the theory, enhancement helps foster that necessary attention to forms with low salience. Through this manipulation, the form becomes perceptually more salient to the learner than it otherwise would be (Barcroft, 2003; Wong, 2003). Second, explicit explanation of the target structure from frequent exemplars is often provided to the learners. With these two differences, input enhancement is more likely to encourage intentional learning by the learners since it directs their attention to target form (Sharwood Smith, 1991, 1993).

Previous Findings in Input Enrichment and Input Enhancement

In instructed second language acquisition, studies that have investigated the differential gains of these two types of input draw on Schmidt's "noticing hypothesis" (1990, 1995, 2001), that SLA only occurs with attention (Hama & Leow, 2010; Leow, 2000). Due to space limitations, this part reviews findings only in the area of grammar (for a more extensive survey, see Reinders & R. Ellis, 2009). An important question in studies that examined the role of input enrichment is whether L2 learners can notice the target form when they are flooded with abundant exemplars. Studies have reported mixed findings. For example, Balcom and Bouffard (2015) found that input flooding, when combined with form-focused instruction, influenced knowledge of adverb placement in French by L1 Arabic learners. The findings concluded that exposing learners to input flooding along with explicit explanation had a positive effect on the learning of the position of adverbs of aspect. Also, the effects were stronger in cases of positive adverbs rather than negative adverbs. Similarly, Rikhtegar and Gholami (2015) found evidence for the influence of input enrichment through reading, in enhancing Iranian ESL learners' grammar knowledge of simple-past tense acquisition. Using accuracy as a measure, they found a statistical difference between the pretest and the posttest scores particularly when students used a dictogloss.

The findings of other studies conducted by researchers including Hernández (2011) and Zyzik and Marques Pascal (2012) document a positive impact of input flooding on grammar knowledge. Yet, the results of Hernández (2011) and Hernández and Rodríguez-González (2012) showed no significant differences in the scores between a group that was exposed to input flooding and one that was not. Trahey and White (1993) examined whether an "input flood" (viewed as "positive input") was sufficient to enable francophone learners of L2 English to learn that English permits adverb placement between the subject and the verb (French does not), but does not permit placement between the verb and object (French does). Exposure occurred one hour a day for ten days. The target structure was not highlighted in any way. The learners succeeded in learning grammatical position in the subject–adverb–verb (SAV) word order, but failed to "unlearn" the ungrammatical position in the subject–verb–adverb–object (SVAO) word order.

Another line of studies, however very limited, distinguished multiple enriched and enhanced group conditions to better characterize the learning effects. Three important studies addressed this need. Alanen (1995) differentiated four conditions: (1) an "enhancement group" that received input in two 15-minute instructional periods, (2) a "rule group" that received just explicit instruction, (3) a "rule + enhanced group" that received both enriched input and explicit instruction, and (4) a control group. They found that the explicit-instruction group that received the rules, and the group that received the rule in addition to enhanced input, outperformed the enhancement only and the control groups. One weakness in this study was that the instructional periods were too short (a total of 30 minutes seems insufficient).

Rosa and O'Neill (1999) compared the effects of instruction directed at learning the Spanish contrary to fact conditional (a complex structure) by university-level learners of L2 Spanish. Four types of instruction were included in this study: (1) rule explanation + rule search, (2) rule explanation + no rule search, (3) no rule explanation + rule search, (4) no rule explanation + no rule search. The learning condition in (3) corresponds to what we have called "enhanced input," and the one in (4) corresponds to "enriched input." Acquisition was measured by means of a time-pressured multiple-choice recognition task, while think-aloud protocols were used to measure awareness of the rule. Awareness was operationalized as a verbal reference to the target feature during task execution, which thus might be considered a measure of intake. Two types of awareness were distinguished: "noticing" if no reference was made to the underlying rules and "understanding" if there was. All the groups improved from pre- to posttest. The instructed condition (i.e., (1)) proved superior to the enriched-input-only condition (i.e., (4)). Also, more aware participants, both those showing greater "noticing" and those showing greater "understanding," performed better on the multiple-choice recognition task. One weakness in this study is that it did not include measures of implicit knowledge.

Radwan (2005) also investigated the effects of instruction involving a focus on meaning only, compared with input enhancement and rule provision on learning and awareness of English-dative alternation. The study also investigated if differences in awareness affected learning. Forty-two lower-intermediate participants were pretested for prior knowledge of the target structure, and one day later given a short story to read that contained a high number of datives. Reading of the short story was followed by comprehension questions. The next day, a similar treatment was administered, but in addition, participants were given a narration task that involved describing a set of pictures. Participants were asked to think aloud while completing the task in order for the researcher to gauge their awareness. The treatments were followed by a posttest (one day later) and a delayed posttest (one month later). A control group completed the tests without receiving any of the treatments. Radwan found a significant advantage for the rule- group over the other groups, which failed to make significant progress. This advantage was maintained on the delayed posttest. The study also found that participants showing a greater degree of awareness during the narration task did better on the tests. However, awareness at the level of noticing was not as good a predictor of learning as awareness at the level of understanding.

Input-Processing Instruction

Certain models in instructed SLA have further addressed the role of input in a new light. The processing-instruction (PI) model (see VanPatten, 2004; VanPatten & Wong, 2004) is one such model that has gained increasing interest in ISLA since its inception in VanPatten and Cadierno (1993). PI is a type of pedagogical technique that has been originally designed to correct faulty processing strategies and help L2 learners create strong form-meaning connections while attending to new grammatical structures (VanPatten, 2004). These connections help learners convert new linguistic input into intake.

The theoretical conceptualizations of PI have four essential characteristics. First, PI explores the processing strategies (principles) that learners develop and the problems that arise from incorrect or inefficient ones (e.g., VanPatten, 1996, 2004). These inefficient (and faulty) strategies are corrected through activities called "structured-input" that help learners attend to the grammatical forms more efficiently and assign correct meaning to them. Three important processing principles are discussed in the context of English and Spanish: the First-Noun Principle, the Primacy of Meaning Principle, and the Sentence Location Principle. According to the first principle, learners tend to interpret the first noun they encounter in an utterance as the subject/agent. In word orders of many languages, the object may surface before the subject. For example, in the English sentence *The police officer was killed by the robber*, learners tend to assign the act of killing to the police officer. In this learning scenario, this principle may result in wrong interpretation, especially when world knowledge allows for two plausible interpretations (e.g., *a police officer may kill a robber* and *a robber may kill a police officer*).

For the Primacy of Meaning Principle, learners are expected to process the input for meaning before they process it for form. In doing this, they depend on content words as opposed to grammatical forms (inflections, affixes, and case markers) to get meaning when both encode the same semantic information. For example, in the sentence *Yesterday, I played tennis with John in the park*, learners depend on the lexical item *yesterday* more than the past tense morpheme *-ed* when encoding the past tense. A third principle is the Sentence Location Principle. According to this principle, L2 learners tend to process forms at the initial position of the sentence more than these at the middle and at the end, and these at the end more than those in the middle (see Benati, 2017, for an overview). Learners instead notice formal features that are at the initial position in the sentence.

The second characteristic of PI is the use of structured-input (SI) activities to overcome inefficient processing strategies. The purpose of these activities is to alert inefficient processing strategies and build up effective ones. Therefore, these activities are manipulated in particular ways to draw learner attention to push them away from the less-than-optimal strategies. Some considerations are always followed in the development of these SI activities (Wong, 2004; VanPatten, 1996). First, the processing problems in the language form/structure in question should be first identified. Second, to maximize the form-meaning connections, only one target form/structure should be the focus of the pedagogical treatment. Third, in the presentation of this form/structure, meaning receives primary focus. That is, input that contains referential meaning and communicative intent is presented. Fourth, the SI activities scale up from sentences to connected discourse in both oral and written input.

The third characteristic of PI is that learners are provided with explicit information about the target structure. This information draws their attention to the form of this structure with specific examples. A fourth characteristic is that since PI is primarily input-oriented, in PI treatments learners are pushed to process the formal features of linguistic input during SI activities without producing the target structure or form. This aspect comes in sharp contrast to structured output-based instruction in which learners are provided with explicit information on the target grammatical property followed by output practice through form-based drills. I discuss this next.

Output-Based Instruction

In contrast to input-based instruction that underscores the role of linguistic data that L2 learners are exposed to either intentionally or unintentionally, output-based instruction emphasizes the role of producing the target language. Output-based instruction rests on Swain's (1985) Output Hypothesis that highlights the connection between output practices and (re)structuring the learner linguistic system. As postulated by Swain (1995) and later by R. Ellis (2003, 2005), pushed output practices trigger processes such as noticing, metalinguistic analysis, and hypothesis-testing. These processes play a role in updating learners' interlanguage system, a process that is not necessarily triggered by input alone.

One important dimension of this conceptualization of output is Swain's discussion of "the negotiation of meaning." Initially, it was used to simply refer to "comprehensible output," with focus on notions such as accuracy and correctness that help the learners to get their message across. Recent reconceptualization expands the focus to "include the notions of being pushed toward delivery of a message that is not only conveyed, but that is conveyed precisely, coherently, and appropriately" (Swain, 1985). This conceptualization was further expanded into Mackey's discussions that show the modifications learners can make as a result of interacting with others in language classrooms, whether they are other learners/peers, teachers, or native speakers. Since then, the analysis of the dynamics of "interactive episodes" has become central in reformulation of what the output hypothesis is about. With planning of how to push the learners to consider their language, this offers them the opportunity to "think harder and harder" to come up with the correct forms and integrate it into the interaction (Mackey, 2006). This planning entails using important techniques such as requests for clarification, recasts, comprehension checks, and linguistic reformulations. These result in the modification of learner language as they engage in negotiation moves.

Swain (1985) identifies three functions of output. She terms the first the *noticing function*. It basically refers to the role practicing the language plays in prompting second language learners to be *consciously* aware of their own linguistic problems. This awareness has two sub-functions: it first generates new linguistic knowledge (when they notice the gap between what they initially said and what was fixed as a result in engaging in the interactive episodes). It also consolidates existing knowledge (when they experience multiple occurrences or frequencies of a certain structural linguistic item, whether lexical, morphosyntactic, or even phonetic). Using think-aloud protocols that allow the learners to verbalize their thoughts aloud has been crucial in showing these two functions (Swain & Lapkin, 1995).

The second function is *hypothesis-testing*. When learners produce language samples and receive feedback from their teachers in interaction, they are given the opportunity to test certain hypotheses about the linguistic forms they produce. Studies have shown that teachers' incidental feedback supports the learners to modify their output with focus on form on the semantic and morphosyntactic levels (Loewen, 2020; Mackey, 2006). Such interactions that allowed learners to modify their responses had enhanced their L2 learning compared to learners who did not produce or modify their utterances (McDonough, 2005). Also, these communicative interactions show learners' uptake particularly when teachers pushed for elicitation and clarification requests more than recasts with simply providing students with an answer. Also, the use of think-aloud protocols to explore strategies and processes in writing had demonstrated learners' use of problem-solving during their writing production. These writing tasks pushed the learners to make sense of their linguistic output.

The third is the *metalinguistic function*. This function is rooted in Vygotsky's sociocultural theory of the mind in which he argues that speaking is in itself a mediating tool. Vygotsky's theory also posits that speaking is a source of individual mental and physical regulation that occurs through scaffolding at the beginning stages of learning and could be internalized later on. For example, collaborative dialogue was shown to help learners engage in solving linguistic problems and knowledge building (Swain, 2005). Therefore, learners become engaged in discussion about language where their externalized utterances become an "object" to reflect on. These dialogic interactions also afford them with meaning-making opportunities to construct or deconstruct meanings behind vocabulary and certain metaphorical phrases.

Present–Practice–Produce

One main type of output-based instruction in which learners are prompted to produce the target linguistic features is the present–practice–produce (PPP) technique (Loewen, 2020; Nassaji & Fotos, 2011). In this technique type, there is balance between elements of explicit instruction and production-based activities. Conventionally, this type of instruction begins with the explanation of a grammar point, followed by very controlled production of that grammar structure. Finally, learners engage in freer practice using the grammar structure (Loewen, 2020). For example, in the *present* part, the learners may be provided with the rules of subject–verb agreement in Arabic as a heavily inflected language and how this agreement is determined by the sentence type, whether subject-first or verb-first. After that, the learners are provided with sentence-based activities that may be enhanced with a visual component, such as a storyline in which they form complete sentences with the correct verb form. This represents the *practice* part of this instructional technique. In the final part, *produce*, the learners are provided with the opportunity to work on activities that require the free production of the subject–verb agreement. For example, they may be asked to narrate a story or a trip they went on.

Loewen (2020) outlines some key characteristics of PPP, but also identifies certain concerns. The PPP technique can have *variable* degrees of focus on meaning. It is true that in the presentation stage there is more focus on the target grammar rules, with plans to push the learners to correctly repeat the L2 sentences in order to form good L2 habits. In that sense, the language presented tends to be decontextualized but builds the habits of producing the target structure. However, the practice, and particularly the production activities, may be much more meaning-focused. In certain articulations of PPP, the learners are given task-based activities that engage them in real communicative activities containing specific predetermined linguistic forms (Foster, 2009). This focus on meaning does not eliminate the possibility that at least *some* learners would think that the main goal of these communicative activities is to practice the targeted linguistic forms rather than to engage in genuine meaningful interaction (R. Ellis et al., 2009; Shintani, 2014).

The concerns about PPP relate to two specific issues. First, the principle of the PPP method may not be based on the recognized L2 ordered development. That is, if late-acquired structures are presented early in the learning process, the practice and production activities will not help learners skip steps in the natural order of acquisition (Nassaji & Fotos, 2011). The second concern is the assumption that the explicit instruction of the presentation part of this technique can develop into the ability to use the language for spontaneous production. Certain L2 acquisitionists cast some doubts about this assumption, contending that while explicit instruction could be successful in developing explicit, metalingual knowledge, there are doubts about the usefulness of such knowledge for spontaneous L2 production (N. Ellis, 2005; VanPatten, 2016). This is because, as this line of thought claims (see earlier section on this debate), it is difficult or even impossible for explicit knowledge to become implicit.

Gains of Input-Based and Output-Based Instruction

The effects of structured-input treatments have been compared to those of structured-output treatments in enhancing language interpretation and production of grammatical structures in adult L2 learning in multiple studies (e.g., Cadierno, 1995; Comer & DeBenedette, 2010; VanPatten & Cadierno, 1993; VanPatten & Wong, 2004). Whereas some studies found comparable effects for both types of treatments in interpretation and production, others concluded that structured input treatments had superior effects in interpretation (Cheng, 2002; Collentine, 1998; Farley, 2001a, 2001b; Pereira, 1996; Woodson, 1997). This has led to questions about the generalizability of existing research findings (for an overview, see Benati, 2005). Since the target languages tested in these comparative studies were mostly limited to English and European languages, the focus has recently settled on structural intricacies that cause persistent difficulties for L2 learners in under-researched and less commonly taught languages (see Yamashita & Iizuka, 2017).

VanPatten and Cadierno's seminal 1993 study opened the door for an entire body of research. It compared the effects of input-oriented instruction (that consisted of EI and SI activities) and traditional instruction (that consisted of EI and SO activities) on interpretation and production of object pronouns and word order in Spanish as a second language. Using a pretest–posttest design, the results showed that PI had greater effects than traditional instruction (TI) on sentence interpretation. In language production, both treatments were found to be similarly effective. A very similar pattern of results was found in Cadierno (1995) that compared the effects of the same two treatments but with verb morphology in Spanish (i.e., the *preterit*). Similar effects were found in Cheng (2004), which examined the acquisition of *ser*, *estar*, and copular verbs in Spanish, and in Benati (2004), which examined the acquisition of the Italian future tense. These studies concluded that PI, with its accompanying SI activities, resulted in changes in the learners' developing linguistic systems and internal representations, resulting in enhanced language production.

Although the previous studies support the effectiveness of PI with its accompanying SI activities, when complex grammatical structures were investigated, mixed findings were reported. For example, Collentine (1998) examined the effectiveness of the PI and output-based TI in the acquisition of the *subjunctive* in adjectival clauses in Spanish. He found out that the participants in both groups unexpectedly made similar gains in sentence interpretation. The PI and TI groups did not show differential performances in language production. Also, both groups significantly outperformed a control group that received no instruction. However, Collentine's study was criticized for not following the PI procedure closely. Farley (2001a) examined the same structural property in Collentine's study, but compared PI and a meaning-based output (MOI) treatment. The MOI consists of traditional explicit information about the target structure without information about the default processing strategies used. Also, it required the participants to focus on the meaning in addition to producing the target construction. The results showed that the PI group outperformed the MOI group in the interpretation task, and they made similar gains in the production task.

Farley (2001b) replicated Farley (2001a) with the same target structure, but with a larger sample of participants and a greater number of instructional activities in each treatment. Surprisingly, no significant differences were found between the PI and the MOI groups in either the interpretation or in the production tasks. More exposure to the instructional materials in Farley (2001b) than in Farley (2001a) was speculated as a factor that may explain the difference in findings in the two studies. Using similar comparative designs, Benati (2005) concluded that the PI group was superior to the MOI group in interpretation tasks and equally effective in production tasks. In the same vein, Morgan-Short and Bowden (2006) surprisingly reported no differences between both treatments in language interpretation, and the MOI group outperformed the PI group in language production.

Keating and Farley (2008) explored the effect of PI and MOI against a third treatment, termed meaning-based drills instruction (MDI), on the acquisition of Spanish object pronouns. Two basic differences were drawn between this third condition, PI, and MOI. First, it did not allow for incidental exposure to structured input, and second, it did include mechanical drills. The MDI activities differed from the MOI activities in that they did not require the learners to produce the target structure, as did the IP and the MOI. The results of the study concluded the PI group outperformed the MDI group on the interpretation test. On the production task, results showed that MOI was more effective than the IP. The study concluded overall that PI played the most significant role in restructuring the internal representations that learners make depending on the input they received. The effectiveness of the meaning-based output led Farley (2001b) and Keating and Farley (2008) to call for a hybrid model that builds on both PI and meaning-based-output teaching.

The mixed findings reported in the previous studies called for the systematic exploration of specific components of PI. The contributive roles of EI and SI activities were separated in some studies. VanPatten and Oikkenon (1996) replicated VanPatten and Cadierno (1993). They divided the learners into three groups:

(a) one receiving EI *and* SI activities (PI), (b) another receiving EI only, and (c) another receiving SI only. Using a pretest/posttest design with an interpretation and a sentence-level production test, the authors showed equal effects for the PI and the SI groups. They did not find the same effects for the group that received the explicit information alone. They concluded that the effects obtained in VanPatten and Cadierno (1993) could be attributed to the SI activities. The study of VanPatten and Oikkenon (1996) was replicated in Benati (2004) that examined the acquisition of gender in Italian. The same results were obtained. A similar pattern of findings was reported in Farley (2004) and VanPatten and Fernández (2004), who reported a greater role for the full (i.e., combined SI and EI) treatment. This pattern of results suggests that it is the SI component of PI that caused enhanced interpretation and production in the target structures.

Form-Focused Instruction

The term form-focused instruction (FFI) describes any pedagogical practice undertaken by L2 teachers to explicitly teach and draw the students' attention to language form. The "form" may consist of phonological (sound), morphosyntactic (word form and word order), lexical, pragmatic, or orthographical aspects of language. In providing the previous definitions of ISLA, Nassaji (2016) identified the role of FFI "as an area of SLA that investigates any processes and mechanisms (social and cognitive) involved in any form-focused intervention (explicit or implicit)" (p. 13). Obviously, this definition approaches ISLA in terms of form-focused intervention. Metalinguistic explanations of these target forms and the L1–L2 differences are always provided. Although it is broadly held that FFI develops explicit knowledge of grammar rules (Norris & Ortega, 2000; Spada & Tomita, 2010), studies have reported mixed effects on grammatical forms with variable inherent linguistic characteristics.

In the recognized literature of FFI in ISLA, a distinction is made between *focus on forms* (FoFs) and *focus on form* (FoF). This distinction was established by Long (1991) and further refined by Long and Robinson (1998). Long (1991) defined FoFs as the traditional structural and synthetic approach to language teaching, in which language is presented to learners in an isolated and decontextualized manner. FoF, on the other hand, was defined as instruction that involves drawing learners' attention to linguistic forms that *arise spontaneously* in the context of meaning-focused communication. This distinction has outlined a new line of inquiry that has explored the best way(s) of drawing learners' attention to form in the context of meaning-focused communication and its effects on language learning. The instruction may be *intensive*, targeting a specific language feature or set of features, or it may be *extensive*, addressing a range of problem areas as they arise. The instruction may also vary along a continuum of *explicit* to *implicit* techniques and may involve preplanned or spontaneous (incidental) attention to language.

The concept of FFI has always been understood in such broad terms. Spada (1997) and R. Ellis (2001, 2002), for example, used the term FFI to refer to any instructional strategies that attempt to draw learners' attention to form. Such strategies can occur in a variety of forms, which can differ from one another in a number of important ways. For example, they can occur both implicitly and explicitly, reactively (such as through various forms of interactional and corrective feedback in response to learner errors) or proactively in a predetermined manner, deductively or inductively, integratively or separately, and also through various forms of input, output, and consciousness-raising tasks designed to draw learner attention to specific target features (see Nassaji & Fotos, 2011). The notion of *form* was also expanded to include not only grammatical or syntactic forms but also vocabulary, pronunciation, and pragmatics. Furthermore, the theoretical perspectives underlying instructional studies shifted from a purely cognitive one to those that incorporated more social, cultural, and sociocultural perspectives.

Spada and Lightbown (2008) distinguish between isolated and integrated FFI. Isolated FFI is the provision of instruction in lessons whose primary purpose is to teach students about a particular language feature because the teacher believes that students are unlikely to acquire the feature during communicative activities without an opportunity to learn about the feature in a situation where its form and meaning can be made clear. From the teacher's perspective, isolated FFI always implies intentional learning and explicit instruction. However, classroom observation research shows that even in traditional classrooms in which grammar lessons are based on a structural syllabus, students are not always sure of the teacher's intended focus (Slimani, 1992). That is, the explicitness and intentionality that the teacher has in mind may not be recognized by the students.

Integrated FFI occurs in classroom activities during which the primary focus remains on meaning, but in which feedback or brief explanations are offered to help students express meaning more effectively or more accurately within the communicative interaction. Some writers seem to assume that drawing learners' attention to form during meaning-based activities always involves implicit feedback and incidental learning, but that is not necessarily the case. Again, the perceptions of teachers and learners may be different. Adult learners sometimes show that they interpret the teacher's implicit feedback (e.g., in the form of recasts) as explicit guidance, creating an opportunity for intentional language learning (e.g., Ohta, 2000; Ellis et al., 2001). However, even when they recognize the teacher's implicit feedback as relevant to language form, learners may not correctly identify the object of the teacher's attention (see Mackey et al., 2000, for a related study). Both isolated and integrated FFI can include explicit feedback on error, metalinguistic terminology, the statement of rules, and explanations.

Form-Focused Instruction and L2 Performance

In characterizing the connection between form-focused instruction and L2 task performance, two main issues have been examined: the effects of form-focused instruction on the development of explicit knowledge including metalanguage, and whether L2 learners *really* apply explicit linguistic knowledge while performing L2 tasks.

Although it is widely held that FFI develops explicit knowledge of grammar rules (Norris & Ortega, 2000; Spada, 2011; Spada & Tomita, 2010), studies have reported mixed effects on grammatical forms with variable inherent linguistic characteristics. Xu and Lyster (2014) studied the differential effects of FFI on the development of metalinguistic knowledge of three morpho-syntactic forms (noun plural, regular and irregular past tense, and third-person singular) in oral production by Chinese-speaking learners of English. These three structures show variable complexity and regularity. The study operationalized complexity in a hybrid manner that included semantic complexity, frequency, and syntactic category, arguably due to the lack of consensus in how to conceptualize this construct. According to this operationalization, the third-person singular was considered to be more complex than the noun plural. The study compared the performances of a control group and an experimental group, both in a pretest/posttest design. Metalinguistic explicit knowledge was operationalized in terms of the participants' ability to provide the rules and to correct errors in the target forms. Results showed that FFI had facilitative effects that varied according to the complexity and regularity of the target forms; participants were more successful in using and explaining regular forms (regular past) as opposed to irregular ones (irregular past) and more complex morpho-syntactic forms (third-person singular) as opposed to less complex ones (noun plural).

Serrano (2011) explored the effect of metalinguistic instruction on the development of Spanish-speaking learners' metalinguistic knowledge of less complex forms (English possessive determiners, *his* and *her*), and whether it correlated with overall performance in error correction and oral production tasks. Two groups, identified as the rule group and the comparison group, were contrasted. The rule group received metalinguistic instruction in which the participants were explicitly taught the rule in English and established comparisons between the rule in English and the rule in Spanish/Catalan. The materials used in the treatment consisted of cloze passages provided with pictures, which the participants had to complete using the determiners *his* and *her*. They also included a picture description task that elicited the target forms. The comparison group did not receive such instruction. Metalinguistic knowledge was operationalized in terms of the participants' ability to correct errors in the target forms and to provide meta-comments while correcting these errors. Using a pretest/posttest design, the study concluded that metalinguistic instruction had a slightly positive effect on the development of metalinguistic knowledge of the target forms. It also reported positive correlations between the participants' metalinguistic knowledge in the rule group and their overall task performance.

Other studies reported explicit gains for FFI, only with less complex structures. Robinson (1996) investigated the effects of explicit instruction on the development of metalinguistic knowledge of two grammatical rules: pseudo-clefts of location (more complex rule) and subject–verb inversion (less complex rule). Complexity in this study was conceptualized from a pedagogical perspective that operationalized complexity in terms of difficulty as perceived by language learners. Difficult forms were considered to be more complex than easy forms. The study concluded that FFI was more effective for subject–verb inversion. Similarly, Williams and

Evans (1998) compared the effects of FFI and input flooding on the development of metalinguistic knowledge of participial adjectives (less complex rule) and passive constructions (more complex rule). Results demonstrated that FFI was more effective for participial adjectives. They concluded that the formally simple and easy rules benefited more from FFI.

The second line of inquiry has examined the extent to which L2 learners employ metalinguistic knowledge while performing different L2 tasks. Renou (2001) investigated the extent to which the relationship between metalinguistic awareness and L2 proficiency varied according to the learning approach and the task demands, whether written or oral. The study compared the performances of a grammar group and a communicative group on written and oral grammaticality judgment tasks and on an L2 proficiency test. It couched its theoretical framework in Bialystok and Ryan's model (1985) that proposed that different language tasks involve different levels of analyzed knowledge and control. Written grammaticality judgment tasks that require error correction and justification impose greater demands on analyzed knowledge. Oral grammaticality judgment tasks, on the other hand, require executive control since there is greater focus on meaning while making the judgment. The study reported a significant relation between written and oral grammaticality judgment tests and L2 proficiency for the entire sample. However, when the subjects were divided into groups, the correlation was no longer significant for the communicative group. Furthermore, the study found significant differences in metalinguistic judgment depending on whether the item was presented in the written or in the oral mode. These results were interpreted as support for Bialystok and Ryan's (1985) model.

Gutiérrez (2013) studied the relationship between metalinguistic knowledge (knowledge of grammatical rules) and metalingual knowledge (knowledge of grammatical terms) and L2 proficiency in Spanish as measured by an oral and a written task. Using an untimed metalinguistic test that consisted of 16 sentences with underlined errors in determiner-noun agreement, L2 learners were required to verbalize the rules and explain them using technical terms. The study found that the participants were not able to verbalize adequate rules about the target structure. Furthermore, no correlation between measures of metalinguistic knowledge and metalingual knowledge and scores of oral proficiencies was found. However, a strong positive correlation was found between these two types of knowledge and scores of written proficiency tests.

Another study is particularly relevant because it employed verbal protocol analysis. Roehr (2006) used stimulated verbal protocol analysis to examine how English-speaking learners of German use their metalinguistic knowledge of adjectival inflection during a form-focused task. The author operationalized metalinguistic knowledge in terms of the learners' explanation of the syntactic categories as well as the relations between them. The task first asked ten participants to complete a multiple-choice activity focusing on German adjectival inflection. Then, in semi-structured interviews using stimulated protocol analysis, the researchers sought to identify the participants' thought processes as they made their decisions during the task. Results of the study demonstrated that L2 learners reported using metalinguistic knowledge at different levels of complexity. Success and consistency in item resolution in the multiple-choice task was related to the reported use of metalinguistic knowledge.

Scoping Studies in Implicit and Explicit Instruction

As briefly mentioned, differences of opinion persist about the role of implicit and explicit instruction in the development of implicit and explicit knowledge. To offer a scoping view, four meta-analyses have grouped many of these different instructional interventions into two types of instruction: explicit options and implicit options (Kang et al., 2018; Goo et al., 2015; Norris & Ortega, 2000; Spada & Tomita, 2010). In these scoping studies, an instructional treatment, following Norris and Ortega (2000), was coded *explicit* if rule explanation formed part of the instruction (deductive instruction) or if participants' attention was drawn to specific target items in the L2 input and they were requested to arrive at some metalinguistic rule on their own (explicit inductive instruction). *Implicit* instruction represented the absence of any rule explanation or any request to arrive at the underlying rule. The results of three of these meta-analyses (Goo et al., Norris & Ortega, and Spada & Tomita) came in support of the use of explicit instruction over implicit instruction: all reported larger effect sizes obtained by explicit over implicit instruction on the immediate posttest. On the other hand, a more recent meta-analysis (Kang et al.) reported relatively similar effect sizes on the immediate posttest but larger effect sizes for implicit instruction on the delayed posttest when compared to explicit instruction. Work by Reiders and R. Ellis (2009) gives support to these conclusions, particularly with difficult features (see Chapter 6 in this book for more details).

Summary and Contributions of this Book

In this chapter, the definition and scope of ISLA were overviewed in some detail. Focus was given to the connections between forms of instruction and the development of explicit and implicit knowledge. There are some controversies that continue to generate discussions. Less investigated in the literature is the examination of how L2 learners develop linguistic knowledge of grammatical forms with *variable* degrees of complexity (see Hu, 2002; Xu & Lyster, 2014). This book considers this issue by focusing on grammatical aspects that vary in terms of difficulty, which are agreement symmetries and asymmetries in L2 Arabic. More specifically, it examines the development of explicit and implicit knowledge in asymmetries that vary in feature mismatch. It is imperative to consider to what degree the inherent characteristics of the target features modulate the effectiveness of implicit or explicit instructional conditions. Some features may benefit more from certain learning conditions than others.

In addition, while it may be argued that, in the explicit instructional conditions, some degree of explicit learning would have taken place, what may account for the superiority of the implicit instructional intervention reported in some studies is not clear. For example, it is not known whether the explicit conditions that resulted in a more robust explicit knowledge became automatized over time and became implicit knowledge. Also, it is still likely that in implicit instruction studies, the participants were investing more cognitive effort during the instructional phase. This explanation may be supported by the gains reported in implicit learning conditions that included the provision of salient feedback, which may, in turn, have promoted deeper processing of the target L2 (e.g., Morgan-Short & Bowden, 2006; Rassaei, 2014). The book considers these possibilities in the interventions by juxtaposing a measure of explicit and implicit knowledge in each chapter. This allows for the examination of these aforementioned issues empirically.

Also, as Leow (2018) explains, ISLA researchers are urged to probe deeper into the broader picture in which the ISLA context lies, that is, within (1) the language curriculum, (2) the type of learning (explicit) that does take place in this context and should be promoted in the instructed setting, and (3) the curricular value of pedagogical implications, ideally robust, for the instructed L2 environment. A strong ISLA research agenda to inform practice, according to Leow (2018), "may be to continue probing deeper into different modalities, different instructional interventions, types of tasks, *linguistic* items, and language levels" (p. 487). This book addresses this call by employing written and oral tasks, diverse measures of implicit and explicit knowledge, and recruiting participants at two different proficiency levels. Importantly, in the field of Arabic second language acquisition research, the exploration of these issues in the contexts of agreement asymmetries remains almost entirely unexplored, as the next chapters will show.

3 Instructed Second Language Acquisition of Noun–Adjective Agreement Asymmetry

Input-Based Exposure and Output-Based Present-Produce-Practice

Introduction

Noun–Adjective Agreement Asymmetries in Arabic

The target structure in this chapter is gender disagreement between the head noun and attributive adjective within the noun phrase. The examples in (1)–(4), restated from Chapter 2, show that for singular nouns, human and nonhuman respectively, the Arabic attributive adjective agrees fully with the head noun in terms of four features: gender, number, case, and definiteness.

(1)	*muhandis-(u)-(n)* engineer.s.m-(nom)-(indef) "an Egyptian male engineer"	*miṣri-(u)-(n)* Egyptian.s.m-(nom)-(indef)
(2)	*muhandis-a{t}-(u)-(n)* engineer.s.f-(nom)-(indef) "an Egyptian female teacher"	*miṣriy-a{t}-(u)-(n)* Egyptian.s.f-(nom)-(indef)
(3)	*kitaab-(u)-(n)* book.s.m-(nom)-(indef) "a new book"	*jadiid-(u)-(n)* new.m.s.-(nom)-(indef)
(4)	*qiṣaa{t}-(u)-(n)* story.m.f-(nom)-(indef) "a new story"	*jadiid-a{t}-(u)-(n)* new-s.f-(nom)-(indef)

These examples show the working definition of agreement as a process in which one element controls another. In (1) and (2), an indefinite singular masculine noun in the nominative case takes an indefinite singular masculine with the same case retained. In a similar vein, in (3) and (4), indefinite singular feminine nouns are assigned singular feminine adjectives with the same case retained. This also applies to dual nouns in the examples in (5)–(8):

DOI: 10.4324/9781003055600-4

(5)	*muhandis-aan-(i)*	*miṣṣriyy-aan-(i)*
	engineer-d.m-(nom)	Egyptian-.d.m-(nom)
	"two Egyptian male engineers"	
(6)	*muhandisa-taan-(i)*	*miṣṣriyya-taan-(i)*
	engineer-d.f-(nom)	engineer-d.f-(nom)
	"two Egyptian female engineers"	
(7)	*kitab-aan-(i)*	*jadiid-aan-(i)*
	book-d.m-(nom)	new-d.m-(nom)
	"two new books"	
(8)	*qiṣat-aan-(i)*	*jadiida-taan-(i)*
	story-d.f-(nom)	new-d.f-(nom)
	"two new stories"	

Although the previous explanations show obvious examples of symmetries, adjective agreement with plural and nonhuman head nouns shows no corresponding pattern as illustrated in (9) and (10). That is, plural nonhuman nouns (masculine and feminine) are assigned a singular feminine adjective (see Belnap & Shabaneh, 1992). This phenomenon has traditionally been referred to as feminine singular agreement plural head nouns.

(9)	*kutub-(u)-(n)*	*jadiida{t}-(u)-(n)*
	book.p.m-(nom)-(indef)	new.s.f-(nom)-(indef)
	"new books"	
(10)	*qiṣṣaṣ-(u)-(n)*	*jadiida{t}-(u)-(n)*
	story.p.f-(nom)-(indef)	new.s.f-(nom)-(indef)
	"new stories"	

In (9), the head noun is nonhuman *plural* masculine (books), but the adjective is *singular* feminine. The same rule applies in (10), in which the feminine plural noun is assigned a singular feminine adjective. This shows disagreement between the noun and the adjective in terms of number *and* gender in (9), and number *only* in (10). This pattern of agreement has been referred to as "deflected," as opposed to "strict," agreement (Ferguson, 1989). Strict agreement means that the plural form targets co-occurrence with plural controllers. However, the grammatical genders of the target and controller in these examples are not the same in the case of feminine plurals.

Previous Findings in L2 Arabic

As I alluded to in the introduction of this book, research in L2 acquisition of Arabic morphosyntax in general is still in its infancy. Agreement asymmetries are absent in this research, although they are salient structural properties. Current research has focused exclusively on symmetries in noun–adjective agreement. It has reported persistent difficulties with Arabic grammatical gender. Mann (1992), for example, found that errors in gender agreement formed 85% of the L2 learners' witting errors. Yet only a few studies have been devoted to investigating this problem in Arabic. Two lines of research have been pursued to better explain these difficulties. The first has investigated at what stage symmetrical noun–adjective agreement emerges in the acquisition order of Arabic morphosyntax. The second has examined the effect of the L1 on the acquisition of some grammatical features of the L2 grammatical gender.

Studies in the first line of research, both longitudinal and cross-sectional, have compared learners' production of morphosyntax primarily to the predictions about the order of L2 acquisition of morphosyntax according to a proposed speech-processing hierarchy in Processability Theory (PT), as delineated by Pienemann (1998). This hierarchy entails three morpheme types: lexical, phrasal, and interphrasal/clausal. PT proposes that these are acquired in an implicational set order across four stages: (1) absence of any language-specific procedures (acquisition of separate new words); (2) development of category procedures (acquisition of grammatical categories such as nouns, adjectives, verbs, etc.); (3) development of phrasal procedures (acquisition of phrasal morphemes that denote features such as number and gender at the phrase level, as in noun–adjective agreement); and (4) development of sentence or interphrasal procedures (such as subject–verb agreement).

Nielsen (1997) compared the predictions of the PT, as outlined previously, with the acquisition order of two Danish-speaking learners of Arabic in a longitudinal study over a 15-month period. The study focused on agreement morphology in four structures: noun–adjective agreement, demonstrative–head noun agreement, iḍaafa [literally, addition or annexation] (all characterized as stage 3 constructions), and subject–verb agreement (characterized as a stage 4 construction). Analysis of data from three different oral tasks (interviews, role-plays, and presentations on different topics) showed that subject–verb agreement was acquired earlier than noun–adjective agreement by one of the two participants. The analysis also showed that neither learner seemed to acquire the agreement procedures within constituents (stage 3 structures) although they initiated the acquisition of agreement procedures between constituents (stage 4 structures). Nielsen (1997) concluded that other factors, such as first-language (L1) effects, need to be considered in charting out the acquisition order in Arabic.

Mansouri (2000) tested the PT claims in the acquisition order of four Australian English-speaking learners of Arabic. Two learners were at the beginning level and two were at the intermediate level. After collecting two data sample sets from each participant, Mansouri concluded that noun–adjective agreement emerged in the first data set and subject–verb agreement emerged in the second data set. This result was seemingly consistent with the predictions of the PT. Agreement features for first-person singular, third-person singular masculine, and third-person singular feminine emerged in the first data set. However, third-person plural agreement only emerged in the second data set. Mansouri's findings were considered inconclusive for two reasons: first, they were not based on reliable emergence criteria. Second, the data samples were collected from a very small number of participants.

The second notable line of research that seeks to explain difficulties in the acquisition of Arabic grammatical gender has characterized the potential role of the L1 in shaping the acquisition order in the Arabic morphosyntax of agreement, with focus on noun–adjective and subject–verb agreement. This line of inquiry was primarily conducted by Alhawary in a set of studies. In one study, Alhawary (2002) examined the role of L1 English effects in the acquisition of number (singular) and gender (masculine and feminine) in subject–verb agreement morphology: *ʔal-walad-(u)* (def-boy-(nom)) *ya-shrab(u)* (3ms-drink) [the boy drinks] and *ʔal-bint-(u)* (def-girl-(nom)) *ta-shrab(u)* (3fs-drink) [the girl drinks]; and noun–adjective (attributive) agreement: *ṭaalib-(un)* (student.sm-(nom)) *ṭawiil-(un)* (tall.ms-(nom)) [a tall male student] and *ṭaalib-at-(un)* (student-sf-(nom)) *ṭawiil-a-(tun)* (tall.sf-(nom)) [a tall female student]. Data drawn from oral interviews with eight participants (ten interviews each) that were conducted every two weeks throughout a school year to elicit semi-spontaneous production data showed two main patterns. First, the subjects tended to acquire subject–verb agreement earlier than noun–adjective agreement, although the latter was formally taught first in the Arabic classroom. Second, there was a more noticeable "backsliding" pattern with respect to the noun–adjective agreement compared to the subject–verb agreement (p. 236). The differential performance on the two structures was explained in terms of the L1 effects: whereas subject–verb agreement is congruent with agreement in English in which number is marked, noun–adjective agreement in Arabic differs from English (incongruent with English).

In another study, Alhawary (2003) tested the predictions of PT (Pienemann, 1998) in light of the Arabic SLA data reported in Alhawary (2002). According to PT phases of morphosyntactic development, noun–adjective agreement is expected to emerge earlier than subject–verb agreement in the acquisition order in Arabic. However, the longitudinal data in Alhawary (2002) exhibited the opposite pattern: subject–verb agreement emerged earlier in the order. Alhawary (2003) concluded that the Arabic production data offered counterevidence to the predictions of PT and posited that PT did not consider the potential effects of the L1 in constraining L2 development of morphosyntax.

Alhawary (2005) further addressed the role of L1 effects on the acquisition of subject–verb and noun–adjective agreement from three theoretical SLA perspectives: (1) the local impairment hypothesis, which claims permanent impairment in the acquisition of any L2 features system, irrespective of the L1; (2) the failed functional features hypothesis, which claims that the L2 system is constrained by the L1 features; and (3) the missing surface inflection hypothesis (MSIH), which claims only temporary impairment in the L2 morphological features system, irrespective of the L1. The MSIH further claims that overcoming this impairment is determined by learners' mapping of the L1–L2 features. The resulting study drew on cross-sectional data from English-speaking ($n = 27$) and French-speaking ($n = 26$) learners in three different classroom levels. Using picture description, picture differences, and picture sequencing tasks, the results overall showed that the French-speaking groups outperformed their English-speaking counterparts in the production of subject–verb and noun–adjective agreement markings in Arabic. This implied a greater role for the L1 in the acquisition of the L2 features system. More important, the study found that, regardless of their L1, the participants were able to acquire noun–adjective word order. These overall results were taken to support the MSIH (p. 302).

However, a more recent investigation of the effect of L1 transfer is Al-Amry's (2014) study. It examined the acquisition of the subject–verb gender agreement structure in Arabic by adult L2 learners who have different L1 backgrounds that vary in their gender system. The results of the study were contradictory to Alhawary's (2005, 2019) findings. No significant difference in acquiring the verbal gender agreement structure was found between learners who have a grammatical gender system in their L1 language and those who do not.

The Current Study

In summary, studies that examined noun–adjective agreement in Standard Arabic have focused mostly on the production of the symmetrical pattern. The goal was, *first*, to place subject–verb agreement in its respective stage in the acquisition order of Arabic morphosyntax; and *second*, to examine the role of L1 effects in shaping this order. The asymmetrical agreement type, however common in the system of Arabic when the noun is nonhuman plural, was not examined in these studies. As I fully explained in Chapter 2, a common observation in the ISLA literature is that incidental and intentional learning appears prominently in the domain of vocabulary and only occasionally appears in the area of grammar (Hulstijn, 2003). Also, it is not clear in this literature whether incidental exposure develops implicit and/or explicit knowledge of the target grammatical feature(s).

To advance knowledge about the acquisition of the morphosyntax of subject–verb agreement in L2 Arabic, the present chapter examines whether the asymmetrical pattern of agreement can be acquired incidentally when L2 learners are flooded with input enriched with instances of this asymmetry with no explicit instruction. It also compares learning gains in this case of asymmetry to the present–practice–produce techniques (Nassaji & Fotos, 2011; Shintani, 2013) in which a combination of explicit instruction and output-based practice are provided. Importantly, in the asymmetrical pattern of noun–adjective agreement, there is mismatch in terms of one feature (*number)* in case of feminine nonhuman plural (takes feminine singular marking) and mismatch in terms of two features (*number* and *gender*) in case of masculine nonhuman plural (takes feminine singular marking). One might predict that learners would perform better on the symmetrical type than on the asymmetrical one because the latter runs counter to the predominant symmetrical agreement system in Arabic in general. Also, they would encounter variable difficulties in the asymmetrical pattern based on mismatch (in terms of one feature or two). To address these related issues, feature mismatches are teased apart in the analysis and discussion.

Research Questions

Motivated by the gaps identified previously, this chapter seeks to answer these questions:

1. Are there differential gains between input-enhanced incidental exposure and output-based present–practice–produce in the development of implicit and explicit knowledge of noun–adjective agreement asymmetries in Standard Arabic by beginner English learners of Arabic?
2. Are there differential gains between input-enhanced incidental exposure and output-based present–practice–produce in the development of implicit and explicit knowledge of noun–adjective agreement asymmetries with differential degrees of feature mismatch?

Participants

A total of 75 beginning learners participated in this study. They were divided into three experimental groups: IE group ($n = 25$), PPP group ($n = 25$), and a control group ($n = 25$). At the beginning of testing, these L2 groups were three sections of elementary Arabic (Arabic 101) at two Arabic programs in two large public universities in the United States. Their biographic information is provided in Table 3.1.

These participants were at the end of their first semester of Arabic study and had been exposed to a total of about 65 contact hours of instruction (13 weeks, five hours a week). In their regular classrooms, the three experimental groups were taught by three different instructors who followed a handout prepared by the researcher. They were tested three times. The pretesting was completed two days before the intervention, and the posttesting was completed twice: immediately after the end of the intervention and ten days later.

At the time of testing, the three groups had covered the introductory part and completed five lessons from Part 1 (3rd edition) of the Al-Kitaab book series (Brustad et al., 2011). They also had been taught basic grammatical aspects of Standard Arabic that included gender marking (at the phrasal and inter-phrasal level), question formation, the definite article, subject pronouns, plural marking, noun phrase structure, possessive and demonstrative pronouns, superlatives, and present tense with common verb patterns in nominal and verbal sentences. Importantly, at the time of testing, only the symmetrical noun–adjective agreement pattern was presented and frequently consolidated. The learners were *minimally*

Table 3.1 Participant Demographic Data and Proficiency Ratings

Learner group	*Number*	*Age range/mean*	*Proficiency ratings*
Control	25 (10 males and 15 females)	18–21 (mean: 20.5)	1.5/6.0
IE	25 (12 males and 13 females)	18–21 (mean: 19.5)	1.5/6.0
PPP	25 (11 males and 14 females)	17–20 (mean: 18.5)	1.5/6.0

introduced to the asymmetrical pattern of agreement in the context of plural formation in lesson 2 in Part 1, and it had not been explicitly taught nor consolidated at any point in their instruction before the study was conducted.

Design and Procedure

Instruction took a full session of around 50 minutes in each intervention. Students were asked not to review the learning materials before they did the posttesting. The control group continued their regular classes with no instruction of the target grammatical feature. For consistency, they completed all testing following the same timeline of the two experimental groups. In total, the study took around three hours (pretest, treatment, and two posttests), and they were compensated for their participation from a research grant awarded to the researcher. Details of the materials used in the chapter are provided next.

Instructional Treatments

INPUT-BASED INCIDENTAL EXPOSURE

The first treatment group, the incidental exposure (IE), received extensive exposure to the target structure of this chapter (*actual* target), which is the noun–adjective agreement asymmetry, while the learners' attention was directed to another linguistic feature, which is subject–verb agreement symmetry in the present tense (*apparent* target). This structure was taught by input-based instruction that entailed the presentation of structured-input activities. In these activities, learner attention was directed to the subject–verb agreement; meanwhile, they were exposed to multiple instances of noun–adjective agreement asymmetries. Thus, where the learners were focused on the subject–verb agreement affixations (prefixes and suffixes), there was extensive exposure to noun–adjective agreement asymmetries. The italicized words in the following examples show the apparent target, whereas the underlined words show the actual target.

(10)	*fii*	*ʕamriika*	*ʔal-ṭulaab-(u)*	*yu-ḥibb-uu-na*	*jaamiʕat*	*harvard.*
	in	America	def-students.p.m-(nom)	3.p.m-like.imperf-indic	university	Harvard.

In America, students like Harvard University.

hiya	*fiihaa*	<u>*kuliyaat-(u)-(n)*</u>	<u>*kabiira{t}-(u)-(n).*</u>
it	has	college.p.f-(nom)-(indef)	big{t}-(u)-(n).

It has big colleges.

The IE instruction proceeded as follows. The students were first given explicit instruction of how subject–verb agreement works in the system of Arabic in the present tense. They were guided with clear examples to the affixation system highlighted in color on the board. They were also told that the system is considerably different from English, which does not have a rich inflectional system like Arabic does. This was demonstrated by the conjugation of the verb *daras* "study" with multiple pronouns. Also, the underpinnings of agreement in terms of the linguistic features of number and gender were fully explained.

Second, they worked at input activities that aimed to help them process subject–verb agreement in oral and written input, but did not require them at any time to engage in producing linguistic output with this feature. For example, in one activity they were given 25 statements about student life, family, and daily life, and were asked to indicate whether they agreed with each one or not, by checking the box whether the statement applies or does not apply to their life and study. An example is provided in the underlined sections below:

(11)	*naḥn(u)*	*nu-ḥibb-(u)*	*ʔal-lugha*	*ʔal-ʕarabiyya.*	
	we	1.p-like.imperf-indic	language	Arabic.	
	We love the Arabic language.				
	hiya	*fiiha*	*durus-(u)-(n)*	*sahla{t}-(u)-(n)*	*jiddan.*
	It	has	lesson.p.m-(nom)-(indef)	easy.s.f-(nom)-(indef)	very.
	It has very easy lessons.				
	Apply	______________	Do not Apply	______________	
(12)	*naḥn(u)*	*nu-ḥibb-(u)*	*ʔal-lugha*	*ʔal-ʔisbaaniyya.*	
	we	1.p-like.imperf-(indic)	language	Spanish.	
	We love the Spanish language.				
	hiya	*fiiha*	*durus-(u)-(n)*	*ṣaʕb-a{t}-(u)-(n)*	*jidan.*
	It	has	lesson.p.m-(nom)-(indef)	hard.s.f-(nom)-(indef)	very.
	It has very hard lessons.				
	Apply	______________	Do not Apply	______________	

Importantly, in each of these 25 statements, participants were exposed to sufficient instances of noun–adjective agreement asymmetries (underlined in the previous examples) in oral and written input with no opportunity to produce sentences containing it. They were also exposed to around 25 examples of aural input with the same pattern while completing the study activities. However, the total of examples of written and aural input *probably* underrepresents the amount of exposure that students received to this structure, as it does not include the other examples of the structure that arose as students listened to the teacher explaining, introducing, and giving feedback during the activities completed in class. In addition, an analysis of lesson materials the student studied, before the study was conducted, indicates that they were exposed to 17 examples of noun–adjective agreement asymmetries in the written form. This was mostly during their exposure to adjectives with sound and broken plural nonhuman nouns. In short, although the total exposure time was relatively short, the exposure to exemplars of the target structure was very plentiful. In this way, it was possible to investigate whether and to what extent acquisition of this asymmetrical pattern is driven by incidental exposure only.

OUTPUT-BASED PRESENT–PRACTICE–PRODUCE

The output-based PPP instruction proceeded as follows: first, the instructor started with modeling sentences that included frequent noun–adjective agreement asymmetries. The modelling part started with seven common statements, with each including an instance of the asymmetrical pattern (underlined) as in (13) in which the adjective *jamiila* "beautiful" (singular feminine) disagrees with the noun *mudun* "cities" (plural feminine):

	Transliteration	Translation
(13)	maʕa zamiil/zamiila: ʔana ʔuḥib wilaayat mishigan kathiiran. hiya fiiha <u>*mudun jamiila*</u> jiddan (madina wa-madina wa-madina: mudun). wa-ʔntun hal tuḥibuuna wilaayat mishigan kathiiran? hal fiiha <u>*mudun jamiila*</u>? mithla maadhaa?	With a classmate: I like the state of Michigan very much, it has very <u>*beautiful cities*</u> (a city, and a city and a city: plural cities). What about you: do you like the state of Michigan very much? Does it have <u>*beautiful cities*</u>? Such as what?

Second, being a form of output-based instruction, PPP contained explicit instruction in which the learners were made aware of the asymmetry included in the target noun–adjective structure. They were explicitly told that nonhuman plural nouns are always followed by singular feminine adjectives, regardless of gender (the rule applies to masculine and feminine). They were given examples of frequent noun–adjective phrases in which the feminine marker {a}was highlighted in contextualized sentences, as in (14):

(14)	ʔakhi yaskun fii wilaayat mishigan, wa-hiyaa fiiha <u>*jamiiʕaat kabiira*</u>. fii haadhii ʔal-wilaaya huwa yuhibu madiinat laansing. hiyaa fiiha *biyuut jamiila* wa-<u>*shawaariʕ waasiʕa.*</u>	My brother lives in the state of Michigan. It has <u>*big universities*</u>. In this state, he likes the city of Lansing. It has *nice homes* and <u>*wide streets.*</u>

Third, related to the second step, the students were given multiple instances of nonhuman plurals (sound and broken types) along with multiple adjectives (13 of them) in the feminine form that go with them. This was meant to consolidate the asymmetry entailed, as in (15) and (16):

(15)	wilaaya wa-wilaaya: wilaayaat. <u>*wilaayaat ʔamriikiyya*</u>, *wilaayaat kaabiira*, *wilaayaat ṣaghiira*, *wilaayaat ghaaliya*	a state and a state and a state: states. <u>*American states*</u>, <u>*big states*</u>, <u>*small states*</u>, <u>*expensive states*</u>
(16)	kitaab, wa-kitaab, wa-kitaab: kutub, <u>*kutub jadiida*</u>, *kutub qadiima.*	a book and a book and a book, <u>*new books*</u>, <u>*old books.*</u>

After that, controlled production of the target grammar structure was initiated. The learners were specifically asked to engage in groups in two sentence-combination activities in which they were given two sentences to combine using a noun–adjective sequence that has the symmetrical pattern of agreement. In one of these, they were asked to describe their city and university in a short paragraph using as many adjectives as they can. They were given singular nouns and masculine adjectives that they were to reformulate to come up with the sentences. Finally, they had the opportunity to engage in activities that involve freer production of the target structure. This was in the form of a task in which they compared living in a small city to living in a big city. They were asked to state which one they liked and explain the reasons. They were asked to record their response and upload it to a folder. They were asked not to read any notes or prepare anything in advance, but they were also requested to be as communicative as possible in their recordings.

This procedure helps promote balance between form and meaning. The explicit instruction part consolidated the specific predetermined linguistic form. At the same time, the production part pushed the learners to practice the targeted form while being engaged in meaning-focused interaction (Foster, 2009; Shintani, 2013).

Measures of Instructional Outcomes

Participants completed three tests in each of the three testing episodes (pretest, immediate posttest, delayed posttest): multiple-choice and grammaticality-judgment (tested for explicit knowledge) and elicitation test (tested for implicit knowledge). These tests and the theoretical rationale that has informed their design have been described in Chapter 2 of this book. Specific details of each test are provided next.

Multiple-Choice Test

The multiple-choice test included 45 high-frequency items that were equally distributed into two categories: (a) 15 items that targeted the asymmetrical pattern of noun–adjective agreement; (b) 15 items that included the symmetrical pattern; and (c) 15 irrelevant items. In each item, the participants were asked to choose the correct item that fills out the gap in contextualized sentences. A sample item for each category (symmetrical and asymmetrical) is provided in (17) and (18):

(17) *ʔanaa lii ʔaṣḥaab* __________ *min madinat ʔal-qahiraa.*

(a) miṣrii	*(b) miṣriyaat*	*(c) miṣriyya*	*(d) miṣriyuun*
Egyptian.s.m	Egyptian.p.f	Egyptian.s.f	Egyptian.p.m

I have Egyptian male friends from Cairo.

(18) *hal ʕindaka ʔakhbaar* __________ *ʔal-yawm?*

(a) mumtaaz	*(b) mumtaaz-a*	*(c) mumtaaz-uun*	*(d) mumtaaz-aat*
excellent.s.m	excellent.s.f	excellent.p.m	excellent.p.m

Do you have excellent news today?

For each one of these items, a correct choice was given a value of 0.0 and the correct one was given 1. Scores of the test were calculated and presented as percentages.

Grammaticality-Judgment Test

The grammaticality-judgment test consisted of 45 sentences. A total of 30 sentences created an obligatory context for use of a noun–adjective combination. In 15 sentences, the asymmetrical noun–adjective agreement was grammatically correct. The remaining 15 sentences were ungrammatical with respect to the adjective form. That is, the symmetrical adjective form was provided instead of the asymmetrical one. In addition, a total of 15 sentences created a context for something else (filler items). Wherever possible, the target structure was not placed initially in the sentence to avoid drawing learner attention to it. Examples of the asymmetrical and symmetrical categories are provided in (19)–(21):

(19) *madiinat niyuu yuurk madiina jamiila jiddan. haadhihi ʔal-madiina fiiha binaayaat ʕaalii jiddan fii kul makan. [Ungrammatical]*
(a) Grammatical ____________ (b) Ungrammatical ____________
New York City is a very beautiful city. This city has high buildings everywhere.

(20) *ḥabiibati layst saʕiida. hiyaa ʕindaha ṣufuuf ṣaʕba jiddan [Grammatical]*
(a) Grammatical ____________ (b) Ungrammatical ____________
My darling is not happy. She has difficult lessons.

(21) *naḥnu nuḥibu haadhihi ʔal-minṭaqa kathiiran liʔana fiiha ṭullaab miṣriyuuun min ʔal-qaahira. [Grammatical]*
(a) Grammatical ____________ (b) Ungrammatical ____________
We like this area very much because it has Egyptian (male) students from Cairo.

The test was developed and administered in a paper–pencil format, and the participants were told not to review previous test items. Test-takers were asked to indicate by checking the relevant box whether each sentence was grammatical or ungrammatical. Once again, one version of the test was used over all three testing sessions but with a different order of presentation of items for each test administration. For each one of these items, a correct judgment was given a value of 0 and the correct one was given 1. Scores of the test were calculated and presented as percentages.

Elicitation Test

The three groups were given a narrative task, Facebook (FB) friend task, in which they were told that one of their FB friends in Egypt wanted to know some information about them: the state where they live and the university where they study. They were asked to record a message in Standard Arabic in which they gave as much information divided into segments as they could. They were asked to write the message that they recorded to double check the morphosyntactic features they meant in the recording. The task was promoted with a visual component that triggered the use of nonhuman plurals with accompanying adjectives. The participants were expected to use noun–adjective constructions in their narrative. They were also told to write accurately to check whether they produced the feminine marker {a} when needed. For each one of these items, an incorrect response was given a value of 0 and the correct one was given 1. Scores of the test were calculated and presented as percentages.

Results

Answer to the First Research Question: Differential Effects on the Development of Explicit Knowledge

Results of Choice Test

In the forced choice task, participants were asked to choose the single correct form of the adjective after considering four options that modulated agreement symmetries and asymmetries. Descriptive statistics for the forced choice are presented in Table 3.2.

Obviously, as shown in Table 3.2, across the three learner groups, the mean scores of the symmetrical pattern were relatively high, including the control group. This is an expected pattern since they were taught the symmetrical pattern before the study was conducted. The asymmetrical-pattern pretest scores, on the other hand, were relatively low for the three groups. A sample of these responses by one participant in the IE group is provided in (22):

Table 3.2 Descriptive Statistics of the Choice Test

	Symmetrical pattern					
	Pretest		*Posttest1*		*Posttest2*	
	%	*SD*	*%*	*SD*	*%*	*SD*
Control	78.50	13.00	72.20	16.00	75.50	16.00
IE	75.40	09.00	93.30	14.00	91.20	14.00
PPP	82.10	10.00	88.50	18.00	85.20	12.00
	Asymmetrical pattern					
	Pretest		*Posttest1*		*Posttest2*	
	%	*SD*	*%*	*SD*	*%*	*SD*
Control	19.60	20.91	20.20	20.18	21.00	19.94
IE	12.80	23.89	23.60	27.36	33.80	18.94
PPP	32.43	8.47	72.60	09.58	74.77	18.66

(22)

هل عندك صُوَر pictures __________ للعائلة؟

(أ) قديمون (ب) قديم (ج) قديمة (د) قديمات

هل عندك طاولات tables __________ في البيت؟

(أ) كبير (ب) كبيرة (ج) كبيرات (د) كبيران

Also, the two posttests for the IE and the PPP groups showed strikingly variable degrees of gains, with the PPP group scoring higher. Samples of the PPP responses by one participant from the pretest and posttest1 are provided in (23):

(23)

Pretest

أنا عندي صُفُوف classes __________.

(أ) كبير (ب) كبيرون (ج) كبيرات (د) كبيرة

هل هناك كُليات colleges __________ عة ميشجان؟

(أ) جيدة (ب) جيدات (ج) جيدون (د) جيد

أنا عندي كُتب books __________.

(أ) جديد (ب) جديدة (ج) جديدات (د) جديدون

هل عندك صُوَر pictures __________ للعائلة؟

(أ) قديمون (ب) قديم) (ج) قديمة (د) قديمات

هل عندك طاولات tables __________ في البيت؟

(أ) كبير (ب) كبيرة (ج) كبيرات (د) كبيران

هل هناك بنايات buildings __________ في مدينة ديترويت؟

(أ) كبيرة (ب) كبير (ج) كبيرات (د) كبيران

هل عندك دُرُوس lessons __________ في اللغة العربية؟

(أ) سهلة (ب) سهل (ج) سهلات (د) سهلان

هل في جامعة ميشجان مَكْتَبات libraries __________؟

(أ) كبير (ب) كبيرة (ج) كبيرات (د) كبيران

Post-tes1

أنا عندي صُفُوف classes __________.

(أ) كبير (ب) كبيرون (ج) كبيرات (د) كبيرة

هل هناك كُليات colleges __________ في جامعة ميشجان؟

(أ) جيدة (ب) جيدات (ج) جيدون (د) جيد

أنا عندي كُتب books ___________.

(أ) جديد (ب) جديدة (ج) جديدات (د) جديدون

هل عندك صُوَر pictures ___________ للعائلة؟

(أ) قديمون (ب) قديم (ج) قديمة (د) قديمات

هل عندك طاوِلات tables ___________ في البيت؟

(أ) كبير (ب) كبيرة (ج) كبيرات (د) كبيران

هل هناك بِنايات buildings ___________ في مدينة ديترويت؟

(أ) كبيرة (ب) كبير (ج) كبيرات (د) كبيران

هل عندك دُرُوس lessons ___________ في اللغة العربية؟

(أ) سهلة (ب) سهل (ج) سهلات (د) سهلان

هل في جامعة ميشجان مَكْتَبات libraries ___________؟

(أ) كبير (ب) كبيرة (ج) كبيرات (د) كبيران

With a close look at the participant pretest responses, it was clear that adjectives with symmetrical agreement were more likely to be chosen, compared to ones with the asymmetrical one, regardless of whether the noun required either. To evaluate the results for statistical significance in the asymmetrical condition, the participants' accuracy scores were submitted to a series of mixed-model ANOVAs (3 X 3) with group (control, IE, PPP) as a between-subject independent variable, test time (pretest, posttest1, and posttest 2) as a within-subject independent variable, and accuracy score as a dependent variable. The ANOVA results (alpha = .05) showed a statistically significant mean effect for group: $F(2, 72) = 43.379$, $p < .001$, $\eta p^2 = .546$. Also, there was a statistically significant mean effect for test time: $F(1.72, 124.24) = 64.263$, $p < .001$, $\eta p^2 = .472$ and for the interaction between test time and group: $F(3.45, 124.24) = 23.7990$, $p < .001$, $\eta p^2 = .398$.

Pairwise comparisons using post hoc tests were run to determine specifically which group differed significantly in the posttests. They showed that there was no difference between the IE and the control group on posttest1 ($p = .557$) and a marginal difference on posttest2 ($p = .021$). They also showed that there was a robust, significant difference between the IE and the PPP groups for posttest1 and posttest2 ($p < .001$ for both). These results support the conclusion that the PPP had a higher maintained gain over a ten-day period. However, as shown by the low-accuracy scores in the IE condition, it seems very likely that extensive exposure alone did not result in substantial learning gains, in this case of agreement asymmetry.

It is worth mentioning that the IE group made some gains that are statistically significant. The post hoc tests showed a significant within-group difference between their accuracy scores on the pretest (12.80%) and posttest1 and posttest2 (23.60% and 33.80% respectively: $p < .001$ for both tests). These results support the conclusion that extensive exposure can result in *some* degree of learning, but it was not comparable to that obtained in the PPP condition.

Results of Grammaticality-Judgment Test

As illustrated in Table 3.3, the results of the pretest in the judgment tests showed overall that, for the symmetrical condition, there was a tendency to opt for accurate response whether "grammatical" or "ungrammatical" across the three groups. This is expected performance that confirms that they acquired this pattern of agreement. A sample of responses is provided in (24) by a participant in the EI group:

(24)

أنا عندي أصحاب من مدينة بغداد، عندي أصحاب عراقيات.

Grammatical .... <u>Ungrammatical</u> ....

In contrast, the participants were significantly more likely to make the wrong judgment across the three groups between "grammatical" or "ungrammatical" in the asymmetrical condition. As expected, this result suggests that this pattern of agreement is harder to acquire than the symmetrical one. A sample of responses is provided in (25) by a participant in the PPP group:

(25)

بيتي جميل جدا، هذا البيت فيه طاولات كبيرة في كل غرفة.

Grammatical .... <u>Ungrammatical</u> ....

صاحبيتي ساره طالبة ممتازة جدا، هي تتكلم لُغات كثيرات جدا.

Grammatical .... Ungrammatical ....

Table 3.3 Descriptive Statistics of the Grammaticality-Judgment Test

	Symmetrical pattern—total					
	Pretest		*Posttest1*		*Posttest2*	
	%	*SD*	*%*	*SD*	*%*	*SD*
Control	90.40	18.00	92.00	13.00	82.00	10.00
IE	83.20	15.00	88.00	20.00	75.00	15.00
PPP	87.00	10.50	90.00	10.00	81.00	10.00
	Symmetrical pattern—ungrammatical					
	Pretest		*Posttest1*		*Posttest2*	
	%	*SD*	*%*	*SD*	*%*	*SD*
Control	77.50	18.00	88.15	13.00	75.00	10.00
IE	78.30	15.00	78.20	20.00	70.20	15.00
PPP	74.20	10.50	85.65	10.00	80.30	10.00

Table 3.3 (Continued)

	Asymmetrical pattern—total					
	Pretest		*Posttest1*		*Posttest2*	
	%	*SD*	%	*SD*	%	*SD*
Control	18.60	21.53	24.20	20.13	19.40	19.96
IE	22.20	21.16	30.16	19.45	34.40	18.89
PPP	23.60	27.36	78.68	20.63	72.50	17.75
	Asymmetrical pattern—ungrammatical					
	Pretest		*Posttest1*		*Posttest2*	
	%	*SD*	%	*SD*	%	*SD*
Control	15.60	12.93	19.00	19.84	19.80	19.65
IE	27.80	19.89	29.76	19.56	33.80	18.45
PPP	23.60	27.36	78.17	20.75	74.77	18.66

The accuracy scores for the three groups in the asymmetrical condition were analyzed separately to know the effect of the intervention on the accuracy to opt for the correct judgment, whether "Grammatical" or "Ungrammatical." In consistence with standard practice in the analysis of GJ tests (Ellis et al., 2009), for each test, two scores were differentiated: total scores and ungrammatical scores. For the total scores, the ANOVA results showed a statistically mean effect for group: F (2, 72) = 30.108, $p < .001$, $\eta p^2 = .807$. Also, there was a statistically mean effect for test time: F (1.52, 110.076) = 69.41, $p < .001$, $\eta p^2 = .491$ and a statistically mean effect for the interaction between test time and group: F (3.05, 110.076) = 34.98, $p < .001$, $\eta p^2 = .493$. Pairwise comparisons using the post hoc Tukey's HSD showed that there was no difference between the IE and the control group on posttest1 (p = .298) nor on posttest2 (p = .455), but there was a significant difference between the EI and the PPP groups on posttest1 and posttest2 (p < .001 for both tests).

The ungrammatical scores of the GJ test reflected the same pattern: a repeated measures ANOVA found a statistically significant effect for group: F (2, 72) = 37.449, $p = .002$, $\eta p^2 = .821$ and a similar effect for test time F (1.16, 83.64) = 61.72., $p < .003$, $\eta p^2 = .462$ with interaction between group and test time F (2.32, 83.64) = 40.76, $p < .000$, $\eta p^2 = .531$. Pairwise comparisons showed that there was no difference between the EI and the control group on posttest1 (p = .062) nor on posttest2 (p = .181). They showed that there was a significant difference between the EI and the PPP groups for posttest1 and posttest2 ($p < .001$ for both tests). These findings support the conclusion that the EI treatment did not result in comparable substantial improvement in making accurate judgments in asymmetrical patterns. This result is corroborated by the lack of difference between the control group and the EI group. Echoing the result of the choice test, the PPP has a higher influence than EI for both posttest1 and posttest2.

Table 3.4 Descriptive Statistics for Elicitation Test

	Asymmetrical pattern					
	Pretest		*Posttest1*		*Posttest2*	
	M	*SD*	*M*	*SD*	*M*	*SD*
Control	19.60	20.91	19.00	20.46	17.40	21.12
IE	23.00	22.82	29.76	19.56	31.00	18.76
PPP	24.40	26.78	73.46	19.79	52.88	33.79

Differential Effects on the Development of Implicit Knowledge

Results of Elicitation Test

In this task, the participants were expected to produce in speaking, then in writing, the asymmetrical pattern of agreement, as promoted with a visual component. Their mean scores are presented in Table 3.4.

There was some variation among the participants, as shown by the standard deviation, but the participants in each group provided sufficient tokens. As anticipated, the participants' accuracy scores in the asymmetrical condition in the pretest were strikingly low, as seen in Table 3.4. Representative samples from elicited responses by four participants in the PPP group are provided in (26)–(29):

(26) waalidati tuḥib ʔal-wilaaya min mishigan. It has binayaat jamilaat wa-tayilaat.

(27) ṣaaḥibii yuḥibb ʔal-jaamiya wilaayit mishigan. fiiha maktabaat jmilaat wa-mumtazaat.

(28) ṣaaḥiba tuḥib ʔal-madiina. fiiha bunuuk kabiir.

(29) waalidi yuḥibb ʔal-wilaaya mishigan. hunaaka madinaat jamilaat.

Two main patterns of responses are notable in these samples. The first was the provision of full agreement on the adjectives to agree in number and gender with the plural nouns (samples in (26), (27), and (29)). The second, and it was less ubiquitous, was to use the masculine singular form of the adjective (sample in (28)). Importantly, as shown by the accuracy scores of the posttests in the table, only the PPP group made significant gains across time. The sample of elicited responses in (30)–(33) are by four participants in the PPP group from posttest1. Obviously, the learners were able to produce the asymmetrical pattern of agreement, marking the adjectives only in the feminine singular form.

(30) baba yuḥibb wilaayat Michigan. ladiiha mudun jamiilah.

(31) ṣaaḥibii laa yuḥibb jaamiʕat wilayat Michigan. ʔaḥyaanan ʕindanaa ʔimtihanaat ṣaʕba. fii MSU, ʔadrus kalimaat jaddida fii ʔal-faṣl ʔal-ʕarabii kula yawm.

(32) fii Lansing fii Michigan, ʕaaʔilatii ʕanduun <u>*sayaraat jamiila.*</u>

(33) ṣaaḥibii yuḥibb jaamiʕat wilayat Michigan. hunaaka <u>*maktabaat jamiila wa-jiidda*</u>. Classmate yuḥibb Lansing, hunaaka <u>*ʔal-shawaariʔ ʔal-waasiʔa*</u>.

The ANOVA showed a statistically significant mean effect for group: F (2, 72) = 219.3416, $p < .000$, $\eta p^2 = .340$. Also, there was a statistically significant mean effect for test time: F (1.96, 122.34) = 24.23, $p < .000$, $\eta p^2 = .252$ and a significant interaction between test time and group: F (3.39, 122.34) = 17.20, $p < .000$, $\eta p^2 = .323$. Pairwise comparisons yielded no difference between the EI and the control group on posttest1 ($p = .060$) or posttest 2 ($p = .063$). However, they returned a robust significant difference between the IE and PPP groups for posttest1 and posttest2 ($p < .000$ for both posttests).

Answer to the Second Research Question: Differential Gains in Differential Feature Mismatch

I now turn to the question of whether there are differential gains between input-enhanced incidental exposure and output-based present–practice–produce in the development of implicit and explicit knowledge of noun–adjective agreement asymmetries with differential degrees of feature mismatch. To address this question, accuracy scores in the pretest and posttest1 in the three tests were subcategorized into disagreement in one feature (number in case of nonhuman feminine plurals with singular feminine adjectives) and disagreement in two (number and gender as in case of nonhuman masculine plural that takes singular feminine adjectives). The total means in each were calculated. The results are reported in Table 3.5.

The general pattern in Table 3.5 is that there is no real difference between two subcategories of agreement asymmetries in the pretests for the three groups (control: $p = .887$; EI: $p = .421$; PPP: $p = .645$). This suggests that beginner L2 learners of Arabic do not actually approach these asymmetries in terms of whether disagreement is one feature or two. They seem to generalize that all nonhuman plurals, regardless of their gender, are assigned singular feminine agreement. The posttest1 offered a corresponding pattern with similar scores in asymmetries with one or two features for the two groups of (control: $p = 1.000$; IE: p = .227), but a significant one for the PPP ($p = .002$).

Table 3.5 Differential Feature Mismatch Across Three Tests

	Pretest				*Posttest1*			
	1 Feature		*2 Features*		*1 Feature*		*2 Features*	
	M	*SD*	*M*	*SD*	*M*	*SD*	*M*	*SD*
Control	17.60	14.22	17.60	14.22	19.60	11.80	19.60	19.60
IE	15.60	12.93	15.60	12.94	15.600	12.93	19.00	19.00
PPP	29.72	06.48	29.73	06.48	77.200	09.25	67.40	07.40

Table 3.6 Differential Feature Mismatch Across Three Tests for the PPP Group

1 Feature			*2 Features*		
Tokens	*Pretest (%)*	*Posttest 1 (%)*	*Tokens*	*Pretest (%)*	*Posttest 1 (%)*
kutuub jaddida	40.54	75.00	*kuliiyaat kathiira*	27.03	70.00
fusuul ṣaʕba	32.43	60.00	*ṭaawilaat kabiira*	43.24	75.00
bunuuk jaddida	24.32	70.00	*ṣuwar qadiima*	24.32	60.00
shawaariʕ waasiʕa	32.43	70.00	*binayaat ʕaaliyaat*	32.43	75.00
makaatib kabiira	27.03	75.00	*maktaabat kabiira*	32.43	95.00
ʔabwaab jamiila	27.03	50.00	*sayaraat mumtaaza*	21.62	75.00
karaasi jaddida	29.73	70.00	*kalimaat jaddida*	27.03	80.00
imtiḥanaat kathiira	35.14	70.00	*lughaat kathiira*	37.84	85.00
ʔashiyaaʔ jaddida	40.54	65.00	*jamiʕaat jayyida*	29.73	90.00
Total	32.13	67.22	Total	29.73	77.73

Table 3.6 shows the distribution of tokens with difference in one feature and tokens with difference in two features in posttest1 for the PPP group.

These findings suggest the earlier finding that beginner learners do not approach these asymmetries in terms of whether disagreement is one or in two features either in instructed or in uninstructed L2 settings. They apply the rule of thumb that simply "nonhuman plurals take singular feminine adjectives."

Discussion

The goal of this chapter has been twofold: first, it examined the differential gains of intensive input exposure and the present–practice–produce technique on the development of explicit and implicit knowledge of asymmetrical noun–adjective agreement. In determining the effect of intensive input, this question answers whether learners were able to acquire a feature while the focus of their attention was directed elsewhere. Second, the chapter asked whether these effects differ with differential feature mismatches.

Through two measures of explicit knowledge and a measure of implicit knowledge, the results showed evidence that input-based IE alone does not result in restructuring L2 noun–adjective agreement asymmetry. Consistently across the three tests with variable degrees of influence, the PPP technique that combined an explicit instruction component with output-based practice had a stronger influence on developing learner performance. So, the answer to the first research question is clearly yes. In answering the second question, the results found that the L2 learners in the control and IE groups were not sensitive to whether the nouns mismatched their corresponding adjectives in number only or in both number and gender. Comparatively, learners in the PPP group made greater gains in asymmetries of one feature than in asymmetries with two.

Part of the results of this chapter are in line with Ellis et al. (2009) that found that intensive incidental exposure does not lead to the development of implicit or explicit knowledge of morphological features. In their study, no difference in mean accuracy scores was reported between an input flood and a control group in the judgment and the provision of the third-person *-s* in English. The results of this study also found no *real* difference between the intensive incidental-exposure group and the control group in their acquisition of noun–adjective agreement asymmetry. They added that this difference was more robust in the case of the PPP group. DeKeyser (2007a) underlines the limitation of current research in its use of controlled or nonspontaneous assessment tasks to measure second language development. Also, Toth (2006) states that assessment of implicit knowledge could help us know whether the L2 system is susceptible to restructuring through input- or output-based language processing. This chapter employed a measure of implicit knowledge (an elicitation task) and two measures of explicit knowledge. The results of the EI group did not show learning gains in the asymmetrical case in question. Although they were exposed to numerous instances of agreement symmetries, they could not notice and consequently internalize the noun–adjective asymmetry entailed at the phrasal level.

One plausible explanation for the marginal success of the L2 learners in the EI group to improve their knowledge of noun–adjective agreement asymmetry from intensive input-based exposure is that they were forced to *dual-task* two aspects of Arabic morphology: subject–verb agreement and noun–adjective disagreement. Their executive system of attention could not maintain constant control of the two grammatical features in this dual tasking (see Verhaeghen & Cerella, 2002). They were quite unsuccessful in efficiently noticing that incongruence in the feature marking in the extensive instances presented with the given rule underlying the asymmetry. This does not eliminate the possibility that learners could pick up agreement asymmetries from the input alone. In one task (choice test), they were able to make some progress from 12.80% in the pretest to 27.36% in the posttest. However, this improvement was minimal, and the effect was not maintained in the other two tests.

In the ISLA literature, there is ongoing controversy around the roles of input- and output-based instruction. One step in resolving this controversy is to examine the relative impacts of each type through the use of measures of implicit and explicit language knowledge. A number of researchers have been unanimous in specifying the contribution that a more precise assessment of explicit and implicit knowledge could make to this debate (Muranoi, 2007). The current study addresses this call. It suggests that output-based instruction, when combined with explicit instruction, had a considerable influence in the development of both types of knowledge in the case in question.

Another way of contributing to our understanding of whether output-based instruction enables learners to internalize new language is to investigate whether there is a transfer of knowledge to novel test items. No research has looked at this question in output-based instruction, and only one study of input-based instruction has addressed the issue (Farley, 2004). This study found that input-based instruction led to significant gains for the interpretation and production of forms to which students *had not* been introduced during instruction. Although transfer of learning was evident with respect to regular subjunctive forms, there was no evidence of generalization of learning to irregular subjunctive forms. The results of this chapter echo the finding by Farley (2004). The learners were not able to generalize their exposure to the noun–adjective agreement asymmetry as supported with the *negligible* degree of success.

As discussed in Chapter 2 of this book, grammaticality-judgment and choice tests are often taken as purer measures of explicit linguistic knowledge. The results of the judgment and choice tests in this chapter suggest that input-based EI did not result in developing explicit knowledge of the asymmetry case in question. It seems very likely overall that explicit instruction that was followed by the controlled production of the target feature was more effective in enhancing the spontaneous production of the target structure. The EI intervention, although it offered many instances of the target structure, did not result in implicit linguistic knowledge in spontaneous production. The PPP intervention resulted in developing the participants' explicit knowledge, which arguably developed into implicit knowledge. This explanation is supported by skill-acquisition theory (DeKeyser, 2007b), which suggests that the ability to produce meaningful language spontaneously (a measure of implicit knowledge) is dependent upon declarative/explicit knowledge. The judicious use of rules and examples had likely helped to develop implicit knowledge of the asymmetrical case in question. Importantly, the L2 learners in this group were found to accurately produce the target asymmetry in speaking spontaneously. This is evidence (at least partial) that their declarative knowledge became proceduralized through slow and deliberate practice.

Conclusion

The results presented in this chapter provide ample evidence that a method of instruction that provides an explicit explanation and gives learners the opportunity to engage in producing language output results in the development of implicit language knowledge of agreement asymmetries. In this study, the fact that the learners did not perform well in the oral narrative task in the pretest confirms that they did not acquire this target feature in L2 Arabic. The gains made in the PPP group challenge the position that there is no specific role for output in creating underlying representations in the interlanguage (VanPatten, 2004). The gains made in the oral narrative task suggest that explicit explanation combined with oral practice may lead to the processing of form-meaning mappings and impact on the L2 developing system of irregular or asymmetrical structures. The results of this study also suggest that PPP is more effective than implicit exposure in the development of explicit knowledge. However, this does not exclude the possibility of developing explicit representations of the target structure from implicit exposure. The results of the choice task have shown *some* development of explicit knowledge that were not apparent in the judgment task. This may suggest that some gains are more apparent in certain tasks and not others, given the fact that their demands are different. Future research needs to investigate the variable task demands and to what degree learning effects are demonstrated in them.

4 Instructed Second Language Acquisition of Referential Agreement Asymmetries

Incidental Focus on Form and Planned Focus on Form

Introduction

Referential Asymmetries in Arabic

As demonstrated in Chapter 2, the rule that nonhuman plural head nouns are treated as singular feminine nouns manifests in several ways in the grammatical system of Standard Arabic. Chapter 3 focused on noun–adjective agreement asymmetries as one of these cases. This chapter focuses on another case, which is the assignment of singular feminine demonstrative pronouns to refer to nonhuman plural heads regardless of their gender, as illustrated in (1) and (2):

(1)	*haadhihi*	*ʔal-kutub*
	this.s.f	def-books.p.m
	"these books"	
(2)	*haadhihi*	*ʔal-qiṣaṣ*
	this.s.f	def-stories.p.f
	"these stories"	

In (1), the demonstrative pronoun *haadhihi* and the nonhuman masculine plural head noun *ʔal-kutub* disagree in terms of number (a plural head is assigned a singular demonstrative) and gender (a masculine head noun took a feminine demonstrative). In (2), demonstrative (*haadhihi*) and the nonhuman feminine plurals noun (*ʔal-qiṣaṣ*) disagree in terms of number only (a plural head noun is assigned a singular demonstrative).

This asymmetrical pattern also manifests in demonstratives, as illustrated in (3) and (4), when they bind nonhuman plural predicates. The demonstrative *haadhihi* (singular feminine) binds a nonhuman plural (masculine or feminine, *jaamiʕaat* and *kutub*, respectively).

DOI: 10.4324/9781003055600-5

(3)	*haadhihi*	*jaamiʕ-aat*	*mumtaaz-a.*
	this.s.f	universities-p.f	excellent-s.f
	"These are excellent universities."		
(4)	*haadhihi*	*kutub*	*jadiid-a.*
	this.s.f.	book.p.m	new-s.f
	"These are new books."		

The same phenomenon manifests in object clitics, as illustrated in (5) and (6), in the imperfective:

(5)	*Ahmad*	*ʕindahu*	*kutub*	*jadiid-a.*	*huwa*	*yaqaraʔu-haa*	*kathiiran.*
	Ahmad	has	books.p.m	new.p.f.	He	reads.3-s.f	a lot.
	"Ahmad has new books. He reads them a lot."						
(6)	*Ahmad*	*ʕindahu*	*qiṣaṣ*	*jadiid-a.*	*huwa*	*yaqaraʔu-haa*	*kathiiran.*
	Ahmad	has	stories.p.f	new-p.f.	He	reads.3-s.f	a lot.
	"Ahmad has new stories. He reads them a lot."						

In (5), the anaphoric object pronoun ({*-haa*}, singular feminine) and its plural nonhuman masculine plural antecedent *kutub* "books" disagree in number and gender. The same pattern appears in (6) in which the anaphoric object pronoun (*{-haa}*, singular feminine) disagrees with its plural nonhuman feminine plural antecedent *qiṣaṣ* "stories" in number. The same disagreement pattern extends to oblique/prepositional clitics in (7):

(7)	*jaamiʕ-aat*	*ʔamriika*	*mumtaaz-a.*	*ʔuriid*	*ʔan*	*ʔadrus*	*fii-haa.*
	universities-p.f	America	excellent-s.f.	I want	to	study	in-her.3.s.f
	"Universities of America are excellent. I want to study in them."						

As illustrated by these examples, there is disagreement between the anaphoric oblique (*{-haa}*, third-person feminine singular) that is affixed to the preposition, and its plural nonhuman feminine antecedent *jaamiʕ-aat* "universities."

Salience of Grammatical Features

These two cases of referential asymmetry offer differences in terms of their salience or prominence to the learners. Salience refers to how easy it is to perceive a given language form. Recently, this construct has attracted attention in SLA studies (e.g., Hanulíková et al., 2012; Hanulíková & Weber, 2012). In this literature, a distinction is made between top-down and bottom-up views of salience (see Summerfield & Egner, 2009). Whereas the "top-down" refers to the perceiver's cognitive underpinnings (i.e., a language form can be salient because it is cognitively pre-activated in the perceiver's mind), "bottom-up" refers to the *intrinsic* characteristics of the language forms that cause the perceiver to attend to them. Research in language studies has focused on the second view. For example, Kerswill and Williams (2002) approach salience as "the property of a linguistic item or feature that makes it in some way perceptually and cognitively prominent" (p. 81). Similarly, to Siegel (2010), salience "refers to the characteristic of being easily noticeable, prominent, or conspicuous" (p. 129).

The role of salience has been examined in SLA studies particularly concerned with acquisition orders (Larsen-Freeman, 1975). Dulay and Burt (1978) identified two ways to approach salience: the inherent characteristics of the linguistic forms and the extralinguistic factors such as frequency that cause some parts of these forms to be salient. For Brown (1973), the former entails variables such as the amount of phonetic substance, stress level, and the serial position of the form in a sentence. Others (see Goldschneider & DeKeyser, 2001) have operationalized salience of morpho-syntactic forms in terms of their number of phones, syllabicity, and phonetic properties. Grammatical forms that have more phones and syllables are considered more salient than forms that have fewer phones and syllables.

A review of acquisition-order studies that examined the role of salience is certainly beyond the scope of this chapter (Gass et al., 2017). An important conclusion in this literature is that salience is a possible determiner of why certain morpho-syntactic forms are acquired earlier than others. For example, the syllabic progressive {*–ing*} is acquired earlier in English than the past tense regular {*–ed*} morpheme, which is non-syllabic (Brown, 1973). Additionally, Collins and Ellis (2009) concluded that salience is a valid explanation why the regular past morpheme {*–ed*} is acquired later than the lexical items that mark the tense, such as yesterday and last week, when presented in the same sentence.

Previous Findings in L2 Arabic

Previous research in the L2 acquisition of referential agreement in Arabic is very scarce. The focus of this research is on the role of L1 effects in shaping the trajectories of language development. Alhawary (2009) compared between the longitudinal data on subject–verb agreement and demonstrative–predicate gender agreement: *haadha (this.m.s) ṭaalib-(un) (student.ms-(nom))* [This is a male student] and *haadhihi (this.f.s) ṭaaliba-(t-un) (student.f.s-(nom))* [This is a female student] by L1 English and French learners of Arabic.

Demonstrative–predicate gender agreement is important because French exhibits gender agreement between demonstrative pronouns and their predicate adjectives while English does not. According to the processability theory, gender agreement between demonstrative pronouns and their predicate adjectives is expected to emerge at stage 4 (the same stage for subject–verb agreement). The longitudinal data showed that English-speaking learners seemed to encounter more problems with demonstrative–predicate agreement than with subject–verb agreement. Second, he compared the longitudinal data with the cross-sectional data from the two groups of learners in the 2005 study. Again, the French participants were found to outperform their English counterparts in the demonstrative–predicate agreement. This role of L1 transfer was confirmed in a recent study by Alhawary (2019) with Chinese and Russian learners of Arabic, whose first languages offer typological differences to Arabic.

Aljadani (2019) investigated the acquisition of noun–demonstrative agreement symmetries by English L1 speakers at the intermediate level (pre- and upper). Using a grammaticality judgment as a measure of explicit knowledge, the researcher also compared their performance to native speakers. Due to typological gender differentiations, English speakers were expected to have *some* difficulties in learning this feature. The study found a difference between native speakers and pre-intermediate learners in their judgment of ungrammatical sentences as well as a significant difference between pre- and upper-intermediate learners. Importantly, the study also detected a difference between upper-intermediate and native speakers in terms of their accuracy OR grammaticality judgments. With these results, this study offers a different pattern of findings from the results reported by Alhawary (2009). It concludes that the lack of gender differentiations in English *did not* result in impeding the acquisition of this aspect of agreement symmetry. This result *is not* in line with the transfer explanation.

The Current Study

Studies that examined demonstrative–noun agreement in Standard Arabic, however scarce, have focused mostly on the symmetrical pattern. The goal was to examine the role of L1 effects. The asymmetrical-agreement type, however common in the system of Arabic when the noun is nonhuman plural, was not examined in these studies. Further, in line with the literature on salience, the two target cases of referential agreement asymmetry (demonstratives and clitics) can be differentiated in terms of their prominence.

Demonstratives are considered to be more perceptually salient than clitics. Demonstratives stand alone before the plural head noun. Clitics also disagree with the head antecedents, are graphically affixed to verbs and prepositions, and do not stand independently as a word. Therefore, they are less prominent or salient to the learner. Less investigated in the ISLA literature is how L2 learners develop implicit and explicit knowledge of grammar forms with variable salience under different instruction techniques (see Hu, 2002; Xu & Lyster, 2014).

To advance knowledge about the acquisition of referential agreement asymmetries in L2 Arabic, this chapter presents the design and results of a classroom intervention that compares the effects of planned and incidental FoF in the acquisition of referential asymmetries (demonstratives and clitics). As explained in Chapter 2, although it is broadly agreed that FoFs develops explicit knowledge of grammar rules, studies have reported mixed effects with regard to the effect of FoF. Using a pretest–posttest design, the chapter presents the effects of each type in the development of explicit and implicit knowledge. Importantly, to determine whether the effect of each type of FoF varies according to the feature's inherent salience, gains in demonstratives (stand-alone) and object and prepositional clitics (affixed) were separated in the analysis.

Research Questions

To address these research gaps, this chapter answers two questions:

1. Are there differential gains for planned and incidental FoF in the development of explicit and implicit knowledge of asymmetrical referential agreement in Standard Arabic by early-intermediate English learners of Arabic?
2. Are there differential gains for planned and incidental FoF in the development of explicit and implicit knowledge of asymmetrical referential agreement in Standard Arabic with differential salience (high salience in demonstratives versus low salience in clitics) by early-intermediate English learners of Arabic?

Participants

A total of 57 early-intermediate learners participated in this study. They were divided into three experimental groups: control (*n* = 19), planned FoF (*n* = 19), and incidental FoF (*n* = 19). At the beginning of testing, the three L2 groups were recruited from sections of intermediate Arabic at an Arabic program at a large public university in the United States. Their biographic information is provided in Table 4.1.

The participants were in the middle of their third semester of Arabic, and they had been exposed to a total of about 185 contact hours of instruction (73 weeks, five hours each). In their regular classrooms, they were taught by different instructors who followed handouts prepared by the researcher. They were tested three times. The pretesting was completed two days before the intervention, and the posttesting was completed twice: immediately after the end of the intervention and a week later. At the time of testing, the two groups had completed several sections from the Al-Kitaab book series (Brustad et al., 2011): the Introductory Part, Part 1 (third edition), and two lessons of Part II.

Participants had been taught basic grammatical aspects of Standard Arabic that included gender marking (at the phrasal and inter-phrasal level), question formation, the definite article, subject pronouns, plural marking, noun phrase structure, possessive and demonstrative pronouns, superlatives, present tense with common

Table 4.1 Participant Demographic Data and Proficiency Ratings

Learner group	*Number*	*Age range/mean*	*Proficiency ratings*
Control	19 (12 males and 8 females)	18–20 (mean: 19.00)	2.0/6.0
Planned FoF	19 (12 males and 8 females)	19–20 (mean: 19.5)	2.0/6.0
Incidental FoF	19 (11 males and 9 females)	19–22 (mean: 19.5)	2.0/6.0

verb patterns in nominal and verbal sentences, adverbs, the numeric system, superlatives, verb tenses, and sentence complements. Importantly, at the time of testing, only the symmetrical agreement pattern of reference had been presented and frequently consolidated. The learners were *minimally* introduced to the asymmetrical pattern of agreement between nouns and demonstratives and nouns and referential clitics. This minimal exposure was in the context of plural formation in lesson 2 and lesson 5 in Part 1 of Al-Kitaab. Thus, this grammatical feature of agreement had neither been explicitly taught nor consolidated at any point in their instruction before the study was conducted. This minimized the effect of previous exposure to the target asymmetries.

Design and Procedure

The three learner groups were pretested two days before they received the instruction that took place at the beginning of the week. Instruction took a full session of around 50 minutes in each intervention. Students were asked not to review any learning materials before they did the posttesting that took place in individualized sessions. In total, the study took around two hours (pretest, treatment, and two posttests), and they were paid research compensation for their participation from a research grant awarded to the researcher. Details of the materials used in the chapter are provided next.

Instructional Treatments

PLANNED FOF

Instruction in planned FoF depended primarily on a *focused* task-based lesson plan: *The Cities in the Pictures*. The teacher encouraged the learners to work in five small groups to negotiate meaning in some detail about features of four cities from picture sets. To facilitate the interaction, the students were given a list of ten vocabulary items with content words (nouns, verbs, and adjectives). They were asked to use them as guides in their interactions or conversations. The teacher modeled the negotiation of meaning with the students earlier in the lesson plan.

The underlying task design and picture selection involved the *two* target forms of asymmetry (demonstratives and object clitics) that arose spontaneously in the context of meaning-focused communication. For example, they were required to contrast certain aspects (*these cities are big* versus *these cities are small*). In this case, then, the FoF was predetermined. Also, the conversation about the picture sets triggered the use of demonstratives and object clitics (target features) in the process of communicating if these are good or bad cities to live in. For example, they would have to produce complete sentences such as “I like to live in these small cities because. . .” The sequence of the lesson plan is depicted in Figure 4.1.

Figure 4.1 Sequence of the Lesson Plan

Step 1	*Step 2*	*Step 3*	*Step 4*	*Step 5*
Task introduction	Brainstorming	Modelling interactions (*teacher-initiated)*	Group work *(learner-initiated)*	Interactive episodes *(teacher-initiated or learner-initiated)*

With this sequence, this type of FoF instruction was similar to FoFs instruction in that a specific form was preselected for treatment, but it differed in two respects. First, the attention to the form occurred in interaction where the primary focus was on meaning. Second, the learners were not made aware that a specific form was being targeted and thus were expected to function primarily as "language users" rather than as "learners" when they performed the task. The teacher provided feedback on these language forms as they arose in the conversation using multiple techniques. As they engaged in the conversation with the teacher in the task, the learners were allowed to ask the teacher about the meaning of key words that they do not know. An example of an interactive episode is provided in (8); the two target features are underlined:

(8)

Turn	*Transliteration*	*Translation*
1: T	*mumkin taquul haadha ʕal-juzʔ marra ʔuhktaa yaa (ʔism ʔal-ṭaalib)*	Could you just try to say this part again, (student's name)?
2: S	*naʕam, laa ʔuḥib ʔan yashtari maal, maal kathiir fii maṭʕim liʔanahum ʔal-mataaʕim khaaliyya or it should be liʔanahaa ʔal-mataaʕim khaaliyya?*	Yes, I do not like to buy money, a lot of money in restaurants because they the restaurants are expensive or it should be because it is the restaurants expensive?
3: T	*liʔanahaa mataaʕim ghaaliyya. ṭayyib yaa (student's name), ʔanaa laa ʔuḥib ʔan ʔashtarii maal kathiir, ʔal-fiʕl "ʔashtarii" means to purchase or buy, but if you are thinking of the verb "to spend money"*	. . . because they are expensive restaurants. Okay, (student's name), I do not like to purchase or buy money, the verb "ʔashtarii" means to purchase or buy, but you are thinking of the verb to spend money.
4: S	*naʕam, laa ʔaʕriff* the verb to spend money. No, sorry, I was trying to think of a way to restructure it.	I do not know the verb for "to spend money." No, sorry, I was trying to think of a way to restructure it.
5: T	*ʔunfiq, ʔunfiq. ṭayyib ʔitfaḍal.*	Spend, spend. Okay, go ahead.

6: S	*laa ʔuḥib ʔan ʔunfiq, the verb to spend money.*	I do not like to spend, the verb to spend money.
7: S	*ʔunfiq ʔunfiq, ʔalif nuun faaʔ qaaf, laa ʔuḥib ʔan ʔinfiq maal kathiir fii haadhihi ʔal-maṭaaʕim ʔal-khaaliyya.*	Spend, spend, ʔalif nuun faaʔ qaaf (spelling of the new verb), I do not like to spend a lot of money in these expensive restaurants.
8: T	*ʔunfiq, okay.*	Spend, okay.

In this episode, the learner is negotiating part of the focused task to explain why they cannot live in one of the cities in the pictures. The learner thinks that they cannot live in these expensive cities because the restaurants are expensive. In Turn 1, the learner is *fluctuating* between symmetrical and asymmetrical referential agreement. Learning toward the asymmetrical pattern, they asked the teacher whether it should be *liʔanahaa ʔal-maṭaaʕim khaaliyya* (they used *kh* instead of *gh*) "because they are expensive restaurants" with the correct clitic. The teacher confirmed the asymmetrical agreement using rising intonation, and then the teacher moves to negotiate the lexical collocate "to spend money" after they noticed that the student made a mistake using the verb "purchase money" instead of "spend money." The student was able to produce asymmetrical referential agreement in turn 8 using the correct demonstrative pronoun in *haadhihi ʔal-maṭaaʕim ʔal-khaaliyya* "these expensive restaurants" after they learned the word for to "spend."

INCIDENTAL FoF

The incidental-FoF instruction involved the use of an *unfocused* task that was communicative in essence. It was designed to elicit a general language sample of a good number of grammatical forms including the two target features. It asked the learners to engage in a conversation about a picture-promoted task (the Roommate Task) about things to do with their roommates and friends. It followed the same sequence of the *focused* task in the planned FoF group. They were guided to talk about what they do with their roommates and friends openly and freely. As the students engaged in the conversation, the teacher elected to incidentally attend to various forms while performing the task. In this case, of course, attention to form was *extensive* rather than *intensive*—that is, many different forms were treated briefly rather than the two target forms repeatedly.

These forms included subject–verb agreement, noun–adjective agreement, plural marking, superlatives, adverbs, and numbers. During this unfocused task, the students made a good number of errors in these grammatical forms in addition to the two target features of asymmetry. The teacher corrected errors in these language forms as they arose in the conversation using multiple feedback techniques. Like the scenario in the planned FoF, the students were also allowed to ask the teacher about the meaning of key words that they did not know as they worked on the task. An example of an interactive episode is provided in (9); one of the target features is underlined.

(9)

Turn	*Transliteration*	*Translation*
1: T	*Sawfaa nantaqil ʔilaa raqam thalaatha, ṭayyib zamiil ʔalif yuḥib mushaahadat al-ʔaflaam, wa-zamiil baaʔ yuḥib al-qiraaʔa. maadhaa tuḥibiina ʔakthar?*	We will move now to item number three, number three. Okay, classmate (a) likes watching movies and classmate (b) likes reading. What do you like more?
2: S	*ʔanaa ʔuriid ʔaqraʔ wa-laakin ʔuriid mushaahadat al-film, wa-zamiil ʔalif yuḥib mushaahadat al-film ʔakthar min yuḥib min ʔaqraʔ*	I want to read but I want to watch the movie and classmate (a) likes watching the movies more than reading.
3: T	*ʔakthar min ʔan yaqraʔ. ṣaḥḥ? ṭayyib mumtaaz, maadha tushaahidiina fii al-tilifizyuun? ʔaii nawʕ min haadhihi ʔal-ʔaflaam tushaahidiin? hal tuḥibbiina al-ʔaflaam al-diraamiyya? al-ruumansiyya? al-kuumidiyya? ʔai nawʕ min al- ʔaflaam?*	More than to read, right. Okay, this is excellent. What do you watch in TV? Which movies? Which kind of these movies do you watch? Do you like watching drama, romance, comedy? What kind of movies?
4: S	*naʕam, ʔuḥib ʔan ʔushaahid haadhaa ʔal-ʔaflaam ʔal-ruumansiyya wa-ʔaflaam action.*	Yes, I like to watch these romantic movies and action movies.
5: T	*haadhaa ʔal-ʔaflaam al-ruumansiyya wa-ʔaflaam action?*	This romantic movies and action movies?
6: S	*naʕam, ʔuriid zameel alif. hwaa yuḥibb haadhihi ʔal-ʔaflaam ʔal-ruumansiyya.*	Yes, I want classmate (a). He likes these romantic movies.
7: T	*jamiil ṭayyib mumtaaz mumtaaz. ṭayyib, ʔantii tuḥibiin zamiil ʔalif.*	Great, okay this is excellent. Okay, you like classmate (a).

This excerpt is taken from a negotiation-of-meaning episode in which the teacher and the student are discussing the kind of classmate they would live with and to what degree their daily habits would match theirs. The teacher-initiated interaction focused on two grammatical features: the subjective and the target asymmetrical agreement in the demonstratives. In turn 2, the student made two instances of the same mistake in the correct form of the subjective, missing the subjective particle *ʔan* "to."

The teacher reformulated the utterance in turn 3, providing the correct configuration of the subjunctive using *ʔan*. They used the rhetorical question marker, *ṣaḥ* "right" to draw the learner's attention to the accurate form. In turn 4, the student was able to produce the accurate subjective structure, but they made a mistake in the demonstrative *haadhaa ʔal-ʔaflaam* "this movies." The teacher, having noticed this mistake, uses recasting in turn 5 with rising intonation *haadhaa ʔal-ʕaflaam al-ruumaansiyya ʔaflaam ʔal-ʔakshan* "this romantic and action movies?" The student realized that the demonstrative links to the word "movies" and corrected it into *haadhihi* that disagrees with the nonhuman plural noun *ʔaflaam* "movies."

Reactive Versus Preemptive FoF in the Treatments

In both types of treatments, *reactive* and *preemptive* focus on form were used in the interactive episodes (teacher–student and student–student) in the classroom (R. Ellis et al., 2002). The first kind was used when the learners made an error in any of the grammatical forms, including the two cases of agreement asymmetries. The second was used when no errors were made, but the teacher decides to make a particular form for the topic of the conversation in which there is negotiation of form as part of the negotiation of meaning that is occurring. The frequency of the episodes in which reactive and preemptive FoF were used was different given the *intensive* versus the *extensive* focus on the target cases of asymmetry.

This *reactive* focus on form took different forms in the task-based interaction. The teacher negotiated the meaning, conversationally using requests for confirmation or for clarification when an error was made in Standard Arabic. The request for confirmation was made by having the teacher repeat the problematic utterance with or without formulating it. The request for clarification, on the other hand, was made by having the learners of Arabic deal with the problematic utterance and reformulate it, producing the accurate form. Also, corrective feedback was given to the students in the interactions through recasts (implicit) and through direct signalizing (explicit) that an error was made. Such techniques are exemplified in the two previous excerpts.

The *preemptive* focus on form was typically learner-initiated. The learner made a query to the teacher about a particular linguistic form that became the topic of the conversation even though no error (or perceived error) in the use of that form had occurred. The fact that this was in the *context* of the task completion where the primary focus was on meaning makes it quite different from the traditional focus on forms. The excerpt in Turn 4 and 5 in (8) is an apt example.

The advantage of student-initiated preemptive focus on form is that it addresses gaps in the students' linguistic knowledge, which are presumed to be significant to them, and which they are therefore strongly motivated to try to fill. A disadvantage of student-initiated attention to form, however, is that it can detract from the communicative activity (R. Ellis et al., 2002). This is one reason why teachers may decline to answer a student query.

Table 4.2 shows the difference between the two types of FoF.

Table 4.2 Differences Between Planned and Incidental Focus on Form

	Planned	*Incidental*
Task	Focused	Unfocused
Features	Predetermined	Spontaneous
Focus	Intensive	Extensive
Initiation	Teacher- and student-initiated	Teacher- and student-initiated
Reactive or preemptive	Mostly reactive	Mostly reactive

Measures of Instructional Outcomes

Participants completed two tests in each of the three testing episodes (pre-test, immediate posttest, delayed posttest): grammaticality metalinguistic test (assesses for explicit knowledge) and oral elicitation test (assesses for implicit knowledge). These tests and the theoretical rationale that has informed their design have been described in Chapter 2 of this book. Details of each test are provided next.

Metalinguistic-Knowledge Test (MKT)

To assess the learner's explicit knowledge of referential asymmetries, a metalinguistic-knowledge test was developed. It was meant to be an analytical rather than an intuitive tool that measures the learner's declarative facts they built about the two target cases of asymmetry. This analytical tool (as in Chapter 2) is supported by research that has showed that learners were able to offer detailed accounts of the explicit knowledge base that they were drawing on while resolving form-focused tasks (see Roehr, 2006). The assumption behind the use of this test was that if the learners were found to provide such accounts, it seems reasonable to assume that they may also be able to estimate their level of metalinguistic knowledge more accurately than would be the case with implicit, automated knowledge, of which they may not be conscious.

The MKT was developed in line with a previous measure developed by Alderson et al. (1997). It focused on learners' knowledge of the rules of the target asymmetrical cases. It presented test-takers in the three groups with 17 ungrammatical sentences. As indicated in the examples in (10) and (11), the learners were not required to judge the grammaticality of each sentence or even to supply the correct form. The sentences were all incorrect and the erroneous part of each sentence was underlined. The learners were told that the sentences are ungrammatical and presented with multiple-choice options offering explanations (accurate and inaccurate) of the target language rule violated in each case. In this respect, the test format departs from the format used by Alderson et al. (1997), in that it measures passive metalinguistic knowledge rather than the ability to *actively* verbalize target language rules. Two items from the test with its accompanying distractors are shown in (10) and (11):

(10) *ʔakhii muḥammad yatakalam thalaath lughaat: ʔal-ʕarabiyya wa-ʔal-injliziyya wa-ʔal-faransiyya. huwa yuhib haaʔulaaʔ ʔal-lughaat kathiiran.*

(a) The pronoun *haaʔulaaʔ* is wrong because the subject *ʔakhii* is singular. It should be replaced with *huwa*.

(b) The pronoun *haaʔulaaʔ* should not come before a noun with the definite article.

(c) Replace the pronoun *haaʔulaaʔ* with the pronoun *haadhaa* because the word *lughaat* is masculine.

(d) Replace the pronoun *haaʔulaaʔ* with the *haadhihi* because the word *lughaat* is nonhuman plural and it should take a singular feminine pronoun.

(11) *hunaaka jaamiʕaat mumtaaza mithla harvard wa-kurniil wa-yiil. ʔana ʔuriid ʔan ʔdrus fiihm fii ʔ al-mustaqabal ʔin shaaʔ allah.*
(a) The word *fiihim* refers to singular and the sentence is about a plural noun *jaamiʕaat.*
(b) The word *fiihim* does not match with the pronoun *ʔana.*
(c) Replace the word *fiihim* with the word *fiiha* because the word *jaamiʕaat* is singular.
(d) The word *fiihim* refers to the word *jaamiʕaa,* which is nonhuman plural. So, it must be replaced with *fiiha* because a nonhuman plural noun takes a singular feminine pronoun.

The test was conducted in a paper–pencil format and the participants were told that they could not turn back to look at previous test items. Test-takers were asked to indicate their answer by checking the correct option for each item. Once again, one version of the test was used for all three testing sessions but with the order of presentation of items different for each test administration. For each one of these items, a correct choice was given a value of 0 and the correct one was given 1. Scores of the test were calculated and presented as percentages.

Oral Narrative Test

The three groups were given an oral narrative task, Facebook (FB) friend task, in which they were told that one of their FB friends in Egypt wanted to know information about them: the state and city where they live, its attractions, and the university where they study. They were asked to record a message in Standard Arabic in which they gave as much information as they could. The task was promoted with a visual component that triggered the use of nonhuman plurals with accompanying adjectives, and required them to produce sentences in their narratives with the two target cases of asymmetry: demonstratives and clitics. They were also told to communicate their thoughts about seven segments in the task: houses, streets, universities, classes, libraries, cities, and hospitals. A sample segment of the task is represented in (12), in which sample sentences were provided. However, it was not easy to balance between instances of the two cases of asymmetries.

(12) Expected sample sentences:

- *Also, I like the colleges in my state. These are not cheap, but they are very good.*
- *I study in these colleges because . . .*
- *I go to these libraries to . . .*
- *kuliiyaat fii wilaayatik—cheap or expensive, good or bad.*
- *maktabaat wa-mudun fii wilaayatik—which ones do you like and why?*

Results

Answer to the First Research Question: Differential Effects on the Development of Explicit Knowledge

Results of MKT

The scores for the three groups were analyzed to know the effect of the two target techniques on the selection of accurate justification for the ungrammatical sentences. As illustrated in Table 4.3, the results of the pretest showed overall that the participants were significantly more likely to select the wrong justification across the three groups in the test items.

The remarkably low scores in the pretest for the three groups suggest that this pattern of disagreement had not emerged in the learners' developing L2 linguistic system. A sample response is provided in (13) by a participant from the planned FoF group in which they opted for the wrong justification. They concluded that, since the head noun is plural, the demonstrative pronoun should accordingly be plural.

(13)

ولاية كاليفورنيا فيها الكثير من المدن الجميلة مثل سان دييجو ولوس انجليز وسان فرانسيسكو. أنا أسافر إلى هذا المدن في الصيف.

(a) The pronoun هذا should be followed by a singular noun and the word المدن is plural.
(b) The first clause tells us about المدن. Since it refers to nonhuman plural, the pronoun should be singular feminine هذه.
<u>(c)</u> المدن is plural and the sentence should use the plural pronoun هؤلاء.
(d) The pronoun هذا is followed by a singular noun and the clause is about a plural noun المدن. It should be replaced with the pronoun هم.

The ANOVA results indicated a statistically significant mean effect for group on mean accuracy scores: F (2, 53) = 43.116, p = .001, ηp^2 = .704. Also, there was

Table 4.3 Descriptive Statistics of MKT

	Referential asymmetrical agreement					
	Pretest		*Posttest1*		*Posttest2*	
	%	*SD*	*%*	*SD*	*%*	*SD*
Control	15.00	18.60	19.00	20.00	22.00	18.80
Incidental FoF	16.40	14.50	27.40	19.20	20.70	18.00
Planned FoF	18.20	16.90	67.00	22.30	63.80	20.80

a statistically significant effect for test time: F (1.52, 114.06) = 57.31, $p < .001$, $\eta p^2 = .542$ as well as a statistically significant mean effect for the interaction between test time and group: F (3.05, 101.041) = 31.73, $p < .001$, $\eta p^2 = .619$. Pairwise comparisons returned a significant difference between the planned FoF group and the control group on posttest1 ($p < .001$) and on posttest2 ($p < .001$). Also, it returned a significant difference between the planned FoF group and the incidental FoF group on posttest 1 and posttest 2 ($p < .001$ for both tests), but no difference between the incidental FoF group and the control group ($p = .116$). A sample of responses is provided in (14) by a participant in the Planned FoF group from posttest 1:

(14)

ولاية كاليفورنيا فيها الكثير من المدن الجميلة مثل سان دييجو ولوس انجليز وسان فرانسيسكو. أنا أسافر إلى هذا المدن في الصيف.

(a) The pronoun هذا should be followed by a singular noun and the word المدن is plural.
(b) The first clause tells us about المدن. Since it refers to nonhuman plural, the pronoun should be singular feminine هذه.
(c) المدن is plural and the sentence should use the plural pronoun هؤلاء.
(d) The pronoun هذا is followed by a singular noun and the clause is about a plural noun المدن. It should be replaced with the pronoun هم.

These findings indicate that the incidental-FoF treatment did not result in substantial improvement in accurate justifications for the errors in asymmetrical pattern for the two posttests. This is supported by the difference between the accuracy scores of the control and the incidental-FoF groups. However, the planned-FoF group had a higher influence than the incidental-FoF group for both posttest 1 and posttest 2.

Results of the Oral Narrative Test

In this task, the participants orally produced the target two referential asymmetrical cases in a recorded message. Their mean accuracy scores were calculated by dividing the accurate instances of referential asymmetries by the total number of tokens. The tokens per group ranged from 140 to 200 items, which was sufficient data for analysis. The mean scores of accurate productions are presented in Table 4.4.

Table 4.4 Descriptive Statistics for Oral Narrative Test

	Referential asymmetrical agreement					
	Pretest		*Posttest1*		*Posttest2*	
	%	*SD*	*%*	*SD*	*%*	*SD*
Control	10.00	28.00	11.00	20.00	13.00	18.00
Incidental FoF	13.00	30.62	31.00	19.00	25.70	22.00
Planned FoF	15.00	32.00	66.00	20.20	57.00	20.00

Overall, the participants' accuracy scores in the pretest were strikingly low, as shown in the table. This is demonstrated in the two samples in (15) and (16) by two participants in the planned- and incidental-FoF groups, respectively.

(15) مرحبا، أسكن في ولاية أريزونا. أحب ولايتي جدا (م م م . . .)، هذا البيوت في ولايتي
ولايتك. أيضا أحب الشارع في ولايتي بسبب هذا هادي جدا. و sorry وأيضا، أحب
الجامعات في ولايتي. هذا (هذو) الجامعات (م م م . . .) جدا جديدة. أحب أدرس هذا
اليوم، أحب أقرأ كتب والقصص (م م م . . .)، الكتاب إنجليزي واسباني.

(16) أعيش في ولاية أريزونا، أريزونا ولاية جميلة. في ولايتي الكثير من البيوت، هذا
البيوت جميلة وقريبة من الجبل. هناك جامعات جديدة في ولايتي، أحسن جامعة في
ال . . . جامعة أريزونا . . . هناك مدين (تقصد المدن) جميل مثل توسان وفينكس، وهذا
المدين (تقصد المدن) غالي، لكن الطقس لطيف طويل السنة. يوجد الكثير من المباني في
مدينة فينكس، أنا لا أحب المستشفيات الولايتي لأنها ليست جديدة.

A clear pattern in these samples is that the participants tended to produce the masculine demonstrative *haadhaa* "this" to refer to plural nonhuman plurals, whether masculine (*haadhaa ʔal-biyuut)* or feminine plurals (*haadhaa ʔal-mudun)*. Importantly, as shown by the accuracy scores of the posttests in the table, the planned-FoF group made more significant gains than the incidental-FoF group over time. Obviously, the learners were able to produce the referential asymmetrical pattern of agreement, particularly for demonstratives. The sample responses in (17) and (18) by two participants in the planned-FoF group from the posttest show this.

(17) أسكن في ولاية كولورادو والبيوت في ولايتي جميلة جدا بسبب بعضهم كبير جدا. أنا
أحب هذه البيوت بسبب لديها جوانب بالنسبة لهم، أنا أحب الشوارع في ولايتي لأنهم
قريب من الشجرة كبيرة. الجامعتي والكليات في ولايتي جميلة جدا لأنهم جديدة وأنا
أدرس فيهم في جامعة قريب من بيتي في سنة ٢٠١٧. المكتبات في ولايتي جميلة جدا
أيضا لأنهم كبيرة جدا، وأنا أحب المدن في ولايتي كبيرة وصغيرة أيضا . . . . أنا أحب
أن أزورهم . . . . البنايات قديمة وجديدة وعالية جدا والمستشفيات في ولايتي
غالية لكن بعضهم رخيص.

(18) أعيش في ولاية أريزونا. أنا أحب ولايتي كثيرا. في ولايتي هناك العديد من البيوت، هذه
البيوت جميلة جدا، أحبهم قريبون من الجبل، كما أني أحب الشوارع في ولايتي لأنهم
جميلة. أنا أحب الجامعة في ولايتي هؤلاء الجامعات جيدة جدا، أحب أن أدرس فيهم في
المستقبل، كما غني أحب الكليات في ولايتي، هذه ليست رخيصة لكنها رخيصة جدا. أنا
أدرس اللغة العربية والعلوم السياسية في هذه الكليات. أيضا في ولايتي أحب المكتبات. أنا
قرأت كتاب جديدة في هذا المكتبات كل يوم. ولايتي ولايتي عندها العديد من المدن الجميلة
مثل توسان وفينيكس. هذه المدن مكلف للغاية لكني أحب ذلك. تعيش فيها لأن الطقس فيها
جميل في الشتاء. أيضا في هذا في هذه المدن هناك طويلة البنايات، أنا أحبهم كثيرا. أنا
أحب المستشفيات في ولايتي، هذه المستشفيات ليس رخيصة، هم أنهم غالية جدا.

The ANOVA returned a statistically significant mean effect for group: F (2, 54) = 38.213, p = .001, ηp^2 = .635. Also, it returned a statistically significant mean effect for test time: F (1.52, 109.03) = 39.41, p < .001, ηp^2 = .539 and a statistically significant mean effect for the interaction between test time and group: F (3.05, 98.041) = 29.61, p < .001, ηp^2 = .610. Pairwise comparisons yielded a significant difference between the planned-FoF group and the control group on posttest1 (p = .001) and posttest2 (p < .001). Also, there was a significant difference between the planned-FoF group and the incidental-FoF group on posttest1 and posttest2 (p < .001 for both tests). Surprisingly, there was a significant difference between the control group and incidental-FoF group: (p < .001 for both tests), which supports the effects of the incidental focus on form on having *some* gains.

Table 4.5 Accuracy Scores in Asymmetrical Demonstratives and Clitics in the Metalinguistic Test

	Posttest1			*Posttest2*		
	Demonstratives	*Clitics*	*p value*	*Demonstratives*	*Clitics*	*p value*
	M (%)	*M (%)*		*M (%)*	*M(%)*	
Incidental FoF	21.00	06.00	< .001	17.00	03.00	*p* < .001
Planned FoF	49.00	18.00	< .001	50.00	13.00	*p* < .001

Table 4.6 Item Distribution in the MKT for the Planned-FoF Group

Demonstratives			*Clitics*		
Tokens	*Posttest1 (%)*	*Posttest2 (%)*	*Tokens*	*Posttest1 (%)*	*Posttest2 (%)*
haadhihi ʔal-buyuut	50	50	*ʔadrus fiiha (ʔal-jaamiʕaat)*	20	20
haadhihi ʔal-mudun	60	60	*ʔuḥibuhaa (ʔal-lughaat)*	30	30
haadhihi ʔal-maktabaat	42	42	*ʔusaafir ʔilihaa (ʔal-wilayaat)*	10	10
haadhihi ʔal-mustas hfayaat	52	52	*ʔdrusuhaa (ʔal-lughaat)*	15	10
haadhihi ʔal-kutub	61	61	*ʔqraaʔu ʕanhaa (ʔal-ʔasmaaʔ)*	10	0
haadhihi ʔal-wilayaat	43	43	*ʔaskuna fiiha (ʔal-guraf)*	20	20
haadhihi ʔal-bunuuk	46	46	*ʔaqraʔuhaa (ʔal-kutub)*	20	10
haadhihi ʔal-shawaariʕ	52	58	*ʔarsumuhaa (ʔal-ṣuwarr)*	25	5
haadhihi ʔal-binayaat	40	40	*ʔaskuna fiiha (ʔal-wilayaat?)*	15	15
Mean	49.00	50.00	Mean	18.00	13.00

Table 4.7 Accuracy Scores in Asymmetrical Demonstratives and Clitics in the Oral Narrative Test

	Posttest1			*Posttest2*		
	Demonstratives	*Clitics*	*p value*	*Demonstratives*	*Clitics*	*p value*
	M (%)	*M (%)*		*M (%)*	*M (%)*	
Incidental FoF	28.00	03.00	< .001	21.00	05.00	< .001
Planned FoF	52.00	16.00	< .001	43.00	14.00	< .001

Table 4.8 Item Distribution in the Oral Narrative Test for the Planned FoF

Demonstratives			*Clitics*		
Tokens	*Posttest1 (%)*	*Posttest2 (%)*	*Tokens*	*Posttest1 (%)*	*Posttest2 (%)*
haadhihi ʔal-maktabaat	50	45	*ʔadrus fiiha (ʔal-jaamiʕaat)*	0	0
haadhihi ʔal-mustashfayaat	60	50	*ʔuḥibuhaa (ʔal-kughaat)*	10	15
haadhihi ʔal-kutub	42	40	*ʔusaafir ʔilihaa (ʔal-wilayaat)*	10	15
haadhihi ʔal-wilayaat	52	52	*ʔdrusuhaa (ʔal-lughaat)*	0	0
haadhihi ʔal-bunuuk	61	40	*ʔqraaʔu ʕanhaa (ʔal-ʔasmaaʔ)*	0	0
haadhihi ʔal-shawaariʕ	50	35	*ʔaskuna fiiha (ʔal-ghuraf)*	0	0
haadhihi ʔal-kutub	50	40	*ʔqraaʔuhaa (ʔal-kutub)*	0	0
Mean	52	43	Mean	3	5

Answer to the Second Research Question: Differential Effects in Asymmetries with Differential Salience

I now turn to the question of whether there are differential gains for planned FoF and incidental FoF in the development of explicit and implicit knowledge of referential asymmetries with differential degrees of salience (high salience in demonstratives versus low salience in clitics). This question is worth asking given the variation in the participants' accuracy scores in demonstratives in comparison to clitics (object and prepositional) as demonstrated in the previous language samples. To closely address this question, accuracy scores in posttest1 and posttest2 in the two tests for the two intervention groups were subcategorized into scores in demonstratives and scores in clitics. The total means for each were calculated, and the results are reported in the following tables.

The calculated means of the two cases of asymmetry in both tests were entered into ANOVA. It returned a statistical difference between demonstratives and clitics for the two groups in both posttest1 and posttest2 in the two tasks. The results show remarkably low improvement for clitics in particular. Neither the incidental nor the planned focus on form resulted in enhancing the learners' noticing of referential asymmetries entailed in clitics. These results suggest that learning gains made by L1 learners of Arabic varied according to the case of inherent salience (see discussion shortly). They seemed to make more gains as a result of the interventions in demonstratives than clitics. It is argued that the planned FoF had greater effects with the more salient case of referential asymmetry.

Discussion

The results of this chapter show that although incidental focus on form in the *unfocused* task with extensive exposure had *some* effects, planned focus on form with intensive exposure produced more significant gains for the development of implicit and explicit knowledge. Incidental focus on form, although it had *some marginal* effects on implicit knowledge, could not develop explicit knowledge of the target structure. Also, in both types of focus on form, the learners made more gains in the more salient feature (demonstratives) than in the less salient feature (clitics). The tendency to use the masculine demonstrative *haadhaa* to refer to plural nonhuman plurals, whether masculine (*haadhaa ʔal-biyuut)* or feminine plurals (*haadhaa ʔal-mudun)* is consistent with the results found in uninstructed SLA research. For example, Alhawary (2009) found out that L2 learners of Arabic (L1 English) across different classroom levels exhibited far more errors in the feminine demonstrative agreement than their French L1 counterparts. This implies that they tended to use the masculine demonstrative for both masculine and feminine demonstrative agreement. This pattern has been found in the L2 acquisition of other gender languages such as Spanish (White et al., 2004).

Based on the results of the MKT posttest scores by participants in both groups, the main observation is that *incidental* focus on form did not result in developing *explicit* knowledge of the two cases of asymmetry. The improvement in accuracy in selecting the correct justification for the errors in referential asymmetries was negligible (from 16% to 19%), which suggests that engaging in incidental focus on form in *unfocused* tasks did not trigger learner awareness to the disagreement between nonhuman plurals and their referentials. Although it is likely that the learners obtained some cues from the unfocused task and could rehearse it in short-term memory and possibly reproduce it in the interactive episodes, they were unable to integrate it into their interlanguage system of agreement. This result is consistent with Ellis et al. (2009), which found out that *enriched* (not *enhanced*) input did not result in developing explicit knowledge as measured by untimed grammaticality judgment.

The results of the oral narrative task, a characteristic measure of implicit knowledge, suggest that the incidental focus on form can indeed result in the development of implicit knowledge of referential asymmetries. The statistical difference between the control group and the incidental-focus-on-form group (11% compared to 31%) suggests that early-intermediate L2 learners of Arabic can acquire implicit knowledge of an irregular or asymmetric structure from incidental-focus-on-form exposure in a communicative activity. According to Ellis et al. (2009), little is currently known about the acquisitional outcomes of incidental focus on form. The current study contributes to expanding understanding of oral narrative task outcomes in irregular or asymmetrical grammatical structures. Also, the results of this task are consistent with a study by Loewen (2002) that suggests that learners can benefit from incidental focus on form. Loewen identified numerous episodes where the classroom participants attended to form in communicative lessons and could transform this to tests that required them to recognize or supply the correct form. The results of his study are in line with the oral narrative task in the current study.

The results of the *planned*-focus-on-form-group show that asking the students to consciously attend to the target structures can facilitate the acquisition of implicit knowledge. These results seem to be contradictory to some studies in the literature. Reinders and R. Ellis (2009) found that asking the students to consciously attend to the target structures can impede the acquisition of implicit knowledge. N. Ellis (1993) found that incidental instruction consisting of enriched input worked better than a more explicit form of instruction when the structure was a difficult one. In this study, there was a significant difference between the accuracy scores of the incidental and planned groups in the MKT (compare 27% to 67% in posttest1). The weight of evidence suggests that the planned focus on form in the context of communicative activity could strongly result in developing explicit knowledge of structures such as agreement asymmetries. The *intensive* focus on form in a planned task that required the use of the target features repeatedly and frequently could make the learners attend to the target forms. This was transformed into explicit knowledge in the MKT. The planned focus on form seems to be a good technique that can boost the L2 learners' capacity to attend to form while focusing on meaning when performing a communicative activity (VanPatten, 1990). The results of the planned group suggest that the L2 learners were able to build some declarative knowledge from the frequent episodes that focus on specific grammatical forms.

An important finding in this chapter is that both types of instruction had more gains in demonstratives than clitics. One explanation comes from the inherent salience of the two cases. A close look at the accuracy rates for both types of tests shows varied levels knowledge of demonstratives and clitics that can be adequately explained in terms of their inherent perceptual salience (see DeKeyser, 2003; R. Ellis, 2006). English-speaking learners of Arabic demonstrated more explicit knowledge of demonstratives because of their high salience. The fact that demonstratives are more graphically salient than clitics may also have affected learners' selective attention. Following Schmidt (2001), early-intermediate learners in this study developed explicit knowledge of demonstratives, and as a result, they could select the accurate justification of the errors more in demonstratives than in clitics.

In comparison, a different pattern was found in clitics (object and prepositional). The analysis of both tasks in the two groups revealed that the learners developed less sophisticated knowledge of clitics due to the low salience of its marker, {*-haa*}, which is attached to verbs and prepositions. According to the conventions of the Arabic script, clitics do not stand independently. The less sophisticated explicit knowledge of clitics is consistent with Hu's (2002) proposal that "because metalinguistic knowledge is explicit knowledge of *linguistic categories*. . . it is reasonable to hypothesize that acquisition and use of such knowledge can be influenced by the inner structure of these categories" (p. 355, emphasis added). The low salience of clitics caused them to go unnoticed in the interactive episodes. These findings confirm a conclusion by N. Ellis (2006) that salience is a key element that triggers selective attention in L2 learning. Additionally, they also support a broader view that learners demonstrate varied manifestations of linguistic knowledge of structures that vary in terms of their inherent linguistic characteristics (Xu & Lyster, 2014).

Conclusion

The results presented in this chapter provide ample evidence that planned focus on form in focused tasks had more significant gains for the development of implicit and explicit knowledge of referential agreement asymmetries in L2 Arabic. Incidental focus on form, although it had *some marginal* effects on implicit knowledge, it could not develop explicit knowledge of the target structure. Also, in both types of focus on form, the learners made more gains in the more salient feature (demonstratives) than in the less salient feature (clitics).

These findings have important implications for the presentation of L2 forms in Arabic language curricula. They highlight the importance of planned-focus-on-form instruction in the context of meaning-based communicative teaching. In focus-on-form methodologies, instructors need to draw the learners' attention to the less salient features that go unnoticed in linguistic input. Specifically, instructors of Arabic should use pedagogical techniques that draw the learners' attention to less salient features in the Arabic agreement system (and in other constructions as well). Focused tasks (designed to elicit the form of a specific linguistic feature), in the context of meaning-centered methodologies, are important tools that contribute sufficiently to grammatical accuracy in communicative competence. The importance of these tasks remains in pushing learners to attend to form while engaged in meaning-based language use.

The results also imply that the inherent characteristics of L2 forms are important factors to consider. Since learners develop less sophisticated metalinguistic knowledge of less salient forms, textbook writers and curriculum developers need to integrate more focus-on-form activities and materials in presenting these forms. These activities should draw the learners' attention to the position of these forms in the internal structure of bigger syntactic constructions. Furthermore, while performing these focused tasks, instructors need to use corrective recasting, where the instructor first repeats a learner utterance that contains errors in the less salient forms, highlighting the error through emphasis. This gives learners the opportunity to attend to these less salient forms. Since accuracy of these less salient forms contributes to meaningful communication, specific form-meaning connection activities (see VanPatten, 2004) need to be integrated. These activities may include picture description, choosing between alternatives, and detecting errors. The significance of these activities is upheld, which means instructors should encourage foreign-language learners to attend to less salient features (e.g., clitics) so that they internalize them in their developing interlanguage systems.

5 Instructed Second Language Acquisition of Subject–Verb Agreement Asymmetries

Structured Input-Based and Structured Output-Based Activities

Introduction

Subject–Verb Agreement Asymmetries in Standard Arabic

The verb-initial sentence, *ʔal-jumla ʔal-fiʕliyya*, is a common word order in Arabic. As the name suggests, this sentence type starts with a verb. As demonstrated in Chapter 2, when an Arabic sentence contains a lexical subject and an object, this sentence type runs in the verb–subject–object (VSO) word order. According to Ryding (2005), this verb-initial word order in Arabic is the *basic* order. Also, it is “the unmarked” (i.e., frequent) word order (Soltan, 2007, p. 34). This word order may vary to the subject-initial sentence (*al-jumla al-ʔismiyya, nominal sentence*) that runs in the SVO word order, which is also common in Arabic. Other word orders in which the object surfaces before the verb and the subject, such as VOS, OSV, and OVS, can be used under certain pragmatic conditions in extended discourse.

In subject-initial sentences, the subject and the verb exhibit a symmetrical pattern of agreement in terms of person (first, second, or third), number (singular, dual, or plural), and gender (masculine or feminine). This is illustrated in (1), (2), (3), and (4).

(1)	*ʔal-ṭaalib-(u)*	*yu-ḥibb-(u)*	*ʔal-ʔustaadh-(a)*	*kathirann.*
	def-student.m.s-(nom)	3ms-like.imperf-(indic)	def-teacher.m.s-(acc)	a lot.
	“The (male) student likes the (male) teacher a lot.”			
(2)	*ʔal-ṭaalibat-(u)*	*tu-ḥibb-(u)*	*ʔal-ʔustaadh.a{t}-(a)*	*kathirann.*
	def-student.fs-nom	3.f.s-like.imperf-(indic)	def-teacher.f.s-(acc)	a lot.
	“The (female) student likes the (female) teacher a lot.”			
(3)	*ʔal-ṭulaab-u*	*yu-ḥibb-uu-n(a)*	*ʔal-ʔustaadh-(a)*	*kathirann.*
	def-student.m.p.-(nom)	3-like. imperf-m.p.-indic	def-teacher.m.s-(acc)	a lot.
	“The (male) students like the (male) teacher a lot.”			
(4)	*ʔal-ṭaalibaat-(u)*	*yu-ḥibb-na*	*ʔal-ʔustaadh-a{t}-a*	*kathirann.*
	def-student.f.p.-(nom)	3-like.imperf-f.p.-indic	def-teacher.f.s-(acc)	a lot.
	“The (female) students like the (female) teacher a lot.”			

DOI: 10.4324/9781003055600-6

In the verb-initial sentence, when the subject is a lexical noun, it surfaces after the verb to form the VSO word order. When the subject is a singular lexical noun, it continues to show a symmetrical pattern of agreement with the verb agreeing in person (first, second, or third), number (singular, dual, or plural), and gender (masculine or feminine). This is illustrated in (5) and (6).

(5)	*yu-ḥibb-(u)*	*ʔal-ṭaalib-(u)*	*ʔal-ʔustaadh-(a)*	*kathirann.*
	3ms-like. imperf-(indic)	def-student.m.s-(nom)	def-teacher.m.s-(acc)	a lot.
	"The (male) student likes the (male) teacher a lot."			
(6)	*tu-ḥibb-(u)*	*ʔal-ṭaalibat-(u)*	*ʔal-ʔustaadh.a{t}-(a)*	*kathirann.*
	3.f.s-like. imperf-(indic)	def-student. fs-nom	def-teacher.f.s-(acc)	a lot.
	"The (female) student likes the (female) teacher a lot."			

In the verb-initial sentence, when the subject is a dual or plural lexical noun, it shows an asymmetrical pattern of agreement with the verb; they agree in person (first, second, or third), gender (masculine or feminine), but they disagree in number. That is to say, a dual or plural subject will take a singular verb. This asymmetrical pattern of agreement is illustrated in (7) for a plural masculine subject and in (9) for a plural feminine subject. Maintaining the symmetrical pattern of agreement renders the structure ungrammatical, as illustrated in (8) and (10):

(7)	*yu-ḥibb-(u)*	*ʔal-ṭṭulaab-(u)*	*ʔal-ʔustaadh-(a)*	*kathirann.*
	3ms-like. imperf-(indic)	def-student. mp-(nom)	def-teacher.ms-(acc)	a lot.
	"The (male) students like the (male) teacher a lot."			
(8)	**yu-ḥibb-uun-(a)*	*ʔal-ṭulaab-(u)*	*ʔal-ʔustaadh-(a)*	*kathirann.*
	3-like. imperf-mp-(indic)	def-student. mp-(nom)	def-teacher.ms-(acc)	a lot.
	"The (male) students like the (male) teacher a lot."			
(9)	*tu-ḥibb-(u)*	*ʔal-ṭṭaalibat-(u)*	*ʔal-ʔustaadhat-(a)*	*kathirann.*
	3fs-like. imperf-(indic)	def-student. fp.(nom)	def-teacher.fs-(acc)	a lot.
	"The (female) student like the (female) teacher a lot."			
(10)	**yu-ḥibb-na*	*ʔal-ṭṭaalibat-(u)*	*ʔal-ʔustaadhat-(a)*	*kathirann.*
	3-like.imperf-fp	def-student. fp-(nom)	def-teacher.fs-(acc)	a lot.
	"The (female) students like the (female) teacher a lot."			

The agreement pattern exemplified in (7) and (9) is characterized as asymmetrical, non-canonical, or partial in Arabic syntactic studies (Bahloul & Harbert, 1993; Bolotin, 1995; Mohammad, 1990; Soltan, 2007). It is "asymmetrical" and "non-canonical" because the verb and the subject disagree in the linguistic feature of number. It is "partial" because the verb and the subject agree in two linguistic features, which are "person" and "gender." In this case, "partial" agreement is contrasted to "full" agreement in which the subject and the verb agree in terms of person, gender, and number in the subject-initial word order as demonstrated in (3) and (4).

Previous Findings in L2 Arabic

In subject-initial sentences, learners were found to depend on word order to assign agency (Al-Thawahrih, 2018). The verb-initial sentence type is broadly held to be the basic or underlying word order in Arabic. However, agreement asymmetries in this sentence type are under-researched in Arabic SLA studies. Current research has focused mostly on subject–verb agreement to better place it in its respective stage in the acquisition order of Arabic morphosyntax. It has also examined the role of L1 effects in shaping this order (see Chapter 3).

A review of the literature revealed only two studies on this topic, both of which found that asymmetry in the verb-initial word order causes difficulties in interpretation and production at the sentence level for Arabic learners. El-Ghazoly (2013) examined the acquisition of subject–verb agreement (a)symmetries, using three tasks to obtain comprehension and production data: a computer-delivered grammaticality-judgment task, a picture-description task, and a word-and-picture-game task. The study compared the performance of three English learner groups of Arabic (intermediate, upper intermediate, and advanced) in addition to a native speaker group. The study reported difficulties in the production of subject–verb agreement asymmetries by intermediate learners (29.30%). This structure starts to emerge only at the upper-intermediate proficiency (85.90%). In terms of grammaticality judgments, the results for each group were as follows: 55.6%, 82.2%, 84.4%, and 83.3%. The accuracy rates seem to indicate difficulty in fully acquiring this construction even at the advanced level. The study approached the difficulty in the acquisition of numeric constructions in terms of learner inability to detect feature constellations that are complex in nature. In addition, it related its results to the Feature Reassembly Hypothesis (Lardiere, 2008, 2009) that explains difficulty in formal feature acquisition, not in terms of lack of access to the universal feature inventory or to the inability to activate or select the relevant features, but in terms of the challenge of detecting associations between morphological forms and feature distributions and combinations.

In a recent study, Azaz (2018) found that agreement asymmetry conspires to cause incorrect sentence interpretation. The study found that English learners of Arabic tended wrongly to assign the action of the plural subject to the singular object. This wrong assignment was driven primarily by (a) the misleading match between the verb that is inflected for third-person singular and the singular lexical object, and (b) the mismatch between the verb and the plural subject in terms of number. To illustrate, beginning English-speaking learners of Arabic were found to take the sentence in (7) to mean that "It is the male teacher who likes the male students," and not "It is the male students who likes the male teacher." In this sentence, whereas the verbs are in the singular form (*yu-ḥibb-u* "he likes"), the subjects are plural lexical nouns (*ʔaṭ-ṭulaab-u* "the male students").

Also, the same study found that English learners of Arabic were found to have persistent difficulties in the production of the asymmetrical pattern of agreement in verb-initial sentences. They were found to mark the verb *fully* (for person, gender, and number) in a prompted sentence-completion task in situations in which *partial* marking (only in terms of person and gender) was the correct response. To follow up with the example in (7), they were found to mark the verb fully for number, person, and gender (i.e., they produced *yu-ḥibb-uu-na* instead of *yu-ḥibb-u*). The study attributed these difficulties to how this case of asymmetry is presented in Arabic textbooks. The authors recommended designing *focused* input-based materials and integrate them into communicative activities that require the use of this target case of asymmetry.

The Current Study

Studies that have examined subject–verb agreement asymmetries in Standard Arabic did not adopt an instructed SLA approach. For example, they have not examined the differential effects of certain instructional interventions, but rather have tested the adequacy of certain theoretical hypotheses in SLA, particularly the Processability Theory (Pienemann, 1998), Full Transfer (Schwartz & Sprouse, 1994, 1996), and Feature (Re)Assembly (Lardiere, 2008) accounts. Chapter 2 of this book has fully reviewed comparable effects of structured input and structured output. Mixed findings have been reported in these comparative studies. A number of factors were proposed as explanations: the complexity of the target construction and the specific procedures in the pedagogical treatments. The target languages tested in these comparative studies were mostly limited to English and other European languages. This has called into question the generalizability of research findings (Benati, 2001) and opened up the venue to explore other structural phenomena in less explored languages, especially those that offer grammatical intricacies in their systems (Yamashita & Iizuka, 2017).

Using a pretest/posttest design, the study described in this chapter examines the differential gains of structured-input and structured-output activities on the interpretation and production of asymmetrical subject–verb agreement in verb-initial sentences in Arabic. On top of the fact that this structural aspect is under-investigated in instructed Arabic SLA in general, it also has been found to create problems for L2 learners.

Research Questions

Motivated by the gaps identified previously, this chapter seeks to answer the following questions:

1. Are there differential effects for structured-input and structured-output activities in accurate interpretation of subject–verb agreement asymmetries by beginner English learners of Arabic?

2. Are there differential effects for structured-input and structured-output activities in accurate production of subject–verb agreement asymmetries by beginner English learners of Arabic?

Participants

A total of 30 beginner learners participated in this study. They were divided into two experimental groups: the structured-input (SI) group (n = 15) and structured-output (SO) group (n = 15). At the beginning of testing, these two L2 groups were recruited from sections of elementary Arabic (Arabic 102) at a large Arabic program at a southwestern university in the United States. The SI group consisted of nine males and six females. Their ages ranged from 18 to 21 (except for one male learner who was 37 years old) with an average of 20.78 (SD: 4.08), and on a scale ranging from 1.00 (lowest) to 5.00 (highest), their proficiency ratings ranged from 1.00 to 2.00 with an average of 1.25 (SD: 0.50) out of 5.0. The SO group consisted of three males and twelve females, whose ages ranged from 18 to 22 with an average of 20 (SD: 1.58), and whose proficiency ratings ranged from 1.00 to 2.00 with an average of 1.63 (SD: 0.43).

In their regular classrooms, the two experimental groups were taught by two different instructors who followed their lesson plans strictly. The two groups were tested toward the end of the spring semester of Arabic 102 and then immediately after (April–May 2018). Before their Arabic 102 class, the participants of the two groups had covered Arabic 101 in the same institution where the study was conducted. In their Arabic 101 and 102 classes, they were taught five days per week, 50 minutes per day.

At the time of testing, the two groups had covered the introductory part and completed Part 1 (third edition) of the Al-Kitaab book series (Brustad et al., 2011). They had also been taught basic grammatical aspects of Standard Arabic that included gender marking (at the phrasal and inter-phrasal level), question formation, the definite article, subject pronouns, plural marking, noun phrase structure, possessive pronouns, nominal and verbal sentences (symmetrical agreement only), numbers (ordinals and cardinals), adverbs, verbal nouns, superlatives, verb tense (present, past, and future), types of clauses (conditional and adjectival), subjunctives, and verb patterns. Importantly, at the time of testing, asymmetrical subject–verb agreement in verb-initial sentences had been briefly and minimally introduced once, and it had not been explicitly consolidated. Only the symmetrical subject–verb agreement pattern had been fully presented and frequently consolidated.

Table 5.1 Participant Demographic Data and Proficiency Ratings

Learner group	*Number*	*Age range/mean*	*Proficiency ratings*
Structured input	15 (9 males and 6 females)	18–21 (mean: 19.5)	1.25/5.0
Structured output	15 (3 males and 12 females)	17–20 (mean: 18.5)	1.63/5.0

Design and Procedure

After the participants were recruited in classroom visits, they were randomly assigned to their respective groups by the researcher. For logistic and programmatic reasons, the two treatments of SI and SO were conducted with participants in small groups outside the classroom with the researcher in his office. This allowed for a systematic procedure and organized data collection. The study used the classical pretest–posttest methodological design. A week before the treatments were conducted, a sentence interpretation and a sentence production test were administered (see details in the Materials section) to characterize the two groups' performance on the symmetrical and asymmetrical patterns of subject–verb agreement. These constituted the pretests. The participants took around two hours to complete them.

In addition, two instructional packets were prepared with the help of two teaching assistants under the researcher's guidance: the SI packet for the SI group and the SO packet for the SO group. The SI and SO treatments were conducted by the researcher himself, and the participants in each group took approximately an hour and a half to complete them. After that, counterbalanced versions of the interpretation and production tests were immediately administered. These constituted the posttests. The participants took around an hour and fifteen minutes to complete them. In total, the study took around four to five hours (pretest, treatment, and posttests), and the two groups were compensated for their participation from a research grant awarded to the researcher. Further details of the materials used in the study are provided next.

Instructional Treatments

Structured-Input Instruction

The SI packet consisted of two sections: (1) an explicit-information (EI) handout written in English with examples in Arabic, and (2) two referential structured-input activities. The EI handout was divided into two parts. The first provided clear explanation with examples of the symmetrical subject–verb agreement pattern in subject-initial sentences. It told the SI group that the subject and the verb in this sentence type agree in number, gender, and person, and this agreement is marked using prefixes and suffixes. The second part provided clear explanation with examples of the asymmetrical subject–verb agreement pattern in verb-initial sentences. Also, it explained that the verb agrees with the subject in gender and person but disagrees in number. The prefixes and suffixes that mark this asymmetrical agreement pattern were highlighted. The handout concluded with a note that contrasted these two patterns of agreement. The learners were made aware of verb inflections that marked the asymmetrical (i.e., partial) and the symmetrical (i.e., full) agreement.

The two referential structured-input activities consisted of reading activities designed to create form-meaning connections for asymmetrical agreement. To achieve this goal, for each sentence in these activities, a picture and an English prompt were provided. They captured what a group of people (e.g., students, family members, colleagues, teachers, translators, employees, etc.) were doing. The topics in these sentences included daily routines, work, family visits, and hobbies. In the first activity, the participants of the SI group were instructed, after reading the prompt and seeing the picture, to select *all* the correct sentences (whether subject-initial or verb-initial) that describe the action. Sample items are provided in (11) and (12).

This activity included 32 test items in which the subjects were distributed between human masculine plurals ($n = 16$) and human feminine plurals ($n = 16$). For each test item in this activity, six options were provided, out of which only two were correct: (a) subject-initial sentence with the symmetrical subject–verb agreement pattern, and (b) verb-initial sentence with the asymmetrical subject–verb agreement pattern. In two of the remaining incorrect four options, the verb inflections were wrongly manipulated, and in two options, the sentences provided did not accurately describe what the picture and the English prompt captured.

(11)

Prompt: My family members visit my brother during the holiday every year.

١. أخي في العطلة my family members يزور أفراد عائلتي holiday.
٢. يزورون أفراد عائلتي أخي في العطلة.
٣. أفراد عائلتي يزورون أخي في العطلة.
٤. أفراد عائلتي يزور أخي في العطلة.
٥. أخي يزور أفراد عائلتي في العطلة.
٦. يزور أخي أفراد عائلتي في العطلة.

(12)

Prompt: The male students get to know the new student in class.

١. على الطلاب في الصف. gets to know الطالب الجديد يتعرّف
٢. يتعرّف الطلاب على الطالب الجديد في الصف.
٣. يتعرّفون الطلاب على الطالب الجديد في الصف.
٤. يتعرّف الطالب الجديد على الطلاب في الصف.
٥. الطلاب تتعرّف على الطالب الجديد في الصف.
٦. الطلاب يتعرّفون على الطالب الجديد في الصف.

In the second activity, after reading the prompt and seeing the picture, the participants were asked to decide whether the sentence presented was correct or incorrect. This activity included 32 items that were distributed between

(a) subject-initial sentences with the symmetrical subject–verb agreement pattern (n = 16) and (b) verb-initial sentences with the asymmetrical subject–verb agreement pattern (n = 16). Sample items are provided in (13) and (14).

(13)

Prompt: The family members are visiting my brother during the holiday.		يزورون أفراد الأسرة أخي في العطلة.
	Correct	Incorrect (if so, why)?

(14)

Prompt: The male translators ask the new director about the work.		يسألون المترجمون المدير الجديد عن العمل.
	Correct	Incorrect (if so, why)?

The 32 test items were equally distributed between correct and incorrect sentences and the subjects were equally distributed between masculine-human plurals and feminine-human plurals. Importantly, in the incorrect sentences, the verb inflections were wrongly manipulated. In these two activities, the participants were not allowed to change their responses once provided, and no feedback was given after each item.

Structured-Output Instruction

The SO materials also consisted of two parts: the same EI handout that was used in the SI packet, along with two output activities. In these activities, the participants of the SO group were pushed to produce the symmetrical and asymmetrical subject–verb agreement patterns (see Appendix B). In the first activity, the participants were instructed, after reading the English prompt and seeing the picture, to write two sentences that best capture the prompt and the picture. It included 32 items that were distributed between subject-initial sentences with the symmetrical subject–verb agreement pattern (n = 16 items) and verb-initial sentences with the asymmetrical subject–verb agreement pattern (n = 16 items). In these two types of agreement, the subjects were equally distributed between masculine human plurals (n = 8) and feminine human plurals (n = 8).

In the second output activity, the participants were instructed, after reading the prompt and seeing the picture, to reorder a given string of words to create two complete sentences: a complete subject-initial sentence and a complete a verb-initial sentence. The verb forms in the string were in the plural form for both types of sentences. It included 32 items in which the subjects were distributed between human masculine plurals (n = 16) and human feminine plurals (n = 16). Consistent with the two SI activities, participants were not allowed to change their responses once provided, and no feedback was given after each item.

(15)

Prompt: The female students know their female teacher.

الطالباتـــالأستاذةـــتعرفنـــجيدًا

Subject First:

____

Verb First:

____

(16)

Prompt: The members of my family travel every year.

أفرادـــكلـــسنةـــعائلتيـــيسافرون

Subject First:

____

Verb First:

____

Measures of Instructional Outcomes

Sentence-Interpretation Test

The sentence-interpretation test asked the participants in the two experimental groups to determine the correct interpretation of 64 Arabic sentences by underlining one of two options provided in English. These 64 sentences were distributed into (i) subject-initial sentences with the symmetrical subject (human plural)–verb agreement pattern (n = 32 items) and (ii) verb-initial sentences with the asymmetrical subject (human plurals)–verb agreement pattern (n = 32 items). The plural lexical subjects in each of the symmetrical and asymmetrical conditions were equally distributed between masculine human plurals (n = 16 items) and feminine human plurals (n = 16 items). All the verbs and lexical subjects in the test sentences were frequent words, and translations of difficult vocabulary were provided in English to facilitate meaning absorption.

In addition to these 64 items, the sentence-interpretation test included 15 filler sentences. The total sentences in the test were randomly scrambled to counter the effect of strategic guessing. In each of the subject-initial sentences with the symmetrical pattern of agreement, the subject was a human plural (masculine or feminine), and the verb denoted a common or frequent action, and the object was a singular human noun and its gender was congruent with the gender of the plural subject (whether masculine or feminine). World knowledge was controlled for by carefully selecting sentences in which the subject and the object could perform the action. An example test sentence is provided in (11):

(17) *Sample sentence:*

ʔal-ṭulaab-u	*yu-ḥibb-uu-na*	*ʔal-ʔustaadh-a*	*kathirann.*
def-students.m.p-nom	3-like-m.p. imperf-indic	def-teacher.m-acc	a lot.

"The (male) students like the (male) teacher a lot."

Task: Select the correct interpretation:

a. It is the male students who like the male teacher a lot.
b. It is the male teacher who likes the male students a lot.

The expectation for (11) was that participants would select the first interpretation in (a). This decision would be motivated by two reasons. First, it is consistent with the predominant word order in English (SVO). Second, and most importantly, the subject and the verb show a symmetrical pattern of agreement in terms of person (third person), gender (masculine) and number (plural).

In the verb-initial sentences with the asymmetrical pattern of agreement, along the same lines of the symmetrical pattern, the subject in each sentence was a human plural noun (masculine or feminine), the verb denoted a common action, and the object was a singular human noun and its gender was congruent with the gender of the plural subject (whether masculine or feminine). An example test sentence is provided in (12):

(18) *Sample sentence:*

ya-ʕrif-u	*zumalaaʔ-ii*	*ṣadiiq-ii*	*jayyidan.*
3ms-know. present-indic	colleagues.3mp-my	friend.m-my	well.

"My (male) colleagues know my (male) friend well."

Task: Select the correct interpretation:

a. It is my (male) colleagues who know my (male) friend well.
b. It is my (male) friend who knows my (male) colleagues well.

The correct response to (12) is still (a), but it shows an asymmetrical pattern of agreement; the verb agrees with the verb in person and gender, but they disagree in number (a masculine plural noun took a masculine singular verb). As reported in

Azaz (2018), it is predicted that the participants from the two groups will tend to assign the wrong interpretation to the sentence as a result of the agreement asymmetry. They are expected to assign the wrong interpretation in (b). The fact that the object is a third-person masculine singular that shows symmetrical agreement with the verb in person, number, and gender would conspire to motivate the wrong interpretation.

Sentence-Production Test

The sentence-production test was carefully designed to elicit the symmetrical subject–verb agreement pattern in subject-initial sentences (*n* = 32) and the asymmetrical pattern in verb-initial sentences (*n* = 32). Test instructions directed the participants in the two experimental groups to read each sentence to understand the meaning established in each and provide the single missing word (which was a frequent verb) with the help of a picture prompt. Participants were required to provide their responses in Standard Arabic, in writing in a paper–pencil format. The 32 test sentences in each condition were equally distributed into masculine human plurals (*n* = 16 items) and feminine human plurals (*n* = 16 items). In addition, 20 filler sentences were included.

All the test sentences were in the imperfective (present) tense, clarified by frequency adverbs that denote habitual present such as "sometimes," "usually," "always," etc. All the subjects in the test sentences in the two conditions were common and frequent human plural nouns. Furthermore, all the verbs were common everyday life actions. Translations of some difficult vocabulary were provided in English to facilitate reading the test sentences and help the participants to absorb the meaning. Two examples of the symmetrical and asymmetrical agreement pattern in the imperfective are provided in (19) and (20), respectively.

(19)	*ʔaḥyaanan*	*ʔal-ʔawlaad*	**HELP**	*al-waalid*	*fii*	*ʔal-ʕamal.*
	Sometimes	the-boys	________________	the father	at	work.

(20)	*ʔaḥyaanan*	**HELP**	*ʔal-ʔawlaad*	*al-waalid*	*fii*	*ʔal-ʕamal.*
	Sometimes	____________	the-boys	the father	at	work.

In (19), the subject surfaces first and the frequency adverb "sometimes" establishes a habitual present and the plural subject *ʔal-ʔawlaadu* "the boys" surfaces before the verb "to help." The picture that follows the noun denotes the verb or the action "to help." The participants were expected to understand the meaning established in the sentence and provide the correct form of the missing verb, which is "*yu-saaʕid-uu-na.*" This correct form shows a symmetrical agreement pattern between the plural subject and the verb in terms of person (third person), gender (masculine), and number (plural). In the imperfective, the prefix *ya-* marks the third-person masculine and the suffix *-uu-na* marks masculine plural.

In (20), the verb surfaces first followed by the plural subject. The participants were expected to understand the meaning established in the sentence and provide the correct form of the verb "*yu-saaʕid-u*," but not "*yu-saaʕid-uu-na*." In contrast to (15), in this verb form, the prefix *ya-* marks the third-person masculine singular, but the number marker *-uu-na* should not surface on the verb forms. Therefore, the subject and the verb agree in person (third person) and gender (masculine) but disagree in number (the verb remained in the singular form "*yu-saaʕid-u* "he helps," although the subject was a plural noun).

Scoring and Analysis

The interpretation and production scores of the asymmetrical subject–verb agreement pattern for the two participant groups were the focus of this study. Participants' responses to this asymmetrical pattern of agreement were screened to determine the missing items before response categorization and scoring were initiated. The sentence interpretation task forced the L2 learner groups to choose between the correct and the incorrect interpretation, and the participants were asked to make their best guess. No missing items were found either in the pretest or the posttest for the two learner groups. A correct sentence interpretation was given a value of 1 and an incorrect one was given a value of 0.

For the sentence-production task, after raw data in the pretests and the posttests were screened, responses were divided into two categories: (a) invalid and (b) valid. Invalid responses consisted of those left blank and those in which the participant produced a verb conjugated with the wrong subject (i.e., using first and second person instead of third person). Valid responses consisted of those in which the verb was conjugated with the correct third-person subject, whether masculine or feminine, singular or plural. Special attention was given to the prefixes and suffixes that surfaced in the verb form. Only verbs marked with the third-person masculine singular marker {*ya-*} and the third-person feminine singular marker {*ta-*} were considered correct. When the verb was fully inflected for person, number, and gender, the response was scored as incorrect. In addition, if a participant provided features markings, as outlined previously, but in the perfective tense (past), his/her response was considered scorable or valid, and it was distributed into the correct or incorrect categories accordingly.

The distribution of valid and invalid tokens in the asymmetrical pattern of agreement, the focus of this study, is presented in Table 5.1. The total number of the items that was expected for each group was 480 tokens (15 participants * 32 items). In scoring the sentence-production task, a correct verb form was given the value of 1.00 and an incorrect one was given the value of 0.00.

The accuracy scores on the asymmetrical pattern of agreement were averaged per individual participants and across the two learner groups in the interpretation and production tests. These averages were inputted into a repeated measures ANOVA test using version 25 of the SPSS software.

Results

Results of the two learner groups on the asymmetrical pattern of agreement are presented in Table 5.3. The pretest scores were generally very low.

A one-way ANOVA test was conducted to determine whether the two learner groups' pretest scores differed at the beginning of the study. Expectedly, it returned no statistically significant difference between the two groups' pretests either on interpretation (F (1, 28) = 0.424, p = 0.520) or on production (F (1, 28) = 0.441, p = 0.512).

Answer to the First Research Question: Differential Effects in the Interpretation of Subject–Verb Agreement Asymmetries

The first research question asked whether there were differential effects for the SI and SO treatments in English-speaking learners' correct interpretation of verb-initial sentences that show asymmetrical subject–verb agreement in Standard Arabic. Before answering this question, the separate effects of each treatment were calculated using the repeated-measures ANOVA with *Treatment* as an independent factor and *Accuracy* as the dependent factor in the interpretation test. It returned a significant difference between the pretest and the posttest scores of the SI group (F(1, 14) = 294.8, p = 0.000, η^2 = 0.955) and the pretest and the posttest scores of the SO group (F(1, 14) = 180.7, p = 0.000, η^2 = 0.928). This result means that each

Table 5.2 Distribution of Valid and Invalid Tokens in the Production of Asymmetrical Agreement

Group	*Pretest*					*Posttest*				
	Valid		*Invalid*		*Total*	*Valid*		*Invalid*		*Total*
	Count	*%*	*Count*	*%*	*%*	*Count*		*Count*	*%*	*%*
SI	413/480	0.86	67/480	0.14	1.00	466/480	0.97	14/480	0.03	1.00
SO	431/480	0.90	49/480	0.10	1.00	459/480	0.96	21/480	0.04	1.00

Table 5.3 Averages of Correct Responses on the Asymmetrical Subject–Verb Agreement

Group	*N*	*Interpretation*		*Production*	
		Pretest (%)	*Posttest (%)*	*Pretest (%)*	*Posttest (%)*
SI	15	0.12	0.97	0.15	0.95
SO	15	0.07	0.92	0.22	0.93

type of treatment was effective in improving learners' interpretation of verb-initial sentences with the asymmetrical pattern of agreement.

To directly answer the first question, a one-way ANOVA (with factor *Treatment*) was conducted only on the posttest scores of the SI and SO groups on the sentence-interpretation test. It returned no significant difference: ($F(1, 28) = 1.698$, $p = 0.203$). Also, when the ANOVA test was run on both the pretest and the posttest scores of the interpretation test for the two groups, it showed no significant difference for *Treatment* (whether SI or SO) ($F(1, 28) = 1.233$, $p = 0.276$), and there was no significant interaction between *Treatment* (whether SI or SO) and *Time* (whether pretest or posttest): $F(1, 28) = 0.004$, $p = 0.948$). This result suggests that both types of treatments were similarly effective in improving learners' correct interpretation of verb-initial sentences with the asymmetrical type of agreement. The two learner groups made similar gains in assigning the correct interpretation.

Answer to the Second Research Question: Differential Effects in the Interpretation of Subject-Verb Agreement Asymmetries

The second research question asked whether there were differential effects for the SI and SO in English-speaking learners' production of the asymmetrical subject–verb agreement pattern in verb-initial sentences. Before this question was answered, the separate effects of SO and SI treatments were calculated using the repeated-measures ANOVA with *Treatment* as an independent factor and *Accuracy* as the dependent factor. It returned a significant difference between the pretest and the posttest scores of the production test of the SI group ($F(1, 14) = 157.9$, $p = 0.000$, $\eta^2 = 0.919$) and the pretest and the posttest scores of the SO group ($F(1, 14) = 59.3$, $p \leq 0.001$, $\eta^2 = 0.809$).

This result suggests that each type of treatment was significantly effective in improving learners' production of the asymmetrical pattern of agreement. To directly answer the question, a one-way ANOVA (with factor *Treatment*) was run only on the posttest scores of the SI and SO groups on the sentence-production test. It returned no significant difference: ($F(1, 28) = 0.892$, $p = 0.353$). Also, when the pretests and the posttest scores of the production test for the two groups were included in the analysis, it still showed no significant difference for *Treatment* ($F(1, 28) = 0.197$, $p = 0.661$), and there was no significant interaction between *Treatment* (whether SI or SO) and *Time* (pre versus post): $F(1, 28)$, 0.664, $p = 0.422$.

Discussion

The present study examined the effects of SI and SO activities in the acquisition of a single case that exhibits morphosyntactic intricacies in Standard Arabic, which is the asymmetrical subject–verb agreement. As the name suggests, there is disagreement between the subject and the verb in the linguistic feature of a number; the verb is inflected for third-person singular although the subject is a plural noun. The results showed that each treatment type (whether SI or SO) significantly improved learner interpretation and production. Also, there were no significant differences between the two groups either in interpretation or in production, which suggests that both treatments were similarly effective in receptive and productive knowledge.

The pretest scores of the interpretation test showed that the SI group tended to depend on subject–verb agreement to wrongly assign the action denoted by the verb to the singular object instead of the plural subject. The demands of the activities faced by the SI group required them to make a judgment and correctly assign the action to the plural subject instead. In the first activity, they were required to choose all the possible correct sentences (whether subject-initial or verb-initial), and in the second they were required to make decisions about the grammatical accuracy of a set of sentences. In these two types of activities, the sentence types (whether subject-initial or verb-initial) and the agreement pattern (whether symmetrical or asymmetrical) were manipulated.

The correct responses in the posttest scores of the interpretation test suggest that the SI activities helped learners to create strong form-meaning mapping while interpreting the asymmetrical pattern of agreement. They successfully assigned the action of the verb, which is inflected for third-person singular, to a plural subject in verb-initial sentences. This form-meaning connection caused accuracy in interpretation to improve significantly in the posttest. If feature compatibility is considered an underlying characteristic of Arabic morphosyntax that is violated for word-order constraints in verb-initial sentences (Ryding, 2005), the SI activities helped learners to make form-meaning connection in a case that runs against this underlying characteristic. It is highly likely that the structured input they received in the two activities directed their attention to this asymmetrical pattern. Although the treatment in the present study combined the EI and the SI activities, it is unlikely that the obtained effect is attributable to EI alone. Many studies have found evidence that EI alone did not result in similar gains to those obtained when EI and SI were combined (Benati, 2004; VanPatten & Oikkenon, 1996; Wong, 2004).

The SI group's significant gains in the production of the asymmetrical pattern of agreement are compatible with results of studies conducted within the PI framework (e.g., Benati, 2005; Cadierno, 1995; Farley, 2001a, 2001b; VanPatten & Cadierno, 1993). These studies concluded that input-based activities combined with explicit information enhance productive knowledge. The posttest scores of the production test support this conclusion. Learners of the SI group produced the asymmetrical pattern of agreement to a considerable degree of success. This suggests that the target asymmetrical pattern of agreement was accommodated in their developing linguistic system as a result of the SI activities they have engaged in. They did not show fluctuation between verb forms that are *fully* marked for person, number, and gender, and verb forms that are *partially* marked for person and gender. This stability in production is viewed as a window into the accommodation of the asymmetrical agreement pattern in their developing linguistic system.

Although the skill-acquisition theory (DeKeyser, 2007a, 2007b; DeKeyser & Sokalski, 1996) and the output hypothesis (Swain, 1995, 2005) can adequately account for the finding that the SO group made significant improvement in the production test, the result that they also made significant gains in the interpretation of the asymmetrical pattern of agreement is an unexpected finding. In fact, these comparable effects in sentence interpretation are incompatible with studies that showed that SI was more effective than SO in sentence interpretation (see Shintani, 2014, for an overview of these studies). One adequate explanation for this unexpected result is that SO learners obtained incidental cues from the output activities that were sufficient and robust enough to *alter* their incorrect processing strategy for the asymmetrical pattern of agreement. Recall that in the SO activities, word order was manipulated and the participants were requested to correctly form agreement in subject-initial (symmetrical) and verb-initial sentences (asymmetrical). This contrastive pattern of symmetrical versus asymmetrical agreement seems to have offered sufficient or plentiful cues that learners utilized when they were faced with the interpretation test. A number of studies have reported similar gains in interpretation; as a result, this incidental exposure, while the focus, was on production (e.g., Farley, 2001b; Keating & Farley, 2008; Morgan-Short & Bowden, 2006; Yamashita & Iizuka, 2017).

Conclusion

The study described in this chapter provides evidence that instructional methods that give learners the opportunity to engage in producing language output in structured output-based activities leads to the acquisition of irregular or asymmetrical structures in interpretation and production. The learning gains of the SO are notable because they challenge claims that there is no specific role for output in creating an underlying competence (VanPatten, 2004). Indeed, they suggest that output formulation may lead to the processing of form-meaning mappings and impact on the L2 developing system. The results of this study also suggest that SO activities are as effective as SI activities when it allows learners to correctly interpret and produce structures that go against the symmetrical patterns of agreement. The fact that, in this study, students in both instructional groups showed gains in interpretation and production demonstrates that output and input both impact on the developing language system. This may suggest that there are different *routes* to L2 development (Erlam et al., 2009). Future research needs to investigate whether particular structures are more amenable to one type of instruction than the other.

Although the results of this study have not shown which treatment is superior, they have important implications in the instructed second language acquisition of grammatical asymmetries in Arabic and other less commonly taught languages. The scarce research conducted on the acquisition of the agreement asymmetries in Arabic showed that the plentiful instances of the asymmetrical subject–verb agreement in learning materials did not guarantee satisfactory performance in the absence of *focused* instruction (Azaz, 2018). The first implication of this study is that carefully structured linguistic input is crucial to foster form-meaning connections in Arabic grammatical aspects that show asymmetries. Highly structured input has the potential to alter learners' incorrect processing strategies and inculcate target-like ones. Processing instruction is recommended as an effective technique in teaching the intricacies of the grammatical system of Arabic (see Farhat & Benati, 2018). Such system is often categorized under "wild" or "rogue" grammars (Lardiere, 2008) because of the complex ways in which the morpho-syntactic features behave and interact with word order. The manipulation of linguistic input in ways that show Arabic learners how the pattern of agreement (symmetrical versus asymmetrical) changes according to the sentence type (subject-initial versus verb-initial) is highly recommended for teaching Arabic as a foreign language.

Another implication for teachers of Arabic is the pressing need to develop structured output activities that push learners to produce the asymmetrical pattern of agreement. The verb-initial word order in Arabic is incongruent with the canonical subject-initial word order in English. Learners usually tend to escape this incongruency and resort to the alternative subject–verb word order, although it may not be the target-like word order. The structured-output activities offer ample opportunities to push learners to produce this asymmetrical pattern in the verb-initial word order, allowing learners to consult their linguistic knowledge about which form to produce in this word order. Arabic may not be the only less commonly taught language that poses these intricacies for learners. Teachers of other less commonly taught languages need to develop input-based and output-based activities that guide learners to process and produce these grammatical intricacies.

Future studies could address a number of limitations. First, the small number of participants in each treatment in the present study calls for a future study with larger samples. Also, because the present study could not include delayed post-tests, it could not address the question of the durability of effects. A future study will need to consider the delayed effects of the two treatments on the interpretation and production of the asymmetrical pattern of agreement. Finally, the present study used only referential activities. Future studies should expand on the current work by using different types of activities, referential and communicative, and examining their effects on the production of the asymmetrical type of agreement in longer discourse that goes beyond the sentence level.

6 Instructed Second Language Acquisition of Numeral Agreement Asymmetries

Enriched Input-Based and Enhanced Input-Based Instruction

Introduction

Numeral–Noun Agreement Asymmetries

As explained in Chapter 2, numeral–noun constructions in Standard Arabic are known for their remarkable complexity. Cardinals in particular have been subject to considerable attention from both Arabic grammarians and generative linguists due to their symmetrical and asymmetrical realities. Simplex numerals (1–10) are classified into two groups according to their agreement behavior: 1–2 and 3–10. Simplex 1 and 2 are shown, *first*, to occur only post-nominally and, *second*, to agree with the numerated noun in gender, definiteness, and case. The nouns and the number that follow form an adjectival phrase in which singular masculine nouns are assigned numbers in the masculine form, and singular feminine nouns are assigned numbers in the feminine form. This is illustrated in (1) and (2).

(1)	*qaraʔtu*	*kitaab-a-n*	*waaḥid-a-n.*
	I read	book.s.m-acc-indef	one.s.m-acc-indef
	I read one book.		
(2)	*qaraʔtu*	*qiṣṣat-a-n*	*waaḥida-(t)a-n.*
	I read	story.s.f- acc-indef	one.f.s.-acc-indef
	I read one story.		

In contrast to the symmetrical agreement pattern noticed in simplex numbers 1 and 2, simplex numbers 3–10 show an asymmetrical pattern with their accompanying nouns in terms of gender. In this asymmetrical pattern (also known as gender reversal), masculine plural nouns are assigned numbers in the feminine form, and

DOI: 10.4324/9781003055600-7

feminine plural nouns are assigned numbers in the masculine form. This is illustrated in (3) and (4):

(3)	*qaraʔtu*	*thalaath-a(t)-a*	*kutuub-i-n.*
	I read	three-s.f-acc	book.p.m-gen-indef.
	I read three books.		
(4)	*qaraʔtu*	*thalaath-a*	*qiṣṣaṣ-i-n.*
	I read	three.s.m-acc	stories.s.f-gen-indef.
	I read three stories.		

Some essential observations were made about these two examples in Chapter 1. *First*, the number precedes the noun. *Second*, they show reverse gender agreement that is determined by the gender of the singular form of the enumerated noun rather than by the gender of the plural form. This is clear in cases involving broken plurals of inanimate objects (notice that in *kitaab* "book" is masculine, but *kutub* "books" is feminine). *Third*, the plural noun is consistently assigned the genitive case because the number and the noun form a construct state or annexation phrase (*ʔiḍaafa)* in which the second noun must be assigned a genitive case. Also, whereas the counted noun can be definite or indefinite, the numerals can have neither the definite article *ʔal-* nor the indefinite article *-n*. In this regard, in case of numeric-masculine plurals, the feminine marker {a} that is attached to the numbers in writing as *taaʔ marbuuṭa* is pronounced as *open taaʔ* (note that it is normally pronounced as {a}).

Previous Findings in L2 Arabic

To the author's knowledge, El-Ghazoly (2013) is the only study in L2 Arabic research that has examined the acquisition of numeric asymmetries. The study used three tasks (a computer-delivered grammaticality-judgment task, a picture-description task, and a picture game) to obtain comprehension and production data from three learner groups (intermediate, upper intermediate, and advanced) and a native speaker group. Results indicated no significant difference between the native and the advanced groups (72% compared to 80%) in their suppliance of morphosyntactic markings required in asymmetrical numeral–noun constructions, but it found a significant difference between the intermediate and the advanced groups (23% compared to 52%). The accuracy rates seem to indicate considerable difficulty in fully acquiring the construction in question not only at the learner level but also in native speakers.

The study approached the difficulty in the acquisition of numeric constructions in terms of learner inability to detect feature constellations that are complex in nature. In addition, the author related its results to the Feature-Reassembly

Hypothesis by Lardiere (2008, 2009) that explains difficulty in formal feature acquisition not in terms of lack of access to the universal feature inventory or to the inability to activate or select the relevant features, but in terms of the inability to detect associations between morphological forms and feature distributions and combinations.

The Current Study

One of the most important observations about numeric asymmetries in Standard Arabic is gender reversal: the numeral is assigned a masculine marker when defining a feminine noun, and vice versa. In this pattern of inverted gender, disagreement is determined by the gender of the singular form of the enumerated noun rather than by the gender of the plural form as in cases involving broken plurals of inanimate objects (notice that in *kitaab* "book" is masculine, but *kutub* "books" is feminine). This feature mismatch poses challenges for native speakers and L2 learners of Arabic as demonstrated in El-Ghazoly (2013).

This chapter examines the differential gains of two types of input (input enrichment and input enhancement), in the development of explicit and implicit knowledge of the numeric asymmetries outlined previously. Although both types are considered *unobtrusive* techniques that focus on certain language forms, they are differentiated based on the learning conditions under which input is manipulated. Input enrichment, as a form of implicit instruction, is often used in the context of a meaning-focused activity in which L2 learners are provided with input loaded with the target feature without telling them that they will be tested afterwards (Hulstijn, 2003). In the input-enhancement condition, on the other hand, the target feature or form is often manipulated in certain ways such as underlining, bolding, or simply reading it with high intonation to draw the learner's attention.

The differential effects of these two types of input manipulation in the development of explicit and implicit knowledge have been debated (see Chapter 2). As mentioned in the overview of this chapter, Reinders and R. Ellis (2009) found that asking students learning English to consciously attend to the target structure in explicit/direct instruction in which they are provided with metalinguistic explanation of the target feature *can impede* the acquisition of implicit knowledge. They concluded that there is no evidence that a noticing instruction can be effective in assisting acquisition. The same observation was made by N. Ellis (1993) that implicit instruction consisting of enriched input worked better than a more explicit form of instruction consisting of enhanced input when the structure was a difficult one. It is noteworthy that none of the studies conducted on these two types of input condition scrutinized to what degree a combination of enhanced input and explicit instruction could result in the development of explicit knowledge. Also, it is not known whether this combination can result in the development of implicit knowledge that arguably is linked to explicit knowledge.

Research Questions

To address these research gaps, this chapter answers two questions:

1. Are there differential gains for implicit instruction via input enrichment and explicit instruction via input enhancement in the development of *explicit* knowledge of numeral–noun agreement asymmetry in Standard Arabic by intermediate English learners of Arabic?
2. Are there differential gains for implicit instruction via input enrichment and explicit instruction via input enhancement in the development of *implicit* knowledge of numeral–noun agreement asymmetry in Standard Arabic by intermediate English learners of Arabic?

Participants

A total of 45 intermediate learners participated in this study. They were divided into three experimental groups: control group ($n = 15$), enriched-input group ($n = 15$), and enhanced-input group ($n = 15$). These three L2 groups were recruited from sections of intermediate Arabic at the Arabic programs in a large public university in the United States over two years. Their biographic information is provided in Table 6.1.

These participants were recruited toward the end of their third semester of Arabic. They had been exposed to a total of about 215 contact hours of instruction. In their regular classrooms, the three experimental groups were taught by two different instructors who followed a handout prepared by the researcher. They were tested three times. The pretesting was completed two days before the intervention, and the posttesting was completed twice: immediately after the end of the intervention and ten days later. At the time of testing, the three groups had completed the Introductory Part, Part 1 (third edition), the first two lessons of Part II of the Al-Kitaab book series (Brustad et al., 2011). They had studied multiple grammatical aspects of Standard Arabic that included gender marking (at the phrasal and inter-phrasal level), question formation, the definite article, subject pronouns, plural marking, noun phrase structure, possessive and demonstrative pronouns, superlatives, present tense with common verb patterns in nominal and verbal sentences, adverbs, superlatives, verb tenses, and sentence complements.

Table 6.1 Participant Demographic Data and Proficiency Ratings

Learner group	*Number*	*Age range/mean*	*Ratings*
Control	15 (12 males and 3 females)	18–20 (mean: 19.00)	2.0/6.0
Enriched input	15 (10 males and 5 females)	19–20 (mean: 19.5)	2.0/6.0
Enhanced input	15 (11 males and 4 females)	19–22 (mean: 19.5)	2.0/6.0

Importantly, at the time of testing the learners were not introduced to the numeral–noun agreement asymmetries, although they studied Arabic numbers. This grammatical feature of agreement asymmetry was not taught or consolidated in instruction because it is an uninterpretable feature (does not communicate new meaning in the phrase). However, it is quite common in Arabic textbook material to teach Arabic numbers in first and second years. For example, the participants in this study studied numbers from zero to ten in the first year. Consistently, in the material they studied, simplex numbers 1 and 2 appeared in the masculine form and numbers 3–10 appeared in the feminine form (see pages 71–72 in Alif Baa). In the second year, the participants were guided to the case marks in these numeral–noun constructions. For example, there was explicit explanation that these constructions formed a construct phrase in which the number takes nominative, accusative, or genitive cases (based on word order), but the noun is consistently assigned genitive case. However, they did not study gender reversal in the simplex numbers 3–10 (see lesson 7 of Part II of Al-Kitaab) although a few instances of these were provided.

Design and Procedure

The three learner groups were pretested one day before they received the instruction that took place at the beginning of the week. Instruction took a full session of around 50 minutes. Students were asked not to review any learning materials before they did the posttesting that took place in multiple small sessions. In total, the study took around two hours (pretest, treatment, and two posttests), and they were compensated for their participation from a research grant awarded to the researcher ($40 each). The next sections detail the materials used in the intervention and testing.

Instructional Treatments

Implicit Instruction Through Enriched Input

The enriched-input instruction was in the form of a meaning-focused activity in which L2 learners were provided with a reading passage about Cairo and its attractions. Following Hulstijn (2003), they were not told that they would be tested afterwards. The activity consisted of four parts: in the first (individual work), the learners listened to an audio recording of a passage along with the text about Cairo attractions. It included 40 instances of numeric constructions, 30 of which focused on numeric asymmetries with numbers 3–10 with masculine and feminine plurals. They read the passage (individually) for around 20 minutes. The numeric constructions in the passage were not highlighted in any format (highlighted here for reader convenience). In the second part (individual work), they wrote complete sentences on a sheet of paper about Cairo attractions (see sample in (4)).

(4)

مدينة القاهرة

مدينة القاهرة هي مكان واحد لكن فيه عشرة أماكن تاريخية معروفة. وتعتبر من أكبر خمس مدن سياحة في الشرق الأوسط وشمال افريقيا. القاهرة فيها أربعة حدائق رائعة، وسبعة أسواق مميزة، كما أنها تشتهر بثلاثة مقاهي تاريخية منها ما يقع على النيل مباشرة. وللقاهرة تاريخٌ طويل حيث بها أربعة متاحف ذات تراث غني وكذلك تسعة معابد أثرية. تضم العاصمة المصرية القاهرة الكثير من الفنادق، منها ستة فنادق كبيرة جدا على نهر النيل الجميل، منها فندق الفور سيزونز (Four Seasons) وفندق هيلتون. كما أن القاهرة فيها تسع مناطق أثرية تقع على أربعة مناطق تاريخية هامة. ومنطقة الأهرامات هي منطقة واحدة يوجد فيها ثلاثة أهرامات معروفة هو: خوفو وخفرع ومنقرع. في الحقيقة، أنا زرتها منذ ست سنوات وكانت زيارة ممتازة للغاية. وتقع أهرامات الجيزة على هضبة الجيزة في محافظة الجيزة، وهي من أهم الأماكن السياحة في القاهرة التي يمر فيها نيل واحد كبير وهو نهر النيل. وهذه الثلاثة أهرامات هي مقابر ملكية كل منها يحمل اسم الملك kingالذي بناه. هوي بذلك لثلاثة ملوك. كما أنَّ هناك عدد كبير من القرى الفرعونية منها عشر قرى تقع في صعيد مصر، منها أربع قرى في مدينة واحدة فقط وهي الأقصر فقط. أيضا، هناك الكثير من القصور palaces التاريخية في مصر، هناك ستة قصور معروفة، منها قصر عابدين Abdeen Palace من أشهر وأفضل عشرة أماكن سياحية في القاهرة. بني في فترة أسرة محمد علي باشا لمصر من عام 1872 حتى عام 1952. وهذا القصر الآن هو متحف يزوره آلاف السياح من أوروبا وأمريكا.

In the third part of the lesson, they worked in three groups (collaborative work) and engaged in conversations with their classmates about attractions in Cairo. They were asked to pose and answer 10–15 questions in complete sentences. In the last part of the lesson, they read the passage again (individually) as they listened to it. With that sequence, the participants were flooded with numerous instances of the asymmetrical pattern in individual and collaborative activities as they worked on the text reconstruction.

Explicit Instruction Through Enhanced Input

The procedure followed in the enhanced-input group was different from the enriched group, although it used the same text/passage. The learners were told that they were going to read a passage about Cairo and its attractions. They were also told *beforehand* that, in this passage, there is an important rule that they have to pay attention to, which is the gender of the nouns and their numbers. All the instances of this rule were highlighted and underlined in bold. Also, they were not told that they would be tested on this rule after the experiment. These were the instructions provided:

> Read this passage and listen carefully with attention to the form of the numbers and the nouns that are counted. Note that in the numeric system of 1–10 in Standard Arabic there are two categories of numbers: numbers 1 and 2 and numbers 3–10.

These are represented in the examples below:

(5)	*zurtu*	*makaan-a-n*	*waaḥid-a-n.*
	I visited	place.s.m-acc-indef	one.s.m-acc-indef
	I visited one place.		
(6)	*zurtu*	*minṭaqat-a-n*	*waaḥida-(t)a-n.*
	I visited	area.s.f- acc-indef	one.f.s.-acc-indef
	I visited one area.		
(7)	*zurtu*	*ʕashr-a(t)-a*	*ʔamaakin-i-n.*
	I visited	ten-s.f-acc	place.p.m-gen-indef.
	I visited ten places.		
(8)	*zurtu*	ʔarbaʕ*-a(t)-a*	*manaaṭiq-i-n.*
	I visited	four.s.m-acc	area.p.f-gen-indef.
	I visited four areas.		

In the first category, the nouns surface first in the linear order and they are followed by the numbers that must agree with the nouns in gender. As you may have noticed in the passage, a singular masculine noun was followed by a singular masculine number and vice versa; a singular feminine noun was followed by a singular feminine number. This is called symmetrical *agreement* between the number and the noun. In contrast, in the second category, numbers 3–10 depart from numbers 1 and 2 in two respects: the numbers surface first in the linear order followed by the nouns, and the numbers disagree with their corresponding nouns in gender. This disagreement (called also *gender reversal* or *disagreement*) is determined by the gender of the singular form of the noun regardless of being human or nonhuman as in the two examples from the passage. This explanation was followed by the same three steps in the enriched-input group.

Measures of Instructional Outcomes

Participants completed two tests in each of the three testing sessions (pretest, immediate posttest or posttest1, delayed posttest or posttest2) that assessed explicit and implicit knowledge, respectively: a grammaticality-judgment test and an oral narrative test (oral, then written). The theoretical rationale that has informed the design of these tests has been described in Chapter 2 of this book. Specific details are provided next.

Explicit Knowledge: Grammaticality-Judgment Test

The grammaticality-judgment test consisted of 44 sentences. A total of eight items created an obligatory context and tested for the participants' knowledge of the symmetrical pattern in simplex 1 (see examples 5 and 6). They were distributed between grammatical and ungrammatical items. In addition, a total of 32 sentences, distributed equally between grammatical and ungrammatical item, created obligatory contexts and tested for the participants' knowledge of the asymmetrical pattern in numbers 3–10. These balanced between masculine and feminine nouns in the plural form (see examples (7) and (8)). The remaining four items focused on irrelevant structures. Wherever possible, sentence-initial placement of the target structure of the simplex numbers 3–10 was avoided so learner attention would not be drawn to it. The distribution of these items is presented in Table 6.2 below.

Table 6.2 Item Distribution in the Grammaticality-Judgment Test

Category	*Number of items*
Symmetrical: simplex number 1	
• Grammatical	4
• Ungrammatical	4
Asymmetrical: simplex numbers 3–10	
• Masculine plurals—grammatical	8
• Masculine plurals—ungrammatical	8
• Feminine plurals—grammatical	8
• Feminine plurals—ungrammatical	8
Other items—fillers	4
Total items	44

Examples of the grammatical and ungrammatical items for the symmetrical and asymmetrical patterns are provided in (9)–(12):

(9) *madinat tusaan fiiha jaamiʔa waaḥida kabiira faqaṭ fii ʔal-madiina, hiya jaamiʕat ʔarizuuna. [Grammatical]*
Grammatical ____________ Ungrammatical ____________

(10) *fii ʔal-ḥaqiiqa ʔana ʔuḥibb makaan waaḥida fii haadhii ʔal-madiina, wa-huwaa ʔal-jaamiʕa. [Ungrammatical]*
Grammatical ____________ Ungrammatical ____________

(11) *tantashir thalaathatu ʔadyaan haamma fii ʔal-sharq ʔal-ʔawsaṭ, hiyaa ʔal-ʔislaam, wa-ʔalmasiiḥiyya wa-ʔalyahuudiyya. [Grammatical]*
Grammatical ____________ Ungrammatical ____________

(12) *ṣaadiqqi kaan lahu thalaathatu ʕalaqaat ʕaaṭifiyya ʕindama kaana fii ʔal-jaamiʕa. [Ungrammatical]*
Grammatical ____________ Ungrammatical ____________

The test was developed and conducted in an untimed paper–pencil format, and the participants were told not to look at previous test items. Test takers were asked to indicate whether each sentence was "grammatical" or "ungrammatical" by checking the relevant box. Once again, one version of the test was used over all three testing sessions, but with the order of presentation of items different for each test administration. In scoring these items, an incorrect choice was given a value of 0, and a correct one was given 1. Scores of the test were calculated and are presented as percentages.

Implicit Knowledge: Oral Narrative Test

The three groups were given the following oral narrative task in past tense that was prompted with a textual and visual component:

> After you took a very good vacation for two weeks in NY City, one of your new friends in Egypt sent you a message asking how you spent it in some detail. Record a detailed voice message to tell them about what you and your friends

did. Clear textual and visual prompts outline some of the things you did. As you record your message, cover *all* the verbs from the first to the seventh day.

The textual and visual component triggered the use of numbers 3–10 along with their counted entities, as in "On the third day, we visited five places downtown." They were also told to communicate their thoughts to their best ability. A sample recording was expected to have 20 frequencies of the number–noun constructions that were equally split between masculine and feminine plurals. A sample prompt is provided in (13):

(13)
fii ʔal-ʔusbuuʕ ʔal-ʔawaal

fii ʔal-yawm ʔal-ʔawaal
Prompts:
- *Tired after the flight. Slept for eight hours.*
- *Read three books.*

fii ʔal-yawm ʔal-thaani
Prompts:
- *Visited/swam at three beaches*
- *Ate at four restaurants: Italian, Chinese, Mexican, and Middle Eastern*

fii ʔal-yawm ʔal-thaalith
Prompts:
- *Talked to four old college friends*
- *Watched three movies at night*

Remember to use these connectors:

ʔawalann ʔayḍann thumma biʔal-ʔiḍaafa ʔilaa dhaalik kamaa wa-baʕda dhaalik

Results

Answer to the First Research Question: Differential Effects on Explicit Knowledge in Grammaticality Judgment

Symmetrical Pattern in Simplex Number 1

The results of the grammaticality-judgment test are presented in Table 6.3. The pretest means suggest that in the symmetrical condition, the three groups tended to opt for an accurate judgment whether "grammatical" or "ungrammatical." Two sample responses by a participant in the enhanced-input group are provided in (14) and (15):

(14) *ʔakhii yaʔkul fii maṭʕam waaḥid fii madinat tusaan, wa-huaa maṭʕam ʕarabii.*
Grammatical ______✓______ Ungrammatical ____________

(15) *ʔukhtii tuḥib ʔan taqraʔ kathiiran laakin ʔal-youm qaraʔat qiṣṣa waaḥid faqaṭ liʔanahaa kaanat mashghuula jidan.*
Grammatical ____________ Ungrammatical ______✓______

In (14), the participant was aware that the singular masculine noun *maṭʕam* "restaurant" should be followed by a singular masculine numeric adjectival *waaḥid.*

Table 6.3 Descriptive Statistics of the Symmetrical Agreement

	Total Items					
	Pretest		*Posttest1*		*Posttest2*	
	%	*SD*	*%*	*SD*	*%*	*SD*
Control	85.00	15.81	81.67	17.60	80.00	16.90
Enriched	85.00	10.36	95.00	10.36	90.0	12.68
Enhanced	95.00	15.81	96.67	8.80	93.33	11.44
	Ungrammatical items					
	Pretest		*Posttest1*		*Posttest2*	
	%	*SD*	*%*	*SD*	*%*	*SD*
Control	70.00	16.90	70.00	16.90	68.33	17.59
Enriched	83.33	12.20	91.67	12.20	90.00	15.81
Enhanced	81.67	19.98	95.00	910.35	95.00	10.35

In (15), the same participant was aware that the singular feminine noun *qiṣṣa* "story" should be followed by a singular feminine numeric adjective *waaḥida.* It is very likely that this participant was aware that the numeric adjective (*waaḥid* or *waaḥida*) should agree with the noun in terms of gender.

As illustrated in Table 6.3, for posttest1, mean scores of the enriched-input and enhanced-input groups were higher than those of the control group. Also, the enhanced-input and enriched-input groups did not differ considerably in their grammaticality judgments. This trend continued in posttest2. Further, accuracy judgment scores in the grammatical items were higher than the ungrammatical ones. This performance overall suggests that the two experimental groups demonstrated knowledge of symmetrical agreement between the noun and simplex number 1 that surfaces after the noun as an adjective (see discussion section).

Asymmetrical Pattern in Simplex Numbers 3–10

In contrast to the symmetrical pattern, in the initial screening of the asymmetrical pattern it was clear that that the participants were more likely to make wrong judgments across the three groups between the "grammatical" and "ungrammatical" conditions in sentences that entail gender reversal. Two sample responses are provided in (16) and (17) by one participant from the enhanced group in which the learner mistakenly opted for the wrong judgment.

(16) *tariikh miṣr ʔal-ḥadiith fiihi khamsa ruuʔasaaʔ faqaṭ baʕda jamal ʕabd ʔal-naasir.*
Grammatical ____________ Ungrammatical ______✓______

(17) *maḥmuud: yaa muḥammad, kam shaariʕan taʕrif fii madinat tuusaan?*
muḥammad: ʔaʕriff ʕashr shawaariʕ kabiira fii madinat tuusaan.
Grammatical _____✓______ Ungrammatical ____________

In (16), the participant thought that the feminine form of number *khams-a* "five" is ungrammatical with a masculine plural *ruuʔasaaʔ* "presidents." In (17), the same learner thought that a masculine number *ʕashr* "ten" is grammatical when proceeds a masculine plural *shawaariʕ* "streets." This suggests that this pattern of agreement poses greater difficulties in contrast to the symmetrical case. Also, in initial screening it was noticed that there was a difference in accuracy judgment scores between numeral-feminine and numeral-masculine plural constructions. This pattern of results motivated a separate analysis of the two constructions.

Gender Reversal in Numeral-Feminine Plural Constructions

The results of the numeral-feminine plural constructions are presented in Table 6.4. For the pretest means, the scores were strikingly low, particularly in the ungrammatical condition in contrast to the numeral-masculine plural constructions (see next section).

As shown in these tables, the enhanced-input treatment resulted in substantial improvement in making accurate judgments (i.e., explicit knowledge) in asymmetrical numeric agreement patterns with feminine plural nouns. Sample responses from one participant in the enhanced input group are provided in (18) in which they correctly shifted their judgment from *grammatical* in the pretest data to *ungrammatical* in the posttests data.

(18) Pretest
ṣaaḥibatii saara zaarat sittat manaaṭiq fii ʔal-maghrib wa-miṣr wa-ʔal-ʔurdunn ʔal- ʕaam ʔal-maaḍi.
Grammatical _____✓______ Ungrammatical ____________
Posttest 1
ṣaaḥibatii saara zaarat sittat manaaṭiq fii ʔal-maghrib wa-miṣr wa-ʔal-ʔurdunn ʔal- ʕaam ʔal-maaḍi.
Grammatical ____________ Ungrammatical ______✓______
Posttest 2
ṣaaḥibatii saara zaarat sittat manaaṭiq fii ʔal-maghrib wa-miṣr wa-ʔal-ʔurdunn ʔal- ʕaam ʔal-maaḍi.
Grammatical ____________ Ungrammatical ______✓______

Gender Reversal in Numeral-Masculine Plural Constructions

Table 6.5 shows the scores of the enriched-input and enhanced-input groups for numeric asymmetries with masculine plural nouns. In comparison to the numeral-feminine plural constructions, the pretest scores are much higher. Also, the results show some improvement in scores obtained by both groups from the pretest to posttest1 and from posttest1 to posttest2.

Sample responses by a participant from the enhanced-input group are provided in (19) in which they correctly shifted their judgment from *ungrammatical* in the pretest data to *grammatical* in the posttests data, gains which can be attributed to instruction.

Table 6.4 Descriptive Statistics of the Asymmetrical Agreement in Feminine Plurals

	Grammatical items					
	Pretest		*Posttest1*		*Posttest2*	
	%	*SD*	*%*	*SD*	*%*	*SD*
Control	41.67	25.30	38.33	23.84	38.33	23.84
Enriched	36.66	24.30	35.83	23.56	30.00	23.53
Enhanced	30.00	26.22	76.67	14.07	74.17	15.28
	Ungrammatical items					
	Pretest		*Posttest1*		*Posttest2*	
	%	*SD*	*%*	*SD*	*%*	*SD*
Control	29.17	17.47	33.33	16.14	34.16	14.53
Enriched	31.67	16.94	43.33	16.28	45.83	12.20
Enhanced	32.50	17.55	75.83	8.80	71.67	12.01

Table 6.5 Descriptive Statistics of the Asymmetrical Agreement in Masculine Plurals

	Grammatical					
	Pretest		*Posttest1*		*Posttest2*	
	%	*SD*	*%*	*SD*	*%*	*SD*
Control	75.83	14.54	77.50	14.33	78.33	15.28
Enriched	78.33	22.40	76.67	24.03	78.33	22.40
Enhanced	75.00	20.04	93.33	6.45	87.50	12.50
	Ungrammatical					
	Pretest		*Posttest1*		*Posttest2*	
	%	*SD*	*%*	*SD*	*%*	*SD*
Control	60.83	25.38	62.50	24.55	59.17	23.84
Enriched	60.00	26.81	60.83	16.95	58.33	18.09
Enhanced	57.50	25.09	88.33	3.23	80.00	12.32

(19) Pretest

tantashir thalaathatu ʔadyaan haamma fii ʔal-sharq ʔal-ʔawsaṭ, hiyaa ʔal-ʔislaam, wa-ʔalmasiiḥiyya wa-ʔalyahuudiyya.

Grammatical ____________ Ungrammatical _____✓______

Posttest 1

tantashir thalaathatu ʔadyaan haamma fii ʔal-sharq ʔal-ʔawsaṭ, hiyaa ʔal-ʔislaam, wa-ʔalmasiiḥiyya wa-ʔalyahuudiyya.

Grammatical _____✓______ Ungrammatical ____________

Posttest 2
tantashir thalaathatu ʔadyaan haamma fii ʔal-sharq ʔal-ʔawsaṭ, hiyaa ʔal-ʔislaam, wa-ʔalmasiiḥiyya wa-ʔalyahuudiyya.
Grammatical ______✓______ Ungrammatical ____________

Results indicate that participants tended to be more successful in making accurate judgments (grammatical and ungrammatical) in the condition that requires a feminine numeral with masculine plurals. They were more likely to think that the numerals have to be in the feminine form. This could also be arguably due to the memorized default feminine forms of the numbers, and not due to acquiring gender reversal (see discussion section).

To closely establish if there was an effect for instructional treatments and on which items, a four-way repeated measures ANOVA was performed with these factors: group (control, enriched input, and enhanced input), grammaticality (grammatical and ungrammatical), gender (feminine and masculine), and test time (pretest, posttest1 and posttest2). The analysis showed a statistically mean effect for group (F (2, 72) = 30.108, p = .001, ηp^2 = .807) and test time (F (2, 84) = 63.558, p < .001, ηp^2 = 0.602). Also, there was a main effect for grammaticality (F (1, 42) = 13.255, p < .001, ηp^2 = 0.240) and gender (F (1, 42) = 110.580, p < .001, ηp^2 = 0.725). Importantly, the interaction between test time and group was significant: F (4, 84) = 49.620, p < .001, ηp^2 = 0.703. Also, interaction was not statistically significant between gender and group (F (2, 42) = 3.115, p =. 0.055, ηp^2 = 0.129) nor between grammaticality and group (F (2, 42) = 0.655, p =. 0.525, ηp^2 = 0.030). There was a statistically significant four-way interaction between time, group, gender, and grammaticality: F (4, 84) = 4.159, p = .004, ηp^2 = 0.165).

To determine which group differed from which group and in what direction, a pairwise-comparisons post hoc test was used. For the numeral-feminine plural noun items in the grammatical condition, there was no difference between the enriched-input and the control groups on posttest1 (p = .060) or on posttest2 (p = .289), but there was a significant difference between the enriched- and the enhanced-input groups on posttest1 and posttest2 (p < .001 for both tests). For the ungrammatical condition, there was no difference between the enriched-input and the control groups on posttest1 (p = .298) nor on posttest2 (p = .060), but there was a significant difference between the enriched-input and the enhanced-input groups on posttest1 and posttest2 (p < .001 for both tests). For the numeral-masculine plural noun items in the grammatical condition, there was no difference between the enriched-input and the control groups on posttest1 (p = .891) nor on posttest2 (p = 1.000), but there was a significant difference between the enriched- and the enhanced-input groups on posttest1 (p = .009). This difference disappeared on posttest2 (p = .153). For the ungrammatical condition, there was no difference between the enriched-input and the control groups on posttest1 (p = .793) or on posttest2 (p = .903). However, there was a significant difference between the enriched- and the enhannced-input groups on posttest1 ($p \leq .001$) and posttest2 (p = .003).

These findings overall suggest that the enriched-input treatment did not result in making substantial gains in making accurate judgments (i.e., explicit knowledge) in asymmetrical numeric agreement patterns with feminine plural nouns. This result is corroborated by the lack of difference between the control group and the enriched group. Comparatively, the enhanced-input manipulation resulted in greater gains than the enriched-input manipulation in the development of explicit knowledge for both posttest1 and posttest2 for the grammatical and ungrammatical categories, particularly in the feminine plurals that require numerals in the masculine form. The only result that runs against this pattern is the lack of statistically significant difference between performance by the control group and the enhanced-input group in the grammatical condition with masculine plurals.

Answer to the Second Research Question: Differential Effects on Implicit Knowledge

Results of the Oral Narrative Test

In this oral narrative test, the participants were expected to produce in speaking (followed by writing) the asymmetrical pattern of numeric agreement with plural feminine and plural masculine nouns in a task that promoted a visual and textual component. The range of tokens in recordings of the three groups varied from 234 to 290 in total. The mean accuracy scores in percentages for feminine and plural nouns are presented in brief below.

Gender Reversal in Numeral–Plural Noun Constructions

The participants' accuracy scores in the asymmetrical condition of numeral-feminine and numeral-masculine plural noun constructions are presented in the following table:

Table 6.6 Descriptive Statistics of the Asymmetrical Agreement in Feminine Plurals

	Feminine Plurals					
	Pretest		*Posttest1*		*Posttest2*	
	M	*SD*	*M*	*SD*	*M*	*SD*
Control	25.57	14.90	31.74	14.93	28.67	13.46
Enriched	28.17	15.85	43.33	16.27	42.50	14.01
Enhanced	28.17	15.85	42.96	16.17	55.06	6.50
	Masculine Plurals					
	Pretest		*Posttest1*		*Posttest2*	
	M (%)	*SD*	*M (%)*	*SD*	*M (%)*	*SD*
Control	75.76	10.21	74.99	10.74	65.74	20.04
Enriched	66.85	11.55	73.19	9.96	65.19	15.42
Enhanced	70.22	13.88	80.65	14.73	77.43	13.67

The pretest scores for the three groups were strikingly lower in numeral-feminine plural noun constructions than the numeral-masculine constructions. As for the posttest scores, it is clear that the enhanced group made more gains. A representative sample from elicited responses by one participant in the enhanced input group are provided in (20):

(20) Sample Participant Posttest 1 Response

fii ʔal-ʔusbuuʕ ʔal-ʔawaal:

*Hallo sadiiqi, kant madinat niuu uurk mumtaza. fii ʔal-yawm ʔal-ʔawwal min ʔal-ʔusbuuʕ ʔana kuntu taʔbaana baʔda ʔal-riḥlaa, wa-nimtu thamaaniyaa saaʕaat, laakin baʕda dhaalika fii ʔal-masaa? qarʔaat thalaathta kutub, thumma fii ʔal-yawm ʔal-thaani ʔanaa zurtu thalaatha shawaaṭiʔ wa-sabaḥtu fihum. wa-ʔiḍann ʔanna ʔakaltu fii ʔarbaʕat maṭaaʕim ʔal-laadhi kaanat ʔal-ʔiṭaaliyya ʔal-ṣiiniyya miksiiki wa-maṭaaʕim sharq waṣaṭ. fii ʔal-yawm ʔal-thaalith ʔana takalamtu maʕa ʔarbaʕat ʔaṣdiqaaʔ qadiimat mn jaamiʕatii. bi-ʔal-ʔiḍaafa ʔilaa dhaalik ʔana shuftu thalaathat ʔaflaam fii ʔal-masaaʔ. fii ʔal-yawm ʔal-raabiʔ dhahabtu ʔilaa thalaatha makaan taarikhiyya baynama fiiha ʔal-mataaḥif. baʕ*da dhaalik fii *ʔal-yawm khaamis, ʔal-khaamis kaana mutʕabiin wa-ʔana nimt ʕashraa saʕaat ʕalaa ʔal-tawaali thalaathat ʔayaam. wa-fii ʔal-yawm zurna thalaath ʔal-hadaaʔiq wa-ʔal-raabiʕ lil-suuq khamsa maraat lil-tasawuq khamsa maraat. wa-fii ʔal-yawm ʔal-saabiʕ, ʔana ʔakaltu kamsaat taʕaam jadiid thumaa marastu ʔal-riiaaḍah sabʔa saaʕaat.*

fii ʔal-ʔusbuuʕ ʔal-thaani:

fii ʔal-yawm ʔal-ʔawwal maʕa ʔaṣdiqaaʔi ʔistamaʕnaa ʔilaa khamsat ʔalbuumaat jajiida bi-musiiqaa ʔal-riif wa-thumma fii ʔal-yawm ʔal-thaani naḥnu ʔistamtaʕnaa bi-ʔal-dhahaab ʔila khams ḥafalaat musiiqaa musiiqiyya fii markaz ʔal-madiina. fii ʔal-yawm ʔal-thaalith ʔistamtaʔna bi-mushaahadat khams ʔaflaam jaddida wa-ʔiḍann zurna thalaathat biyuut tariikhiyya wa-ʔishtarayynaa khamsat qamiṣaat jadiida. fii ʔal-yawm ʔal-raabiʕ (um . . .) raqasnaa maʕa tisʕaa ʔaṣdiqaaʔii fii ḥaflaa musiiqiyya ḥataa muntaṣaf ʔal-layl. fii ʔal-yawm ʔal-khaamis ʔana wa-ʔaṣdiqaaʔii ʕarafnaa thalaath thaqafaat ʔal-mukhtalifa min thalaath lughaat. fii ʔal-yawm ʔal-saadis ʔakhadhnaa ʔashr ṣuwarr lil-shiitaʔ wa-ʔal-ḥadaaʔiq. fii yawm ʔal-ʔakhiira youm ʔal-saabiʕ qaraʔat khamsa khams qiṣṣas jadiida khilaala riḥla fii ṭariiqa ʕawdatii.

The main pattern in the underlined numeric phrases in this sample is the tendency of the enhanced-input group to *drop* the feminine marker on the numbers with feminine plurals and retain it in case of masculine plural. This successful performance is likely attributable to the effect of the intervention in which the learners were explicitly guided to the numeric asymmetries in the enhanced-input group.

To establish if there was an effect for instructional treatments and on which items, a three-way repeated measures ANOVA was performed with group (control, enriched input, and enhanced input), gender (feminine and masculine), and test time (pretest, postest1, and postest2). The analysis showed a statistically mean effect for group: F (1, 42) = 2741.348, p = .001, ηp^2 = .359. Also, it returned a statistically mean effect for test time: F (2, 84) = 16.617, $p < .001$, $\eta p^2 = 0.283$, and gender: F (1, 42) = 220.115, $p < .001$, $\eta p^2 = 0.840$. Importantly, there was a significant interaction between test time and group: F (4, 84) = 49.620, $p < .001$, $\eta p^2 = 0.703$; gender and group: F (2, 42) = 4.732, $p = 0.014$, $\eta p^2 = 0.184$; but no interaction between gender and time: F (2, 42) = 27.942 $p = 0.055$, $\eta p^2 = 0.129$. Overall, there was a three-way interaction between time, group, and gender: F (4, 84) = 5.486, $p < .001$, $\eta p^2 = 0.400$.

To determine which group differed from which group and in what direction, a pairwise-comparisons post hoc test was used. For the numeral-feminine plural nouns, there was no statistically significant difference between the enriched-input and the control groups on posttest1 ($p = .051$) but there was statistically significant difference on posttest2 ($p = .003$). Also, there was no significant difference between the enriched- and the enhanced-input groups on posttest1 ($p < .949$), but there was a significant difference for posttest2 ($p < .001$). For the numeral-masculine plural nouns, there was no difference between the enriched-input and the control groups on posttest1 ($p = .096$) nor on posttest2 ($p = .050$), but there was a significant difference, however marginal, between the enriched- and the enhanced-input groups on posttest1 and posttest2 ($p = .050$ for both tests).

These comparisons offer a complex pattern. When compared to the control group in feminine plurals, the enriched-input treatment *did* result in the development of implicit knowledge of the numeric asymmetrical agreement pattern in the oral narrative task. This result is corroborated by the significant difference between the two groups in posttest2. Also, the enhanced group seemed to outperform the enriched group on posttest2. For masculine plural nouns, the enhanced-input group with explicit explanation made higher gains than the enriched-input group in the development of implicit knowledge in both posttest1 and posttest2. This finding runs against the observation that asking students to consciously attend to the target structure in explicit/direct instruction in which they are provided with metalinguistic explanation of the target feature can *impede* the acquisition of implicit knowledge (by Reinders & R. Ellis, 2009; see discussion section).

Discussion

There were two central questions in this chapter. The first asked about the differential effects of enriched input and enhanced input combined with explicit explanation on the development of explicit knowledge of numeric asymmetries. Explicit knowledge was measured in terms of the learners' ability to make accurate judgments in an untimed grammaticality test. The untimed set up of the grammaticity test, particularly the ungrammatical portion, was a common measure of explicit knowledge. The *second* question asked about the differential effects of enriched input and enhanced input when combined with explicit explanation on the development of *implicit* knowledge of numeric asymmetries. Implicit knowledge was measured in terms of the learners' ability to produce accurate numeral constructions with gender reversal in a production task that was promoted with a visual and textual component. This technique is commonly utilized as a measure of implicit knowledge.

The answers to the research questions differ depending on the gender and the grammaticality of the plural nouns. In the first question, for feminine plurals that require masculine numbers in the grammatical and ungrammatical condition, the posttest scores of the enriched-input group on the judgment task when compared with the control group shows that the implicit instruction via enriched input had *no* effects on the development of explicit knowledge of the asymmetrical agreement pattern. This is supported with the lack of statistical significance on the gains from pretest to posttest1 and from posttest1 to posttest2. This pattern of gains was strikingly different from the gains made by the enhanced-input group. The posttest scores of this group on the judgment task when compared with the enriched group shows that the enhanced input, when combined with a more explicit instruction, had *a considerable* effect in the development of explicit knowledge of the asymmetrical agreement pattern. The same pattern was mostly maintained with masculine plurals that are assigned feminine numerals.

Reinders and R. Ellis (2009) found that in the case of ungrammatical items in untimed grammaticality judgments (arguably the best measure of explicit knowledge), gain scores of an enhanced-input group in negative adverbs were all *negative* in the absence of explicit explanation. No group differences were found on the grammatical or ungrammatical items in the untimed test. The conceptual difficulty of negative adverbs may have prevented the learners from benefiting from deliberate attention to this structure. They were simply unable to work out the rule. The results of the judgment task in this chapter are complementary to their results. The pattern of results in the current study suggests that enriched input or input flooding does not result in the development of explicit knowledge in the case of asymmetry, but enhanced input, when combined with explanation, can accomplish this. It is argued that direct explanation is key in developing explicit knowledge of low-salience features such as morphemically asymmetric endings. The results of this task are not in line with some previous studies. For example, Leow (1998) found that an orienting (i.e., explicit) instruction had *no* effect on learners' acquisition of *irregular* Spanish verb forms.

For the second research question, the posttest scores on the oral narrative task as a measure of implicit knowledge showed a complex pattern. For feminine plurals that required masculine numerals, there was *no* difference between the control and the enriched groups on posttest1, but there was a difference in posttest2. For masculine plurals that required feminine numerals, no significant differences were found in either posttest. This indicates that the implicit instruction via enriched input had *no* significant effects on the development of implicit knowledge of the asymmetrical agreement pattern. More relevant to the second question, when the results of the enriched-input and enhanced-input groups were compared for feminine plurals, no difference was found between the enriched- and the enhanced-input groups on posttest1 ($p < .949$), but there was a significant difference for posttest2 ($p < .001$). This difference was maintained, although marginal, for masculine plurals.

These results are not in line with some of the previous literature. N. Ellis (1993), for example, found that incidental instruction consisting of enriched input worked *better than* a more explicit form of instruction when the structure was a difficult one. The results obtained here support the premise that enhanced input combined with linguistic explanation results in the development of implicit and explicit knowledge; in other words, it could develop both types of knowledge. This supports the position that explicit knowledge could develop into implicit knowledge.

Also, the results of the pretests in the numeric asymmetrical case show a statistically significant difference between the scores of numeral-masculine plural constructions and numeral-feminine plural constructions with the three groups. Across the three groups, there was a tendency to make the correct judgments and produce the feminine numerals with masculine plurals rather than to make the correct judgments and produce the masculine numerals with feminine plurals. It is very likely that this pattern is because the L2 Arabic learners used the feminine form—probably because L2 Arabic learners tend to memorize these numbers (3–10), which are in the feminine form, early on in their learning. This explanation is more plausible than learning the gender reversal, since the pretest scores in numeral-feminine plural constructions were significantly lower.

Overall, the pretest and posttest results shed light on developmental stages in the L2 acquisition of simplex numeric constructions in Arabic. The pretest data suggest that the symmetrical pattern of agreement in the simplex numbers 1–2 (*waaḥid* and *waaḥid-a*) is easier to acquire than the asymmetrical pattern with the simplex numbers 3–10 in numeric-noun constructions. It is very likely that the simplex *waaḥid* and *waaḥid-a* are easier because they are in concord with the noun–adjective agreement rules in Arabic. Word order in which the nouns surface first (and not the number) makes this feature prominent to the learners. It is plausible to outline these stages as follows: in stage 1, the learners acquire the numbers in the feminine form. In stage 2, they acquire the feminine form of numbers with masculine plurals, and in stage 3, they acquire the masculine form of numbers with feminine plurals that require dropping the feminine marker from the plural nouns. In this sequence, it is very likely that L2 learners of Arabic *learn* the feminine marker earlier in the sequence and *unlearn* it with feminine plurals at a later stage.

Conclusion

In this chapter, results were obtained using separate measures of explicit knowledge (using a grammaticality-judgment test in which grammatical and ungrammatical items were analyzed separately) and implicit knowledge using oral narrative test. The results of this study have shown that enhanced input, when combined with a more explicit instruction, had *a more considerable* effect in the development of explicit knowledge of the asymmetrical agreement pattern. Also, they have shown that implicit instruction via enriched input had *some* effects on the development of implicit knowledge of the asymmetrical agreement pattern. Enriched input in this study did assist the acquisition of implicit knowledge to some degree, but effects were greater when it was combined with enhanced input. The study is supportive of the claims that have been advanced on behalf of focus-on-form instruction (Doughty & Williams, 1998). It shows that even a very unobtrusive focus-on-form strategy *can be* effective. Norris and Ortega's (2000) general finding, namely that explicit instruction is more effective than implicit instruction, is supported by the results of this study, that enhanced input combined with explicit explanation produces the greatest learning gains. This might have been because the noticing instruction provided in this study was sufficiently explicit to assist the learners to notice the asymmetrical pattern.

Finally, one weakness of the current study was a relatively small sample size (the enriched- and enhanced-input groups had only 15 learners each). However, there was a control group as an important point of comparison. Future studies need to recruit larger samples. Also, the total exposure to the target structure was relatively limited, at about 30 exemplars in the reading passage. But then, it did produce a *measurable* effect. Future studies need to increase the number of exemplars, which would then be expected to even further increase the effect. Lastly, one would expect learners at higher proficiency to do better in noticing the asymmetries, but this needs to be tested empirically.

7 Theoretical and Pedagogical Implications

Key Premises and Controversies this Book Addressed

The research reported in this book was motivated by the dearth of studies on agreement asymmetries in Arabic from an instructed second language acquisition lens. As presented in the introduction, agreement asymmetries represent salient aspects that put Arabic among languages with "rogue" or "wild" grammars (Lardiere, 2008). These agreement asymmetries appear in basic grammatical structure, such as noun–adjective and subject–verb agreement. Notably, these asymmetries run against the pervasive symmetrical pattern of Arabic agreement in which a linguistic element (controller) determines the morphosyntactic form of another (target). There is acknowledgment in the scarce L2 Arabic research that these asymmetries pose challenges for learners. These asymmetries are neither systemically taught (El-Ghazoly, 2013) nor properly addressed in textbook materials (Azaz, 2018).

The four studies were premised on key assumptions that were made in the two background chapters of the book (Chapters 1 and 2). The first assumption was that based on their inherent characteristic, the asymmetries in question were not envisioned as equally difficult. The case for this assumption was made in Chapter 1 on agreement asymmetries in Arabic. The basis for the differentiation between symmetrical and asymmetrical agreement patterns rests on well-attested descriptive realities presented in the context of formal features, particularly number and gender. The underlying phenomenon in Standard Arabic that nonhuman plural head nouns are assigned agreement of singular feminine head nouns appear in noun–adjective, subject–verb, and referential agreement (pronominals, demonstratives, and clitics). Some simplex numeral constructions (with numbers 3–10) also reflect asymmetries in gender (known as gender reversal). In some of these structures, asymmetries are reflected in both features (number and gender) or only one (either feature).

The second assumption was that the linguistic units carrying feature instantiations differ in terms of their perceptual salience or prominence (some are more salient than others). The case for this assumption was made in the discussion of referential asymmetries. Based on relevant literature on salience in L2 studies, feature mismatch in demonstratives, for example, was premised to be more salient than feature mismatch in prepositional and object clitics. The less salient feature

DOI: 10.4324/9781003055600-8

was premised to be learned more effectively under more explicit instructional conditions.

The third premise connects the previous two to instructed second language acquisition. It assumes that understanding the effects of certain forms of instruction on the acquisitional outcomes of these asymmetries should be based on the juxtaposition of data from implicit and explicit knowledge, and language interpretation and production. In particular, examining the effects of certain instructional conditions in the development of implicit and explicit knowledge is fundamental to understanding the nature of instructed second language acquisition and developing a theory that can best explain how it takes place in the classroom (R. Ellis, 2009). The case for this assumption was made in Chapter 2. Following R. Ellis (2004, 2009) and DeKeyser (2009), a distinction was made between explicit knowledge and implicit knowledge based on the well-attested fact that users of language

> may be able to use a linguistic feature accurately and fluently without any awareness of what the feature consists of and vice-versa, notably in the case of many classroom learners of an L2, who may be able to verbalize about a feature without being able to use it in communicative language use.
>
> (R. Ellis, 2009, p. 335)

Based on this fact, distinct measures are used to assess for these two types of linguistic knowledge. Following standard practice, explicit knowledge was measured by asking the learners to provide grammaticality judgments, choose the accurate justification for grammatical inaccuracies, or choose the correct linguistic form. Using proper elicitation prompts, both textual and visual, implicit knowledge was measured by examining the fluent and communicative L2 use in written and oral narration.

Scholars extensively disagree whether these two types of knowledge are distinct and dichotomous or continuous or intertwined (see Dienes & Perner, 1999). Whereas implicit knowledge is considered primary in language use, there is controversy regarding the role of explicit knowledge in L2 communicative use and whether it could be converted to implicit knowledge. Three positions were reviewed in Chapter 2. The first is the dismissive view proposing that explicit knowledge plays no role whatsoever in communicative language use (e.g., Alderson et al., 1997). The second is the direct view, establishing straight links between explicit knowledge and L2 communicative use. It proposes that this knowledge is involved in task performance. The third view, a compromise between the two, establishes indirect links between explicit knowledge and implicit knowledge in L2 communicative use. According to this view, explicit linguistic knowledge plays a role when it is proceduralized and automatized through practice (DeKeyser, 1998, 2009; R. Ellis, 1994). In the theoretical discussion that follows, some results in this book are taken to support this third view.

Another important controversy in the ISLA literature is whether incidental learning of grammar could happen in incidental- or implicit-instructional options. Generally, incidental learning was found to appear prominently in the area of vocabulary and only very rarely in grammar (Hulstijn, 2003). Scoping studies seem to support the role of explicit options (Norris & Ortega, 2000; Spada & Tomita, 2010). However, some research reviewed in Chapter 3 and Chapter 4 shows that the more explicit options of instruction can *impede* the development of implicit knowledge of grammar (Reinders & R. Ellis, 2009). These issues were taken up critically in two of the studies reported in this book on asymmetries. The conclusion made in this regard (see next section) is that although incidental learning *could be* possible in asymmetrical structures, more explicit options such as planned form-focused instruction yield more robust effects. In particular, these explicit options have greater learning effects in less salient asymmetrical features, such as prepositional and object clitics.

The last controversy this book contributes to is an old one. Over the course of three decades of research, mixed results have been reported from input-based and output-based instructional options (see Chapter 2). Following the tenets of input-processing instruction (VanPatten, 2004) and the output hypothesis (Swain, 1995, 2005), Chapter 5 provided evidence from production and interpretation data that both approaches can yield comparable results with subject–verb agreement asymmetry. This result supports a *parallel-routing* position that input and output can contribute to interlanguage development (Erlam et al., 2009).

Theoretical Contributions of This Book to Theory of ISLA of Grammar

In this section, the key theoretical contributions of this book are presented in key premises based on the results analyzed in this book. Instead of presenting the contributions of each study separately, the key patterns of the results that emerged in the chapters are couched within the premises and controversies outlined in the previous section. They are expected to contribute to a more complex understanding of ISLA theory of grammar in classroom settings.

Implicit Instruction Has Marginal Effects in Learning Asymmetrical Properties

Implicit learning refers to learning that occurs without awareness (Leow, 2000; Williams, 2005). In common manipulations of the learning conditions, the participants' attention is drawn to a particular feature while another feature is presented in plentiful input. In Chapter 3 of this book, intensive exposure to the noun–adjective agreement asymmetry (actual target) while learner attention was focused on subject–verb agreement (actual target) failed to yield robust results for the development of implicit or explicit knowledge (the target group's accuracy rate improved marginally from 23% to 31% in the oral narrative task). With a control group as a point of comparison, the study yielded evidence that the intensive incidental exposure did not result in significant gains (only a marginal effect was found in the choice test). These findings contribute to the ongoing discussion of whether incidental learning is possible in the area of grammar. Although some research has found evidence for the acquisition of *regular* grammatical properties under implicit input-based conditions (Farley, 2004), the results of the noun–adjective agreement asymmetry suggest that it is not possible. These results suggest that dual learning of two aspects of Arabic morphology (subject–verb agreement and noun–adjective disagreement) is unlikely in beginner learners. Their executive system of attention could not maintain constant control of the two grammatical features (see Verhaeghen & Cerella, 2002, for further discussion).

Also, this marginal learning effect appeared under the incidental focus-on-form condition. In Chapter 4, incidental focus on form, although extensive, did not result in substantial effect (the target group's accuracy rate improved marginally from 13% to 31% in the oral narrative task). Similarly, this marginal gain was replicated in Chapter 6, where implicit instruction via enriched input did not improve the acquisition of gender reversal in numeral asymmetries. This result contributes to a greater understanding of the role of incidental focus on form, from which Ellis et al. (2009) and Loewen (2005) reported acquisitional outcomes. In the context of agreement asymmetries here, these acquisitional outcomes were less significant. It is true that the participants in Chapter 4 could have attended to form in communicative numerous episodes and apply this to tests that required them to recognize or supply the correct form in the narrative task. However, this gain was still marginal in comparison to the planned-focus-on-form group.

An important factor that must be recognized is learners' proficiency. Clearly, the results of implicit or incidental instruction reported in these chapters were obtained from beginner and early-intermediate learners of Arabic. A plausible explanation for their marginal development could come from the threshold hypothesis (Lafford, 2006) that explains gains in grammatical subtleties in terms of internal cognitive resources, such as working memory and span of attention that relate to proficiency. This explanation is plausible, based on findings from a body of research that has approached learner gains from a psycholinguistic perspective (e.g., Harrington & Sawyer, 1992; Hulstijn & Bossers, 1992; Sunderman & Kroll, 2009; Tokowicz et al., 2004). This psycholinguistic research shows that advanced learners are better prepared (than beginner and intermediate learners) to make gains in certain grammatical subtleties. According to this research, the solid lexical and grammatical base for advanced learners leaves more cognitive space to attend to these subtleties, particularly those that do not have much communicative value. One important question is whether implicit instruction with these asymmetrical properties would yield different results with advanced learners. A future study needs to replicate these studies with advanced learners to answer this question.

Explicit Instruction Has Greater Learning Gains in Asymmetrical Properties

As explained in Chapter 2, instruction is deemed explicit under two conditions: the first is when the target rules are provided, a direct rule-giving approach. The second is when the learner's attention is drawn to the underlying rules in the input. An important pattern that appeared in the results of three of the studies in this book is that greater gains were made in learning asymmetrical features when the treatment included one or the two of these conditions. In Chapter 3 on noun–adjective asymmetries, the output-based present–practice–produce treatment made greater gains than the incidental intensive exposure group. Treatment in this group included explicit instruction in the presentation stage in which the participants were made aware of the asymmetries entailed in the adjectives accompanying masculine and feminine plural nouns. A similar pattern was reported in Chapter 6 in which input enhancement combined with explicit instruction resulted in more gains in the development of explicit and implicit knowledge of numeric asymmetries (gender reversal). Although the explicit-instruction component was not isolated so its effect cannot be pinpointed, it is likely that including these conditions contributed to the overall learning gains in the development of *both* explicit and implicit knowledge (see next premise).

These results are in line with recent growing work on "hard to acquire" structures (see Akakura, 2012). They suggest that with difficult structures, such as asymmetries, learners need to be explicitly given the rule(s) underlying the asymmetrical pattern. In addition, the learners in these chapters were guided to contrast symmetrical and asymmetrical patterns of agreement. This contrastive approach contributed at least partially to triggering noticing. This helps them to *notice* the subtleties entailed in the input. Schmidt (1990, 1994, 1995a) advanced this notion of noticing to what has become known as the "noticing hypothesis." This hypothesis claims that for acquisition to take place, learners must *consciously* notice forms (and the meanings these forms realize) in the input. In the current study, the noticing triggered by explicit explanation, while not guaranteeing full acquisition, enabled learners to process the forms and incorporate them into their developing interlanguage.

There Is a Relationship (at Least an Indirect One) Between Explicit and Implicit Knowledge

A primary question in ISLA theory that this book sought to address is whether explicit-instruction options can result in the development of implicit knowledge. This has been a subject of theoretical debate in ISLA theory. With the agreement that explicit instruction results in the development of explicit knowledge, this question can be phrased differently: whether there is a relationship between explicit knowledge and implicit knowledge. Whereas scholars such as VanPatten (2016) strongly believe that explicit knowledge *cannot* become implicit knowledge, other scholars (DeKeyser, 1998, 2009; R. Ellis, 1994) suggest that it could.

The results of three studies in this book offer evidence that there is a relationship between the two types of knowledge. The juxtaposition of explicit-knowledge and implicit-knowledge measures in these three chapters offered opportunities to answer this important question. Results of Chapter 3 provided evidence that learners in the present–practice–produce group were able to produce the target noun–adjective asymmetry in the elicitation task. They did this after demonstrating development of their explicit knowledge in choice and grammaticality-judgment tests. The improvement (from 24% in the pretest to 52% in posttest2) suggests that they have developed implicit knowledge of the target asymmetry. Similarly, results of Chapter 4 provided evidence that the planned-focus-on-form group developed implicit knowledge of referential asymmetries in oral narration (an improvement from 15% in the pretest to 57% in posttest2). In Chapter 6, the enhanced-input intervention that entailed explicit instruction resulted in more developed implicit knowledge of the numeric asymmetry (an improvement from 28% in the pretest to 55% in posttest2).

This pattern of results suggests explicit knowledge, once developed with an explicit-instruction component, has an effect on implicit language knowledge. Contrary to the dismissive view proposing that explicit knowledge plays no role whatsoever in the development of implicit knowledge in L2 communicative use (e.g., Alderson et al., 1997; VanPatten, 2016), the results reported in this work indicate that explicit knowledge can develop into implicit knowledge of asymmetrical forms in "hard to acquire" structures.

It is noteworthy to mention that this pattern of results was reported after explicit knowledge was established using common measures, particularly metalinguistic knowledge and grammaticality judgment. These findings add to the growing evidence in L2 studies on grammar that the two types of knowledge are intertwined and continuous even in hard structures (Akakura, 2012). There is a link (at least indirect) between explicit knowledge and implicit language knowledge that is demonstrated in the capacity of communicative speech in oral narrative (DeKeyser, 1998, 2009; R. Ellis, 1994).

The Effect of Feature Salience Is Real in Instructed Conditions

A key construct that was fundamental in this book is salience of feature asymmetry. In line with L2 studies, this construct was approached as a property of a linguistic item that makes it in some way perceptually and cognitively prominent, noticeable, or conspicuous (Kerswill & Williams, 2002; Siegel, 2010). In morpho-syntactic forms, this property is operationalized in terms of number of phones, syllabicity, and phonetic properties. Grammatical forms that have more phones and syllables are considered to be more salient than forms that have fewer phones and syllables (see Goldschneider & DeKeyser, 2001). With this conceptualization, a difference was established in Chapter 4 between two cases of referential asymmetries: the asymmetrical demonstrative *haadhaa* was determined to be more salient than asymmetrical clitic marker *-haa*. Whereas the former stands alone as a word, the latter is affixed to the verb or preposition that hosts it.

A main question in Chapter 4 was whether learning gains made in these two cases of agreement asymmetries are *different* under the *same* instructional conditions. The analysis of posttest data using a measure for explicit knowledge (metalinguistic test) and a measure for implicit knowledge (oral narrative) in two different learning conditions (incidental focus on form and focused focus on form) showed consistently greater gains in asymmetrical demonstratives than asymmetrical clitics. The focused-focus-on-form-group accuracy rate was 43% in demonstratives and 14% in clitics. The incidental-focus-on-form-group accuracy rate was 21% in demonstratives and only 5% in clitics.

In particular, the results showed a remarkably low improvement for clitics. The planned focus on form resulted in more noticing of referential asymmetries entailed in clitics (compare 14% to 5 % in oral narratives). Although the gains in incidental focus on form were less significant than the gains in the planned focus on form, they still confirm that the learners were more attentive to the more salient feature even in the incidental condition. These results overall add to the growing evidence in the literature that feature salience is a key consideration in L2 developmental trajectories (Gass et al., 2017). They suggest that that the less salient features require a more aggressive rule-giving approach to obtain acquisitional outcomes (Akakura, 2012).

Mismatch in One or Two Features Is Not a Learnability Issue

Another important question in this book was whether learners encounter more difficulties in feature constellations that reflect mismatch in one or two features (number and gender). This question was addressed in Chapter 3 in the context of noun–adjective agreement asymmetries under two learning conditions: input-enhanced incidental exposure and output-based present–practice–produce by beginner learners. Accuracy scores in nonhuman feminine plurals with singular feminine adjectives (mismatch in one feature, i.e., number) and in nonhuman masculine plural that takes singular feminine adjectives (mismatch in two features, i.e., number and gender) were analyzed separately in the pretest and the posttest data in measures of explicit and implicit knowledge. Intriguingly, no real differences were found before or after instruction. This suggests that beginner L2 learners of Arabic were not sensitive to these subtleties of feature mismatches. They used a feminine marker with the adjective in plural nouns equally, regardless of the noun or adjective's gender. In other words, the congruence between the gender of the feminine plural nouns and the adjective form did not result in higher acquisitional outcomes. It is likely that they consider the +/− human as the determining feature, regardless of gender.

Conversational Negotiation of Asymmetrical Forms Is Beneficial in Task-Focused Interaction

In Chapter 2 of this book, form-focused instruction options were contrasted to communicative meaning-focused options (Loewen, 2005). With the result that agreement asymmetries in Arabic are difficult structures for L2 learners of Arabic (Azaz, 2018; El-Ghazoly, 2013), Chapter 4 examined the possibility of acquiring referential asymmetries under two different conditions: incidental focus on form in task-unfocused interaction and planned focus on form in task-focused interaction. Loewen (2020) recommended the examination of the effects of both, "a distinction that has not yet received much specific attention" (p. 67).

Using a measure of explicit knowledge (a metalinguistic test) and measure for implicit knowledge (an oral narrative) that engaged the learners in conversational and didactive episodes, the study described in Chapter 4 provided evidence that planned focus on form in focused tasks had more significant gains for the development of implicit and explicit knowledge. Importantly, planned focus on form is suggested to enhance noticing for the asymmetrical forms while the learners focused on accomplishing the communicative task (Schmidt (1990, 1994, 1995a). This result motivates a good number of practical implications for teachers of Arabic (see next section).

Implications for Arabic Instruction and Material Design

This section of the chapter translates the findings into the Arabic classroom. It makes recommendations for teachers, textbook writers, and material designers when they present the target agreement asymmetries.

Arabic Instruction in the Classroom

The underlying principle in the recommendations for teachers is that morphosyntactic forms that entail agreement asymmetries need to be taught with careful planning in meaning-focused tasks. Instruction with good design matters in the development of implicit and explicit knowledge of these asymmetrical properties. Also, based on the underlying pattern in the results that there is a relationship between explicit and implicit knowledge, an explicit explanation of these asymmetries should be integrated. Loewen (2020) outlines the features of such approach to focus on form as one in which "attention to both meaning and form can be combined to create an optimal learning environment in which both implicit and explicit learning occur, and in which implicit and explicit knowledge are developed" (p. 64). This instruction with good design could be implemented in several ways. Three common ones are discussed in detail, with concrete implications and recommendations for each.

Conversational Form-Focused Instruction in Tasks

Designing Meaning-Focused Tasks

Based on the results of Chapter 4 on referential asymmetries and Chapter 6 on numeral asymmetries, L2 learners of Arabic were found to make greater gains when engaged in meaning-focused tasks. In Chapter 4, they negotiated meaning in a task that required them to compare and contrast cities they would live in. In Chapter 6, they negotiated meaning in a task that required them to discuss city attractions. In both tasks, the target asymmetrical features were seeded intentionally and carefully into the task design. These results are consistent with research indicating that including attention to language items during meaning-focused interaction is generally more beneficial for L2 acquisition than interaction alone. As Loewen (2020) explains,

> Often times in meaning-focused interaction inside the classroom, there is little attention to language form unless there is a breakdown in communication. However, by introducing focus on form into interaction within the classroom, teachers can help draw learners' attention to linguistic items.
>
> (p. 81)

Based on these results and insights from other relevant research, teachers of Arabic should design meaning-focused tasks that create obligatory occasions for using specific linguistic features such as asymmetries (Philp et al., 2010). These tasks should have a communicative goal as well as a linguistic focus. The themes of these tasks should reflect learner needs and previous experiences. Common tasks in this regard include choosing a city to work and live in, choosing a roommate or a Facebook friend, identifying differences between two cities, and choosing between jobs. In all these focused tasks, the design enriched with visual and textual components should reflect target linguistic aspects that learners are expected to produce. Such tasks can be easily seeded with the linguistic asymmetries, with the expectation that learners will need to process them in the input, as well as produce them as they negotiate the task with their peers or their teachers.

Negotiation of Form in Meaning-Focused Interactive Episodes

The results of Chapter 4 showed the benefits of the negotiation of form in meaning-focused interaction. Two types of interactive episodes were distinguished: conversational and didactic. Conversational focus on form by default is more affiliated to communicative activities, as it provides the means for solving communication difficulties whenever these arise. Didactic focus on form reflects the fact that even when performing communicative activities, the classroom participants are motivated to learn the target language (R. Ellis et al., 2002). The learners in the planned-focus-on-form group were able to pick up the asymmetrical forms while they participated in the communicative task. Both types of interactive episodes played their own particular roles.

These results have important implications for teachers as they engage with the learners in communicative activities. The use of recasts and requests for clarifications as a corrective-feedback technique is expected to improve the students' fluency and confidence in using the asymmetrical forms, and consequently help them construct linguistic competence. Didactic focus on form is needed, as it more likely to provide sufficient opportunities for students to attend to form. It is also recommended to give the students the space to ask questions about form during the course of a communicative activity. In the presentation of the interactive scenarios in Chapter 4, there were some interesting episodes in which the students asked about certain forms that they needed to keep the flow of the communication going.

It is not recommended that the teacher ignore their request for certain language forms. Providing the form *at the time of need* during the interaction will be particularly helpful. In addition, since some of these forms are of low salience in the Standard Arabic system, instructors need to direct students' attention to these forms in the interaction.

There is an important cautionary point here: focus on form *while* the learners are negotiating the meaning in the task should not be taken to mean to restrict attention to form at the expense of the communication of the meaning. This can impact learner fluency. The teacher should keep meaningful communication at the center of the interaction. In student presentational modes of communication, it is sometimes recommended that teachers make a note of forms that cause students problems (such as asymmetries) and address them after the presentation. It is recommended not to hinder the flow of the communication during a communicative activity to make learners aware of specific forms at the time they need to use them. Although focus-on-form interactive episodes in Chapter 4 were mostly provided by the teacher, it is possible to train students on how to engage in focus-on-form activities. In group work, with advanced learners in particular, learners can be guided to the benefits of giving feedback to each other during role-plays and subsequent interactive tasks. This has shown to significantly improve their accuracy scores in complex structures (Sato & Ballinger, 2012).

Contextualized Input-Based Instruction

Based on the results of Chapter 5 in this book, significant and comparable gains were made for structured input-based and output-based activities. This has important implications in the instructed second language acquisition of grammatical asymmetries. Carefully structured input activities are crucial to foster form-meaning connections in grammatical aspects that show agreement asymmetries. These structured activities should not be presented in isolation, but they should be integrated into meaningful tasks that students can engage in.

Structured input activities have the potential to alter learners' incorrect processing strategies and instill target-like ones (see Farhat & Benati, 2018). The manipulation of linguistic input in such ways that show Arabic learners how the pattern of agreement (symmetrical versus asymmetrical) changes according to the sentence type (subject-initial versus verb-initial) is highly recommended for teaching Arabic as a foreign language. As Arabic learners were found to assign a wrong interpretation to the verb form in the verb-initial sentences, contextualized and structured input activities are expected to foster the connections between the singular form of the verb and the plural subject. These activities are highly recommended for other cases of agreement asymmetries.

An important factor that has a bearing on the instructed second language acquisition of grammatical asymmetries is the provision of an explicit explanation component. One important question is at what point this explanation can be included. It is recommended to be included *before* the learners work on these structured input activities, which will enhance their noticing of the grammatical intricacies in the input.

Contextualized Output-Based Instruction

Based on the results of Chapter 3 on noun–adjective agreement asymmetries and Chapter 5 on subject–verb agreement asymmetries, output-based activities and practice were found to develop implicit and explicit knowledge. These results have important implications for teachers of Arabic. They need to design structured-output activities that push learners to produce the asymmetrical patterns of agreement.

The verb-initial word order in Arabic is incongruent with the basic subject-initial word order in English. Learners usually tend to escape this incongruency and resort to the alternative subject–verb word order, although it may not be the target-like word order. Similarly, adjectives following nonhuman plurals show mismatches in number and gender. Uninstructed learners tend to use adjectival forms that fully agree with the head nouns.

Teachers need to design structured-output activities such as elicitation activities prompted with pictures. These offer sufficient opportunities that push learners to produce these asymmetrical patterns and allow them to consult their linguistic knowledge about which form to produce. Arabic may not be the only less commonly taught language that poses these intricacies to learners. Teachers of other less commonly taught languages need to develop output-based activities that guide learners to process and produce these grammatical intricacies.

Implications for Curriculum Design and Materials Development

The focus of this book is on agreement asymmetries, which are a related set of structural phenomena in L2 Arabic. These structures, despite being among common and high-frequency forms that are usually presented early on in the sequence of Arabic textbooks, were found to pose difficulties for learners at all levels of proficiency (El-Ghazoly, 2013). The intuitive conclusion from this research is that the way these structures are currently presented in textbooks is not adequate. Based on the results of the four investigations in this book, Arabic curriculum design and material development can be informed about how to present for the first time and how to consolidate them in subsequent materials.

There are three important and generalizable issues that can be learned from the findings of the four studies in this book. First, in learning morphosyntactic intricacies and difficult grammar rules, learner issues will continue to persist when they rely heavily on course materials that do not present these intricacies adequately, although they are common in the system of the language they are learning. Second, without supplemental materials, there is little hope of rectifying these issues. The textbook should not be considered as the only tool for learning intricate morphosyntactic forms and grammar rules.

Third, there has been a debate on which paradigm is more effective in adult learning: explicit instruction or implicit learning, with some empirical support for the implicit learning of regular grammar rules. The results of the present studies show that learners did not notice a pattern that was commonly used in their course materials. These results imply that morphosyntactic intricacies such as agreement asymmetries are difficult structures that need to be taught explicitly but in context. This implication corroborates existing scoping studies, showing that explicit focused instruction has positive effects (Norris & Ortega, 2000; Spada & Tomita, 2010).

Sample Task with Balanced Focus on Form and Meaning

As explained previously, tasks that focus on form and meaning are highly recommended to enrich grammar instruction in context. In Appendix 2, a theme-based sample task (titled *madinatii ʔal-mufaḍḍala* "My Favorite City") is provided. It focuses on teaching the grammatical asymmetries in context and enables learners to create with language. The task starts with the context and shows the students the expectations as they engage with each other in interaction (see Appendix 2). In each segment, more than one asymmetry may be used. Following established pedagogical practice, it did not focus on grammar for the purpose of recognition but for production. In some cases, grammar highlights are provided to activate learner awareness about the form and use of the structures. For certain parts of the prompts, morphosyntactic forms may be colored to draw the learners' attention to the form. This task could be used to engage the learners in meaningful interaction that pushes them to negotiate meaning and while focusing on the agreement asymmetries.

References

Akakura, M. (2012). Evaluating the effectiveness of explicit instruction on implicit and explicit L2 knowledge. *Language Teaching Research, 16*(1), 9–37.

Al-Amry, A. (2014). *The acquisition of gender agreement in adult learners of Arabic* [Unpublished Master's thesis, Carleton University].

Alanen, R. (1995). Input enhancement and rule presentation in second language acquisition. In R. Schmidt (Ed.), *Attention and awareness in foreign language learning and teaching* (pp. 259–302). University of Hawai'i.

Al-Ansari, I. H. (1991). *Mughni Al-Labib* (M. Abd Al-Hamid, Ed.). Al Asriyyah Library. www.alkitab.com/50065.html

Al-Bataineh, H., & Branigan, P. (2020). *The syntax of (complex) numerals in Arabic* [White paper]. www.researchgate.net/profile/Hussein-Al-Bataineh/publication/339281852

Alderson, J. C., Clapham, C., & Steel, D. (1997). Metalinguistic knowledge, language aptitude, and language proficiency. *Language Teaching Research, 1*, 93–121.

Alderson, J. C., & Hudson, R. (2013). The metalinguistic knowledge of undergraduate students of English language or linguistics. *Language Awareness, 22*, 320–337.

Alhawary, M. T. (2002). The role of L1 transfer in L2 acquisition of inflectional morphology. In D. Parkinson & E. Benmamoun (Eds.), *Perspectives on Arabic linguistics* (Vol. 13–14, pp. 219–248). John Benjamins.

Alhawary, M. T. (2003). Processability theory: Counter-evidence from Arabic second language acquisition data. *Al-'Arabiyya, 36*, 107–166.

Alhawary, M. T. (2005). L2 acquisition of Arabic morpho-syntactic features: Temporary or permanent impairment? In M. T. Alhawary & E. Benmamoun (Eds.), *Perspectives on Arabic linguistics* (Vol. 17–18, pp. 273–312). John Benjamins.

Alhawary, M. T. (2009). *Arabic second language acquisition of morphosyntax*. Yale University Press.

Alhawary, M. T. (2011). *Modern standard Arabic grammar: A learner's guide*. John Wiley & Sons.

Alhawary, M. T. (Ed.). (2018). *The Routledge handbook of Arabic second language acquisition*. Routledge.

Alhawary, M. T. (2019). *Arabic second language learning and effects of input, transfer, and typology*. Georgetown University Press.

Aljadani, A. S. (2019). The acquisition of grammatical gender in Arabic demonstratives by English native speakers. *International Journal of Contemporary Education, 2*(1), 78–86.

Al-Mubarrad, M. (1994). *Al-MuqTaḍ ab* (M. ʿAḍ iymah, Ed.). Ministry of Religious Endowments.

Alqarni, M. (2015). *The morphosyntax of numeral-noun constructions in modern standard Arabic* [Doctoral dissertation, University of Florida].

Alqassas, A. (2017). Gender and number polarity in modern standard Arabic numeral phrases. *Canadian Journal of Linguistics/Revue Canadienne de Linguistique*, *62*(1), 1–17.

Al-Thawahrih, J. (2018). Arabic L2 learners' use of word order and subject- verb agreement for actor role assignment. In M. Al-Hawary (Ed.), *The Routledge handbook of Arabic second language acquisition* (pp. 201–221). Routledge.

Aoun, J., Benmamoun, E., & Sportiche, D. (1994). Agreement, word order, and conjunction in some varieties of Arabic. *Linguistic Inquiry*, *25*, 195–220.

Aoun, J. E., Benmamoun, E., & Choueiri, L. (2010). *The syntax of Arabic*. Cambridge University Press.

Aqeel, I. (1980). *Sharh Ibn Aqeel of the Alfiyyah of Ibn Malik* (20th ed.). Dar Masir.

Azaz, M. (2016). Crosslinguistic effects in L2 acquisition: The case of Arabic determiner phrase. *Al-'Arabiyya*, *49*, 1–24.

Azaz, M. (2018). The link between morphosyntactic accuracy and textbook presentation: The morphosyntax of subject-verb agreement in Arabic. *Foreign Language Annals*, *51*(4), 831–851.

Azaz, M. (2019). L1 transfer effects in the production of generic plurals in L2 Arabic. *The Modern Language Journal*, *103*(1), 275–290.

Azaz, M. (2023). *Perspectives on Arabic linguistics XXXIV*. John Benjamins Publishing.

Bahloul, M., & Harbert, W. (1993). Agreement asymmetries in Arabic. In J. Mead (Ed.), *Proceedings of the eleventh West Coast conference on formal linguistics* (pp. 15–31). CSLI Publications.

Balcom, P., & Bouffard, P. (2015). The effect of input flooding and explicit instruction on learning adverb placement in L3 French. *The Canadian Journal of Applied Linguistics*, *18*(2), 1–27.

Barcroft, J. (2003). Distinctiveness and bidirectional effects in input enhancement for vocabulary learning. *Applied Language Learning*, *13*, 47–73.

Belnap, R. K., & Shabaneh, O. (1992). Variable agreement and nonhuman plurals in classical and modern standard Arabic. In Ellen Broselow, Mushira Eid & John McCarthy (Eds.), *Perspectives in Arabic linguistics IV: Papers from the fourth annual symposium on Arabic linguistics* (pp. 245–262). John Benjamins.

Benati, A. (2004). The effects of structured input activities and explicit information on the acquisition of the Italian future tense. In B. VanPatten (Ed.), *Processing instruction: Theory, research and commentary* (pp. 207–226). Lawrence Erlbaum Associates.

Benati, A. (2005). The effects of processing instruction, traditional instruction, and meaningful-based output instruction on the acquisition of the English past tense. *Language Teaching Research*, *9*, 67–93.

Benati, A. (2017). Classroom-oriented research: Processing instruction. *Language Teaching*, *52*(3), 343–359.

Benmamoun, E. (2000). *The feature structure of functional categories: A comparative study of Arabic dialects*. Oxford University Press.

Bialystok, E., & Ryan, E. B. (1985). Toward a definition of metalinguistic skill. *Merrill-Palmer Quarterly*, *31*, 229–251.

Block, D. (2003). *The social turn in second language acquisition*. Edinburgh University Press.

Bolotin, N. (1995). Arabic and parametric VSO agreement. In M. Eid (Ed.), *Perspectives on Arabic linguistics 7* (pp. 7–27). John Benjamins.

Brown, R. (1973). *A first language*. Harvard University Press.
Brustad, K., Al-Batal, M., & Al-Tonsi, A. (2011). *Al-kitaab fii ta'allum Al'Arabiyya: A textbook for Arabic* (Part 1, 3rd ed.). Georgetown University Press.
Bybee, J., & Hopper, P. (Eds.). (2001). *Frequency and the emergence of linguistic structure*. Benjamins.
Cadierno, T. (1995). Formal instruction from a processing perspective: An investigation into the Spanish past tense. *The Modern Language Journal*, *79*, 179–193.
Chaudron, C. (1985). Intake: On methods and models for discovering learners' processing of input. *Studies in Second Language Acquisition*, *7*, 1–14.
Cheng, A. C. (2002). The effects of processing instruction on the acquisition of *ser* and *estar. Hispania*, *85*, 308–323.
Cheng, A. C. (2004). Processing instruction and Spanish *ser* and *estar*: Forms with semantic-aspectual values. In B. VanPatten (Ed.), *Processing instruction: Theory, research and commentary* (pp. 119–42). Lawrence Erlbaum Associates.
Collentine, J. (1998). Processing instruction and the subjunctive. *Hispania*, *81*, 576–587.
Collins, L., & Ellis, N. C. (2009). Input and second language construction learning: Frequency, form, and function [Special issue]. *Modern Language Journal*, *93*(2), 329–335.
Comer, W. J., & DeBenedette, L. (2010). Processing instruction and Russian: Issues, materials, and preliminary experimental results. *Slavic and East European Journal*, *54*, 118–146.
Corbett, G. (2006). *Agreement*. Cambridge University Press.
Corder, S. P. (1967). The significance of learners' errors. *International Review of Applied Linguistics in Language Teaching*, *5*, 161–170.
Danon, G. (2009, April). Grammatical number in numeral-noun constructions. *CGG-19*, 1–3.
DeKeyser, R. (1998). Beyond focus on form: Cognitive perspectives on learning and practicing second language grammar. In C. J. Doughty & J. Williams (Eds.), *Focus on form in second language acquisition* (pp. 42–63). Cambridge University Press.
DeKeyser, R. (2003). Implicit and explicit learning. In C. Doughty & M. Long (Eds.), *Handbook of second language acquisition* (pp. 313–349). Wiley-Blackwell.
DeKeyser, R. (2007a). *Practice in a second language: Perspectives from applied linguistics and cognitive psychology*. Cambridge University Press.
DeKeyser, R. (2007b). Skill acquisition theory. In B. VanPatten & J. Williams (Eds.), *Theories in second language acquisition: An introduction* (pp. 97–113). Lawrence Erlbaum Associates.
DeKeyser, R. (2009). Cognitive-psychological processes in second language learning. In M. H. Long & C. J. Doughty (Eds.), *The handbook of language teaching* (pp. 119–138). Wiley-Blackwell.
DeKeyser, R. (2020). Skill acquisition theory. In B. VanPatten & J. Williams (Eds.), *Theories in second language acquisition* (pp. 83–104). Routledge.
DeKeyser, R., & Sokalski, K. J. (1996). The differential role of comprehension and production practice. *Language Learning*, *46*, 613–642.
Dienes, Z., & Perner, J. (1999). A theory of implicit and explicit knowledge. *Behavioral and Brain Sciences*, *22*, 735–808.
Doughty, C., & Williams, J. (Eds.) (1998). Pedagogical choices in focus on form. In *Focus on form in classroom second language acquisition* (pp. 197–261). Cambridge University Press.
Dulay, H. C., & Burt, M. K. (1978). Some remarks on creativity in language acquisition. In W. C. Ritchie (Ed.), *Second language acquisition research: Issues and implications* (pp. 65–89). Academic Press.

Elder, C., Warren, J., Hajek, J., Manwaring, D., & Davies, A. (1999). Metalinguistic knowledge: How important is it in studying a language at university? *Australian Review of Applied Linguistics*, *22*, 81–95.

El-Ghazoly, B. (2013). *Feature reassembly and forming syntactic ties: The acquisition of non-canonical agreement in Arabic L2* [Doctoral dissertation, Indiana University].

Ellis, N. C. (1993). Rules and instances in foreign language learning: Interactions of explicit and implicit knowledge. *European Journal of Cognitive Psychology*, *5*, 289–318.

Ellis, N. C. (2002). Frequency effects in language processing: A review with implications for theories of implicit and explicit language acquisition. *Studies in Second Language Acquisition*, *24*(2), 143–188.

Ellis, N. C. (2005). At the interface: Dynamic interactions of explicit and implicit language knowledge. *Studies in Second Language Acquisition*, *27*, 305–352.

Ellis, N. C. (2006). Selective attention and transfer phenomena in L2 acquisition: Contingency, cue competition, salience, interference, overshadowing, blocking, and perceptual learning. *Applied Linguistics*, *27*(2), 164–194.

Ellis, N. C. (2015). Implicit and explicit language learning: Their dynamic interface and complexity. In P. Rebuschat (Ed.), *Implicit and explicit learning of languages* (pp. 3–23). John Benjamins.

Ellis, R. (1990). *Instructed second language acquisition*. Basil Blackwell.

Ellis, R. (1994). *The study of second language acquisition*. Oxford University Press.

Ellis, R. (2001). Investigating form-focused instruction. In R. Ellis (Ed.), *Form-focused instruction and second language learning* (pp. 1–46). Wiley-Blackwell.

Ellis, R. (2002). Does form-focused instruction affect the acquisition of implicit knowledge? A review of the research. *Studies in Second Language Acquisition*, *24*, 223–236.

Ellis, R. (2003). *Task-based language learning and teaching*. Oxford University Press.

Ellis, R. (2004). The definition and measurement of explicit knowledge. *Language Learning*, *54*, 227–275.

Ellis, R. (2005). Principles of instructed language learning. *System*, *33*(2), 209–224.

Ellis, R. (2009). Implicit and explicit learning, knowledge and instruction. In R. Ellis, S. Loewen, C. Elder, R. Erlam, J. Philp, & H. Reinders (Eds.), *Implicit and explicit knowledge in second language learning, testing, and teaching* (pp. 3–25). Multilingual Matters.

Ellis, R., Basturkmen, H., & Loewen, S. (2001). Learner uptake in communicative ESL lessons. *Language Learning*, *51*(2), 281–318.

Ellis, R., Basturkmen, H., & Loewen, S. (2002). Doing focus-on-form. *System*, *30*(4), 419–432.

Ellis, R., Loewen, S., Elder, C., Reinders, H., Erlam, R., & Philp, J. (2009). *Implicit and explicit knowledge in second language learning, testing, and teaching*. Multilingual Matters.

Ericsson, A., & Simon, H. (1984). *Protocol analysis: Verbal reports as data*. MIT Press.

Erlam, R., Loewen, S., & Philp, J. (2009). The roles of output-based and input-based instruction in the acquisition of L2 implicit and explicit knowledge. In *Implicit and explicit knowledge in second language learning, testing, and teaching* (pp. 241–261). Multilingual Matters.

Farhat, A., & Benati, A. (2018). The effects of motivation on processing instruction in the acquisition of modern standard Arabic gender agreement. *Instructed Second Language Acquisition*, *2*, 61–82.

Farley, A. P. (2001a). Authentic processing instruction and the Spanish subjunctive. *Hispania*, *84*, 289–299.

Farley, A. P. (2001b). The effects of processing instruction and meaning-based output instruction. *Spanish Applied Linguistics*, *5*, 57–94.

Farley, A. P. (2004). Processing instruction and the Spanish subjunctive: Is explicit information needed. In B. Van Patten (Ed.), *Processing instruction: Theory, research, and commentary* (pp. 227–239). Lawrence Erlbaum.

Fassi Fehri, A. (1993). *Issues in Arabic clauses and words*. Kluwer Academic.

Fassi Fehri, A. (2004). Nominal classes, reference, and functional parameters, with reference to Arabic. *Linguistic Variation Yearbook*, *4*, 41–107.

Fassi Fehri, A. (2017). New roles for gender: Evidence from Arabic, Semitic, Berber, and Romance. In M. Sheehan & L. R. Bailey (Eds.), *Order and structure in syntax II: Subjecthood and argument structure* (pp. 221–256). Language Science Press.

Ferguson, C. A. (1989). Grammatical agreement in classical Arabic and the modern dialects: A response to Versteegh's pidginization hypothesis. *al-'Arabiyya*, 5–17.

Firth, A., & Wagner, J. (2007). Second/foreign language learning as a social accomplishment: Elaborations on a reconceptualized SLA. *The Modern Language Journal*, *91*, 800–819.

Foreign Service Institute (2018). *FSI's experience with language learning*. Retrieved April 2, 2018, from https://www. state.gov/m/fsi/sls/c78549.htm

Foster, P. (2009). Task-based language learning research: Expecting too much or too little? *International Journal of Applied Linguistics*, *19*, 247–263.

Fotos, S., & Ellis, R. (1991). Communicating about grammar: A task-based approach. *TESOL Quarterly*, *25*(4), 605–628.

Freeman, D. E. L. (1975). The acquisition of grammatical morphemes by adult ESL students. *TESOL Quarterly*, *9*(4), 409–419.

Gass, S. M. (1997). *Input, interaction, and the second language learner*. Lawrence Elrbaum.

Gass, S. M., & Mackey, A. (2000). *Stimulated recall methodology in second language research*. Lawrence Erlbaum Associates.

Gass, S. M., & Selinker, L. (1994). *Second language acquisition: An introductory course*. Lawrence Erlbaum Associates.

Gass, S. M., Spinner, P., & Behney, J. (Eds.) (2018). Salience in second language acquisition and related fields. In *Salience in second language acquisition* (pp. 1–18). Routledge.

Goldschneider, J., & DeKeyser, R. (2001). Explaining the "natural order of L2 morpheme acquisition" in English: A meta-analysis of multiple determinants. *Language Learning*, *51*(1), 1–50.

Goo, J., Granena, G., Yilmaz, Y., & Novella, M. (2015). Implicit and explicit instruction in L2 learning: Norris and Ortega (2000) revisited and updated. In P. Rebuschat (Ed.), *Implicit and explicit learning of languages* (pp. 443–483). John Benjamins.

Gutiérrez, X. (2013). Metalinguistic knowledge, metalingual knowledge, and proficiency in L2 Spanish. *Language Awareness*, *22*, 176–191.

Hama, M., & Leow, R. P. (2010). Learning without awareness revisited. *Studies in Second Language Acquisition*, *32*, 465–491.

Han, Z., & Nassaji, H. (2018). Introduction: A snapshot of thirty-five years of instructed second language acquisition. *Language Teaching Research*, *23*(4), 393–402.

Hanulíková, A., van Alphen, P. M., van Goch, M. M., & Weber, A. (2012). When one person's mistake is another's standard usage: The effect of foreign accent on syntactic processing. *Journal of Cognitive Neuroscience*, *24*, 878–887.

Hanulíková, A., & Weber, A. (2012). Sink positive: Linguistic experience with the substitutions influences nonnative word recognition. *Attention, Perception, and Psychophysics*, *74*, 613–629.

Harrington, M., & Sawyer, M. (1992). L2 working memory capacity and L2 reading skill. *Studies in Second Language Acquisition, 14*(1), 25–38.

Hassan, A. (1981). *Al Nahw Al-Waafi [The complete syntax]*. Dar Al-Ma'aref.

Hatch, E. (1983). Simplified input and second language acquisition. In R. W. Andersen (Ed.), *Pidginization and creolization as language acquisition* (pp. 64–88). Newbury House.

Hernández, T. (2011). Re-examining the role of explicit instruction and input flood on the acquisition of Spanish discourse markers. *Language Teaching Research, 15*, 159–182.

Hernández, T., & Rodríguez-González, E. (2012). Impact of instruction on the use of L2 discourse markers. *Journal of Second Language Teaching and Research, 2*, 3–31. http://pops.uclan.ac.uk/index.php/jsltr

Holes, C. (2004). *Modern Arabic: Structures, functions, and varieties*. Georgetown University Press.

Housen, A., & Pierrard, M. (2005). *Investigations in instructed second language acquisition*. Mouton de Gruyter.

Hu, G. (2002). Psychological constraints on the utility of metalinguistic knowledge in second language production. *Studies in Second Language Acquisition, 24*, 347–386.

Hu, G. (2011). Metalinguistic knowledge, metalanguage, and their relationship in L2 learners. *System, 39*, 63–77.

Hulstijn, J. H. (2003). Incidental and intentional learning. In C. Doughty & M. Long (Eds.), *The handbook of second language acquisition* (pp. 349–381). Wiley-Blackwell.

Hulstijn, J. H. (2013). Incidental learning in second language acquisition. In C. A. Chapelle (Ed.), *The encyclopedia of applied linguistics* (pp. 2632–2637). Wiley-Blackwell.

Hulstijn, J. H., & Bossers, B. (1992). Individual differences in L2 proficiency as a function of L1 proficiency. *European Journal of Cognitive Psychology, 4*(4), 341–353.

Husseinali, G. (2016.) *Arabic L2 interlanguage: Syntactic sequences, agreement and variation*. Routledge.

Jarrah, M., & Zibin, A. (2016). Syntactic investigation of nunation in Haili Arabic. *SKY Journal of Linguistics, 29*, 39–61.

Kang, E. K., Sok, S., & Han, Z.-H. (2018). A meta-analysis of 35 years of instructed second language acquisition research. *Language Teaching Research, 23*(4), 403–427.

Keating, G., & Farley, A. (2008). Processing instruction, meaning-based output instruction, and meaning-based drills: Impacts on classroom L2 acquisition of Spanish object pronouns. *Hispania, 91*, 639–650.

Kerswill, P., & Williams, A. (2002). "Salience" as an explanatory factor in language change: Evidence from dialect levelling in urban England. In M. C. Jones & E. Esch (Eds.), *Language change: The interplay between internal, external and extra-linguistic factors (contributions to the sociology of language)* (pp. 81–110). Mouton de Gruyter.

Klein, W. (1986). *Second language acquisition*. Cambridge University Press.

Kouloughli, D. E. (1994). *Grammaire de l'arabe d'aujourd'hui*. Pocket.

Krashen, S. D. (1982). *Principles and practice in second language acquisition*. Pergamon.

Krashen, S. D. (1981). *Second language acquisition and second language learning*. Pergamon.

Krashen, S. D. (1987). *Principles and practice in second language acquisition*. Prentice Hall.

Krashen, S. D. (2003). *Explorations in language acquisition and use: The Taipei lectures*. Heinemann.

Lafford, B. A. (2006). The effects of study abroad vs. classroom contexts on Spanish SLA: Old assumptions, new insights and future research directions. In C. A. Klee & T. L. Face

(Eds.), *Selected proceedings of the 7th conference on the acquisition of Spanish and Portuguese as first and second languages* (pp. 1–25). Cascadilla Proceedings Project.

Lardiere, D. (2008). Feature-assembly in second language acquisition. In J. Liceras, H. Zobl, & H. Goodluck (Eds.), *The role of formal features in second language acquisition* (pp. 106–140). Lawrence Erlbaum Associates.

Lardiere, D. (2009). Further thoughts on parameters and features in second language acquisition: A reply to peer comments on Lardiere's some thoughts on the contrastive analysis of features in second language acquisition' in SLR 25 (2). *Second Language Research, 25*(3), 409–422.

Larsen-Freeman, D., & Long, M. (1991). *An introduction to second language acquisition research.* Longman.

Leow, R. P. (1998). The effects of amount and type of exposure on adult learners' L2 development in SLA. *The Modern Language Journal, 82*(1), 49–68.

Leow, R. P. (2000). A study of the role of awareness in foreign language behavior: Aware versus unaware learners. *Studies in Second Language Acquisition, 22*(4), 557–584.

Leow, R. P. (2001). Do learners notice enhanced forms while interacting with the L2? An online and offline study of the role of written input enhancement in L2 reading. *Hispania, 84*, 496–509.

Leow, R. P. (2015). *Explicit learning in the L2 classroom: A student-centered approach.* Routledge.

Leow, R. P. (2019). ISLA: How implicit or how explicit should it be? Theoretical, empirical, and pedagogical/curricular issues. *Language Teaching Research, 23*(4), 476–493.

Leow, R. P., & Zamora, C. (2017). Intentional and incidental learning. In S. Loewen & M. Sato (Eds.), *Routledge handbook of instructed second language acquisition* (pp. 33–49). Routledge.

Lichtman, K., & VanPatten, B. (2021). Krashen forty years later: Final comments. *Foreign Language Annals*. https://doi.org/10.1111/flan.12543

Loewen, S. (2005). Incidental focus on form and second language learning. *Studies in Second Language Acquisition, 27*(3), 361–386.

Loewen, S. (2013). Instructed second language acquisition. In C. Chapelle (Ed.), *The encyclopedia of applied linguistics* (pp. 2716–2718). Wiley-Blackwell.

Loewen, S. (2015). *Introduction to instructed second language acquisition.* Routledge.

Loewen, S. (2020). *Introduction to instructed second language acquisition.* Routledge.

Loewen, S., & Sato, M. (Eds.) (2017). *The Routledge handbook of instructed second language acquisition.* Routledge.

Long, M. (1991). Focus on form: A design feature in language teaching methodology. In K. de Bot, R. Ginsberg, & C. Kramsch (Eds.), *Foreign language research in cross-cultural perspective* (pp. 39–52). John Benjamin.

Long, M. (2000). Focus on form in task-based language teaching. In R. D. Lambert (Ed.), *Language policy and pedagogy* (pp. 179–192). John Benjamins.

Long, M. (2015). *Second language acquisition and task-based language teaching.* Wiley-Blackwell.

Long, M. (2017). Instructed second language acquisition (ISLA): Geopolitics, methodological issues, and some major research questions. *Instructed Second Language Acquisition, 1*, 7–44.

Long, M., & Robinson, P. (1998). Focus on form: Theory, research, and practice. In C. Doughty & J. Williams (Eds.), *Focus on form in classroom second language acquisition* (pp. 16–42). Cambridge University Press.

Mackey, A. (2006). Feedback, noticing and instructed second language learning. *Applied Linguistics*, *27*, 405–430.
Mackey, A., Gass, S., & McDonough, K. (2000). How do learners perceive interactional feedback? *Studies in Second Language Acquisition*, *22*(4), 471–497.
Mann, S. (1992). *TaHliil l-ʾaxTaaʾ l-lughawiyyah bil-markaz l-ʾiʿdaadii bil-jaamiʿah l-ʾislaamiyyah lʿaalamiyyah bi-maaliiziya: Al-mustawaa l-mutaqaddim. Risalat maajis-tiir*. Maʿhad l-xurTuum l-dawlii lil- lughah l-ʿarabiyyah.
Mansouri, F. (2000). *Grammatical markedness and information processing in the acquisition of Arabic [as] a second language* (Vol. 2). Lincom Europa.
Marcin, M. (2016). Agreement in modern standard Arabic constructions with cardinal numerals over ten. *Lingua Posnaniensis*, *58*(1), 69–88. https://doi.org/10.1515/linpo-2016-0005
McCarthy, J. (1981). A prosodic theory of nonconcatenative morphology. *Linguistic Inquiry*, *12*(3), 373–418.
McCarthy, J., & Prince, A. (1990). Prosodic morphology and templatic morphology. In M. Eid & J. McCarthy (Eds.), *Perspectives on Arabic linguistics II: Papers from the second annual symposium on Arabic linguistics* (pp. 1–54). John Benjamins.
McDonough, K. (2005). Identifying the impact of negative feedback and learners' responses on ESL question development. *Studies in Second Language Acquisition*, *27*, 79–103.
Mohammad, M. A. (1990). The problem of subject-verb agreement in Arabic: Towards a solution. In M. Eid (Ed.), *Perspectives in Arabic linguistics 1* (pp. 95–125). John Benjamins.
Mohammad, M. A. (2000). *Word order, agreement and pronominalization in standard and palestinian Arabic*. John Benjamins.
Morgan-Short, K., & Bowden, H. (2006). Processing instruction and meaningful output-based instruction: Effects on second language development. *Studies in Second Language Acquisition*, *28*, 31–65.
Muranoi, H. (2007). Output practice in the L2 classroom. In R. DeKeyser (Ed.), *Practice in a second language: Perspectives from applied linguistics and cognitive psychology* (pp. 51–84). Cambridge University Press.
Nassaji, H. (2016). Introduction: Recent advances in instructed second language acquisition. *Studies in Second Language Learning and Teaching*, *6*, 13–18.
Nassaji, H. (2017). Grammar acquisition. In S. Loewen & M. Sato (Eds.), *Routledge handbook of instructed second language acquisition* (pp. 205–222). Routledge.
Nassaji, H., & Fotos, S. (2011). *Teaching grammar in second language classrooms: Integrating form-focused instruction in communicative context*. Routledge.
Nielsen, H. L. (1997). On acquisition order of agreement procedures in Arabic learner language. *Al-ʿArabiyya*, *30*, 49–94.
Norris, J. M., & Ortega, L. (2000). Effectiveness of L2 instruction: A research synthesis and quantitative meta-analysis. *Language Learning*, *50*, 417–528.
Ohta, A. S. (2000). Rethinking interaction in SLA: Developmentally appropriate assistance in the zone of proximal development and the acquisition of L2 grammar. *Sociocultural Theory and Second Language Learning*, *4*, 51–78.
Overstreet, M. H. (1998). Text enhancement and content familiarity: The focus of learner attention. *Spanish Applied Linguistics*, *2*, 229–258.
Paradis, M. (1994). Neurolinguistic aspects of implicit and explicit memory: Implications for bilingualism and second language acquisition. In N. Ellis (Ed.), *Implicit and explicit language learning* (pp. 393–419). Academic Press.
Pereira, I. (1996). *Markedness and instructed SLA: An experiment in teaching the Spanish subjunctive* [Unpublished doctoral dissertation, University of Illinois].

Philp, J., Walter, S., & Basturkmen, H. (2010). Peer interaction in the foreign language classroom: What factors foster a focus on form? *Language Awareness*, *19*, 261–279.

Pienemann, M. (1998). *Language processing and second language development: Processability theory*. John Benjamins.

Preminger, O. (2019). What the PCC tells us about "abstract" agreement, head movement, and locality. *Glossa: A Journal of General Linguistics*, *4*(1), 13.

Radwan, A. A. (2005). The effectiveness of explicit attention to form in language learning. *System*, *33*, 69–87.

Rassaei, E. (2014). Scaffolded feedback, recasts, and L2 development: A sociocultural perspective. *The Modern Language Journal*, *98*, 417–431.

Reber, A. S. (1967a). Implicit learning of artificial grammars. *Journal of Verbal Learning and Verbal Behavior*, *77*, 317–27.

Reber A. S. (1967b). Implicit learning of artificial grammars. *Journal of Verbal Learning and Verbal Behavior*, *6*, 855–863.

Reber, A. S. (1989). Implicit learning and tacit knowledge. *Journal of Experimental Psychology: General*, *118*(3).

Rebuschat, P. (2013). Measuring implicit and explicit knowledge in second language research. *Language Learning*, *63*, 595–626.

Rebuschat, P., & Williams, J. (2012). Implicit and explicit knowledge in second language acquisition. *Applied Psycholinguistics*, *33*, 829–856.

Reinders, H., & Ellis, R. (2009). The effects of two types of input on intake and the acquisition of implicit and explicit knowledge. In R. Ellis, S. Loewen, C. Elder, R. Erlam, J. Philp, & H. Reinders (Eds.), *Implicit and explicit knowledge in second language learning, testing, and teaching* (pp. 281–302). Multilingual Matters.

Renou, J. (2001). An examination of the relationship between metalinguistic awareness and second-language proficiency of adult learners of French. *Language Awareness*, *10*(4), 248–267.

Rikhtegar, O., & Gholami, J. (2015). The effects of pre-versus post-presentation input flooding via reading on the young Iranian EFL learners' acquisition of simple past tense. *English Language Teaching*, *8*(3), 80–88.

Robinson, P. (1996). Learning simple and complex second language rules under implicit, incidental, rule-search, and instructed conditions. *Studies in Second Language Acquisition*, *18*, 27–67.

Roehr, K. (2006). Metalinguistic knowledge in L2 task performance: A verbal protocol analysis. *Language Awareness*, *15*, 180–198.

Roehr, K. (2007). Metalinguistic knowledge and language ability in university-level L2 learners. *Applied Linguistics*, *29*, 173–190.

Rosa, E., & O'Neill, D. (1999). Explicitness, intake, and the issue of awareness: Another piece to the puzzle. *Studies in Second Language Acquisition*, *21*, 511–553.

Ryding, K. C. (2005). *A reference grammar of modern standard Arabic*. Cambridge University Press.

Sato, M., & Ballinger, S. (2012). Raising language awareness in peer interaction: A cross-context, cross-methodology examination. *Language Awareness*, *21*(1–2), 157–179.

Saville-Troike, M., & Barto, K. (2006). *Introducing second language acquisition*. Cambridge University Press.

Schacter, D. L. (1989). On the relation between memory and consciousness: Dissociable interactions and conscious experience. In H. L. Roediger & F. I. M. Craik (Eds.), *Varieties of memory and consciousness: Essays in honor of Endel Tulving* (pp. 355–389). LEA.

Schmidt, R. (1990). The role of consciousness in second language learning. *Applied Linguistics, 11*, 129–158.
Schmidt, R. (1994). Implicit learning and the cognitive unconscious: Of artificial grammars and SLA. In N. C. Ellis (Ed.), *Implicit and explicit learning of languages* (pp. 165–209). Academic Press.
Schmidt, R. (1995). Consciousness and foreign language learning: A tutorial on the role of attention and awareness in learning. In R. Schmidt (Ed.), *Attention and awareness in foreign language learning* (pp. 1–63). University of Hawaii, Second Language Teaching & Curriculum Center.
Schmidt, R. (2001). Attention. In P. Robinson (Ed.), *Cognition and second language instruction* (pp. 3–32). Cambridge University Press.
Schwartz, B. D., & Sprouse, R. A. (1994). L2 cognitive states and the full transfer/full access model. *Second Language Research, 12*, 40–72.
Schwartz, B. D., & Sprouse, R. A. (1996). Word order and nominative case in non- native language acquisition: A longitudinal study of (L1 Turkish) German inter- language. In T. Hoekstra & B. D. Schwarts (Eds.), *Language acquisition studies in generative grammar: Papers in honor of Kenneth Wexler from the 1991 GLOW workshops* (pp. 317–68). John Benjamins.
Serrano, R. (2011). From metalinguistic instruction to metalinguistic knowledge, and from metalinguistic knowledge to performance in error correction and oral production tasks. *Language Awareness, 20*, 1–16.
Sharwood Smith, M. (1986). Comprehension versus acquisition: Two ways of processing input. *Applied Linguistics, 7*, 239–256.
Sharwood Smith, M. (1991). Speaking to many minds: On the relevance of different types of language information for the L2 learner. *Second Language Research, 7*, 118–132.
Sharwood Smith, M. (1993). Input enhancement in instructed SLA. *Studies in Second Language Acquisition, 15*, 165–179.
Shintani, N. (2013). The effect of focus on form and focus on forms instruction on the acquisition of productive knowledge of L2 vocabulary by young beginning-level learners. *TESOL Quarterly, 47*, 36–62.
Sibawayh, A. B. (1988). *Al-Kitāb [The Book]* (3rd ed., Vol. 1., A. Haroon, Ed.). Al Khanji Library.
Siegel, J. (2010). *Second dialect acquisition*. Cambridge University Press.
Slimani, A. (1992). Evaluation of classroom interaction. In C. Alderson & A. Beretta (Eds.), *Evaluation in second language education* (pp. 197–220). Cambridge University Press.
Soltan, U. (2007). *On formal feature licensing in minimalism: Aspects of Standard Arabic morpho-syntax* [Unpublished doctoral dissertation, University of Maryland].
Spada, N. (1997). Form-focused instruction and second language acquisition: A review of classroom and laboratory research. *Language Teaching, 30*, 73–87.
Spada, N. (2011). Beyond form-focused instruction: Reflections on past, present and future research. *Language Teaching, 44*(2), 225–236.
Spada, N., & Lightbown, P. M. (2008). Form-focused instruction: Isolated or integrated? *TESOL Quarterly, 42*(2), 181–207.
Spada, N., & Tomita, Y. (2010). Interactions between type of instruction and type of language feature: A meta-analysis. *Language Learning, 60*, 263–308.
Summerfield, C., & Egner, T. (2009). Expectation (and attention) in visual cognition. *Trends in Cognitive Sciences, 13*, 403–409.

Sun, Y. A. (2008). Input processing in second language acquisition: A discussion of four input processing models. *Studies in Applied Linguistics and TESOL, 8*(1).

Sunderman, G., & Kroll, J. F. (2009). When study-abroad experience fails to deliver: The internal resources threshold effect. *Applied Psycholinguistics, 30*(1), 79–99.

Suzuki, Y., & DeKeyser, R. (2017). Exploratory research on second language practice distribution: An aptitude × treatment interaction. *Applied Psycholinguistics, 38*, 27–56.

Swain, M. (1985). Communicative competence: Some roles of comprehensible input and comprehensible output in its development. In S. Gass & C. Madden (Eds.), *Input in second language acquisition* (pp. 235–253). Newbury House.

Swain, M. (1995). Three functions of output in second language learning. In B. Seidlhofer (Ed.), *Principle and practice in applied linguistics: Studies in honor of H.G. Widdowson* (pp. 125–144). Oxford University Press.

Swain, M. (2005). The output hypothesis: Theory and research. In E. Hinkel (Ed.), *Handbook on research in second language teaching and learning* (pp. 471–483). Lawrence Erlbaum Associates.

Swain, M., & Lapkin, S. (1995). Problems in output and the cognitive processes they generate: A step towards second language learning. *Applied Linguistics, 16*, 371–391.

Tokowicz, N., Michael, E. B., & Kroll, J. F. (2004). The roles of study-abroad experience and working-memory capacity in the types of errors made during translation. *Bilingualism: Language and Cognition, 7*(3), 255–272.

Tomlin, R. S., & Villa, V. (1994). Attention in cognitive science and second language acquisition. *Studies in Second Language Acquisition, 16*, 183–203.

Toth, P. D. (2006). Processing instruction and a role for output in second language acquisition. *Language Learning, 56*(2), 319–385.

Trahey, M., & White, L. (1993). Positive evidence and pre-emption in the second language classroom. *Studies in Second Language Acquisition, 15*, 181–204.

Truscott, J. (1998). Noticing in second language acquisition: A critical review. *Second Language Research, 14*, 103–135.

Ullman, M. (2001). The declarative/procedural model of lexicon and grammar. *Journal of Psycholinguistic Research, 30*, 37–69.

Ur, P. (2011). Grammar teaching: Research, theory, and practice. In E. Hinkel (Ed.), *Hand-book of research in second language teaching and learning* (Vol. II, pp. 507–522). Routledge.

VanPatten, B. (1989). Can learners attend to form and content while processing input? *Hispania, 72*, 409–417.

VanPatten, B. (1990). Attending to form and content in the input: An experiment in consciousness. *Studies in Second Language Acquisition, 12*(3), 287–301.

VanPatten, B. (1996). *Input processing and grammar instruction: Theory and research*. Ablex.

VanPatten, B. (1999). Processing instruction as form-meaning connections: Issues in theory and research. In J. Lee & A. Valdman (Eds.), *Form and meaning: Multiple perspectives* (pp. 43–68). Heinle & Heinle.

VanPatten, B. (2000). Thirty years of input. In B. Swierzbin, F. Morris, M. Anderson, C. Klee, & E. Tarone (Eds.), *Social and cognitive factors in second language acquisition: Selected proceedings of the 1999 second language research forum* (pp. 287–311). Cascadilla Press.

VanPatten, B. (2004). *Processing instruction: Theory, research, and commentary*. Lawrence Erlbaum Associates.

VanPatten, B. (2016). Why explicit knowledge cannot become implicit knowledge. *Foreign Language Annals*, *49*(4), 650–657.

VanPatten, B. (2017). Situating instructed language acquisition: Facts about second language acquisition. *Instructed Second Language Acquisition*, *1*, 45–60.

VanPatten, B., & Cadierno, T. (1993). Input processing and second language acquisition: A role for instruction. *The Modern Language Journal*, *77*(1), 45–57.

VanPatten, B., & Fernández, C. (2004). The long-term effects of processing instruction. In B. VanPatten (Ed.), *Processing instruction: Theory, research and commentary* (pp. 273–289). Lawrence Erlbaum Associates.

VanPatten, B., & Oikkenon, S. (1996). Explanation vs. structured input in processing instruction. *Studies in Second Language Acquisition*, *18*, 495–510.

VanPatten, B., & Wong, W. (2004). Processing instruction and the French causative: Another replication. In B. VanPatten (Ed.), *Processing instruction: Theory, research, and commentary* (pp. 97–118). Lawrence Erlbaum Associates.

Verhaeghen, P., & Cerella, J. (2002). Aging, executive control, and attention: A review of meta-analyses. *Neuroscience & Biobehavioral Reviews*, *26*(7), 849–857.

White, L. (2003). *Second language acquisition and universal grammar*. Cambridge University Press.

White, L. (2009). Some questions about feature re-assembly. *Second Language Research*, *25*, 343–348.

White, L., Valenzuela, E., Kozlowska–Macgregor, M., & Leung, Y. K. I. (2004). Gender and number agreement in nonnative Spanish. *Applied Psycholinguistics*, *25*(1), 105–133.

Williams, J. N. (2005). Learning without awareness. *Studies in Second Language Acquisition*, *27*(2), 269–304.

Williams, J. N., & Evans, J. (1998). What kind of focus and on which forms? In C. Doughty & J. Williams (Eds.), *Focus on form in classroom second language acquisition* (pp. 139–155). Cambridge University Press.

Wong, W. (2003). Textual enhancement and simplified input: Effects on L2 comprehension and acquisition of non-meaningful grammatical form. *Applied Language Learning*, *13*, 17–46.

Wong, W. (2004). The nature of processing instruction. In B. VanPatten (Ed.), *Processing instruction: Theory, research, and commentary* (pp. 33–65). Erlbaum.

Wong-Fillmore, L. (1989). Teachability and second language acquisition. In M. Rice & R. Schiefelbusch (Eds.), *The teachability of language* (pp. 311–332). Paul H. Brookes.

Woodson, K. (1997). *Learner-centered input processing: Bridging the gap between foreign language teachers and SLA researchers* [Unpublished doctoral dissertation, Georgetown University].

Wrembel, M. (2015). Metaphonological awareness in multilinguals: A case of L3 Polish. *Language Awareness*, *24*, 60–83.

Wright, W. (1964). *A grammar of the Arabic language* (3rd ed., Vol. 2). Cambridge University Press.

Xu, H., & Lyster, R. (2014). Differential effects of explicit form-focused instruction on morphosyntactic development. *Language Awareness*, *23*, 107–122.

Yamashita, T., & Iizuka, T. (2017). The Effectiveness of structured input and structured output on the acquisition of Japanese comparative sentences. *Foreign Language Annals*, *50*, 387–397.

Yaquub, B. Y. (2001). *Sharal-mufaal l-lzamakhshary*. Daar al-kutub al-ilmiyya.

Yaʾīsh, ʾI. (2001). *Sharḥ Al-mufaSSal Lil-Zamaxsharī* (1st ed., Vol. 4, ʾImīl Yaʾqūb, Ed.). Dar Al-Kotob Al-ilmyah.

Zyzik, E., & Marques Pascal, L. (2012). Spanish differential object marking: An empirical study of implicit and explicit instruction. *Studies in Hispanic and Lusophone Linguistics*, *5*, 387–421.

Appendix 1

Sample Instruments from Chapter 3

Instructed Second Language Acquisition of Noun–Adjective Agreement Asymmetries

Grammaticality Test

(١) أنا عندي أصحاب من مدينة بغداد، عندي أصحاب عراقيات.

Grammatical .... Ungrammatical ....

(٢) أخي لا يعرف أنَّ هناك كليات كثيرات في جامعة ميشجان.

Grammatical .... Ungrammatical ....

(٣) أختي تحب أنَّ تقرا كتب جديدة كل صيف.

Grammatical .... Ungrammatical ....

(٤) في الحقيقة، أنا عندي صفوف كثيرة هذه السنة.

Grammatical .... Ungrammatical ....

(٥) بيتي جميل جدا، هذا البيت فيه طاولات كبيرة في كل غرفة.

Grammatical .... Ungrammatical ....

(٦) لي صديق من مدينة القاهرة وهو عنده صور قديمات لأسرته.

Grammatical .... Ungrammatical ....

(٧) مدينة نيويورك مدينة جميلة جدا، هذه المدينة فيها بنايات عاليات في كل مكان.

Grammatical .... Ungrammatical ....

(٨) حبيبتي ليست سعيدة اليوم، هي عندها دروس صعبة جدا.

Grammatical .... Ungrammatical ....

(٩) جامعة هارفرد فيها مكتبات كبيرات جدا. أنا أقرأ فيها كثيرا.

Grammatical .... Ungrammatical ....

(١٠) أمريكا بلد جميل جدا، فيه سيارات جميلة في كل مكان.

Grammatical .... Ungrammatical ....

(١١) نحن نحب هذه المنطقة كثيرا لأنَّ فيها بيوت كبير وجميل.

Grammatical .... Ungrammatical ....

(١٢) حبيبي سعيد جدا اليوم، هو عنده أخبار ممتاز عن الأسرة.

Grammatical .... Ungrammatical ....

(١٣) والدي يحب ولاية ميشجان كثيرا، هناك مدن جميلة جدا.

Grammatical .... Ungrammatical ....

(١٤) زميلي يحب منطقة الجامعة لأنَّ فيها بنوك جديدات في كل شارع كبير.

Grammatical .... Ungrammatical ....

(١٥) أصحابي يحبون مدينة لانسينج لأنَّ فيها مناطق جميلة.

Grammatical .... Ungrammatical ....

(١٦) والدتي تعمل في شركة يونايتد ايرلينز United Airlines ، هذه الشركة عنها مكاتب كبيرة في كل مدينة.

Grammatical .... Ungrammatical ....

(١٧) زميلي مايكل يدرس اللغة العربية، هو يعرف كلمات جديدة في كل درس.

Grammatical .... Ungrammatical ....

(١٨) صاحبيتي ساره طالبة ممتازة جدا، هي تتكلم لُغات كثيرات جدا

Grammatical .... Ungrammatical ....

(١٩) ولاية كاليفورنيا ولاية كبيرة جدا، فيها جامعات جيدة جدا.

Grammatical .... Ungrammatical ....

(٢٠) أمريكا بلد جميل جدا، فيه ولايات جميل جدا مثل كاليفورنيا ونيويورك.

Grammatical .... Ungrammatical ....

(٢١) أختي تحب هذه المكتبة كثيرا، هي فيها قِصَص جيدة جدا من كل مكان في العالم

Grammatical .... Ungrammatical ....

(٢٢) والدي يحب بيتنا كثيرا، هذا البيت فيه أبواب جميلات في كل غرفة.

Grammatical .... Ungrammatical ....

(٢٣) أخي الصغير عنده غرفة جميلة جدا. هذه الغرفة فيها كراسي جديدة في كل مكان.

Grammatical .... Ungrammatical ....

(٢٤) أختي تحب الثقافة العربية جدا، هي تحب الأسماء العرب جدا جدا.

Grammatical .... Ungrammatical ....

(٢٥) أخي يحب بيتنا كثيرا، هو فيه غُرَف كبيرة جدا جدا.

Grammatical .... Ungrammatical ....

(٢٦) أنا عندي يوم طويل اليوم، أنا عندي إِمتحانات كثيرون في اللغة العربية والإسبانية.

Grammatical .... Ungrammatical ....

(٢٧) أختي الصغيرة عندها غرفة جميلة جدا. هذه الغرفة فيها أشياء جديدة في كل مكان.

Grammatical .... Ungrammatical ....

(٢٨) أنا لي أصحاب في ولاية ميشجان وولاية أريزونا هم مصريون من مدينة القاهرة.

Grammatical .... Ungrammatical ....

Choice Test

(١) أنا لي أصحاب friends __________ من مدينة القاهرة.

(أ) مصريون (ب) مصرية (ج) مصريات (د) مصري

(٢) أنا عندي صُفُوف classes __________.

(أ) كبير (ب) كبيرون (ج) كبيرات (د) كبيرة

(٣) هل هناك كُليات colleges __________ في جامعة ميشجان؟

(أ) جيدة (ب) جيدات (ج) جيدون (د) جيد

(٤) أنا لي أَخْوال uncles __________ من مدينة بغداد.

(أ) عراقي) (ب) عراقية (ج) عراقيات (د) عراقيون

(٥) أنا عندي كُتب books __________.

(أ) جديد (ب) جديدة (ج) جديدات (د) جديدون

(٦) هل عندك صُوَر pictures __________ للعائلة؟

(أ) قديمون (ب) قديم) (ج) قديمة (د) قديمات

(٧) هل عندك طاولات tables __________ في البيت؟

(أ) كبير (ب) كبيرة (ج) كبيرات (د) كبيران

(٨) هل هناك بِنايات buildings __________ في مدينة ديترويت؟

(أ) كبيرة (ب) كبير (ج) كبيرات (د) كبيران

(٩) لي أصْحَاب friends __________ يعملون في أمريكا.

(أ) مترجم (ب) مترجمون (ج) مترجمات (د) مترجمة

(١٠) هل عندك دُرُوس lessons __________؟ في اللغة العربية؟

(أ) سهلة (ب) سهل (ج) سهلات (د) سهلان

(١١) هل في جامعة ميشجان مَكْتَبَات libraries __________ ؟

(أ) كبير (ب) كبيرة (ج) كبيرات (د) كبيران

(١٢) هل في أمريكا سَيَّارات cars __________؟

(أ) يبانية (ب) يبانينون (ج) يابانيات (د) يباني

(١٣) هل عندك أخْبَار news __________ اليوم؟

(أ) ممتاز (ب) ممتازة (ج) ممتازون (د) ممتازات

Sample Instruments from Chapter 4

Instructed Second Language Acquisition of Referential Asymmetries

Metalinguistic Test

(١) الأستاذة أمل تخرج يوم الأحد، هم تخرج مع أصدقائها.

(a) The subject of the sentence is feminine singular الأستاذة أمل and it should be replaced with the pronoun هي that goes/agrees with it.
(b) The subject of the sentence is masculine singular الأستاذة أمل and it should be replaced with the pronoun هو that goes/agrees with it.
(c) The context of the sentence is about Amal's friends who go out with her and therefore it should be هم يخرجون.
(d) The prefix ت in the verb is used with the pronoun "you." So, هم should be replaced with the pronoun أنتِ.

(٢) هناك جامعات ممتازة جدا مثل هارفارد وبوسطن وييل. أنا أريد أن أدرس فيهم في المستقبل إن شاء الله.

(a) The word فيهم refers to singular and the sentence is about a plural noun جامعات.
(b) The word فيهم does not match with the pronoun أنا.
(c) Replace the word فيهم with the word فيها because the word جامعات is singular.
(d) The word فيهم refers to the word جامعات, which is nonhuman plural. So, it must be replaced with فيها because a nonhuman plural noun takes a singular feminine pronoun.

(٣) أخي محمد يتكلم ثلاث لغات: العربية والانجليزية والفرنسية. هو يحب هؤلاء اللغات كثيرا.

(a) The pronoun هؤلاء is wrong because the subject is أخي is singular. It should be replaced with هو.
(b) The pronoun هؤلاء should not come before a noun with the definite article.
(c) Replace the pronoun هؤلاء with the pronoun هذا because the word لغات is masculine.
(d) Replace the pronoun هؤلاء with the pronoun هذه because the word لغات is nonhuman plural and it should take a singular feminine pronoun.

(٤) منطقتنا فيها بيوت جميلة جدا قريب من الجامعة، الكثير من أصدقائي يسكنون في هؤلاء البيوت.

(a) Replace the pronoun هؤلاء with the pronoun هي because we are talking about a plural noun بيوت.
(b) The pronoun هؤلاء should not come before a noun with the definite article.
(c) Replace the pronoun هؤلاء with the pronoun هذا because the word بيت is masculine.
(d) Replace the pronoun هؤلاء with the singular feminine pronoun هذه because the word لغات is nonhuman plural, and it should take a singular feminine pronoun.

(٥) أنا أحب أصحابي محمد ومحمود وأحمد، أنا أخرج معه كل أسبوع.

(a) The word أصحابي is plural, it means "my friends" and therefore the indirect object pronoun ه refers to singular. The correct plural pronoun is هم.
(b) The speaker is "I" and the preposition ـه should be ي to read معي
(c) We never attach the pronoun ـه to prepositions such as مع. So, it should be مع ـه as two separate words.
(d) The correct preposition in the context of the sentence should be في and not مع.

(٦) هناك ولايات جميلة جدا في أمريكا، وأنا أريد أن أسافر إليهم في الصيف إن شاء الله.

(a) The first clause talks about the plural noun ولايات, which is nonhuman, and the word إليهم refers back to people.
(b) Replace the word إليهم, which refers to plural "to them," with the word إليها which refers to singular feminine because the word ولايات is nonhuman plural.
(c) إليهم is wrong; it should be إلي هم as two separate words.
(d) إليهم is the wrong form of the preposition + pronoun, it must be إليك

(٧) ولاية كاليفورنيا فيها الكثير من المدن الجميلة مثل سان دييجو ولوس انجليز وسان فرانسيسكو. أنا أسافر إلى هذا المدن في الصيف

(a) The pronoun هذاshould be followed by a singular noun and the word المدن is plural.
(b) The first clause tells us about المدن. Since it refers to nonhuman plural, the pronoun should be singular feminine هذه.
(c) المدن is plural and the sentence should use the plural pronoun هؤلاء.
(d) the pronoun هذا is followed by a singular noun and the clause is about a plural noun المدن. It should be replaced with the pronoun هم.

(٨) عندنا كليات كثيرة جدا، والطلاب يدرسون فيهم تخصصات كثيرة مثل اللغات والطب والعلوم والهندسة.

(a) The noun كليات is masculine plural and the word فيهم refers to the feminine plural.
(b) We do not combine في and هم in Standard Arabic.
(c) Replace فيهم with فيها because the clause talks about a nonhuman plural noun كليات and in Standard Arabic should be treated as a singular feminine noun.
(d) The sentence starts with a verb conjugated with "we," and so the word فيهم should be replaced with فينا.

(٩) زميلي محمد يتكلم اللغات الأوربية مثل الاسبانية والفرنسية، هو يدرسهم الأن في الجامعة.

(a) The first clause is about Mohamed and so يدرسهم should be replaced with يدرسه.
(b) The sentence is about the past, and so the verb يدرسهم should be درسهم.
(c) We must not combine the verb with the direct object in Arabic, so it should read يدرس هم.
(d) It is true that object pronoun in يدرسهم refers to a plural noun, but it refers to nonhuman plural that takes singular feminine in Standard Arabic. So, يدرسهم should be replaced with يدرسها.

(١٠) بعض الطلاب في جامعة أريزونا من كل مكان في العالم، مثلاً، هي من أسيا وأروبا وإفريقيا وأستراليا.

(a) أسيا وأروبا وإفريقيا وأستراليا are plural and therefore the correct pronoun should be هم instead of هي.
(b) The sentence is about كل مكان في العالم, and it is singular. Therefore, the correct pronoun should be هو instead of هي.
(c) The sentence is about جامعة أريزونا and the pronoun that refers to it should be هذه instead of هي.
(d) The sentence is about بعض الطلاب, which is plural, it means "some students." The correct plural pronoun should be هم instead of هي.

(١١) والدي ووالدتي وأخي كلهم يعملون في بنوك كبيرة. هؤلاء البنوك في وسط المدينة.

(a) The word البنوك is singular masculine and so the pronoun هؤلاء should be replaced with the pronoun هذا.
(b) Never use هؤلاء with nonhuman plural, and use the singular feminine demonstrative pronoun هذه consistently in Standard Arabic.
(c) The sentence talks about والدي ووالدتي وأخي and therefore the pronoun هؤلاء should be replaced with the pronoun هم.
(d) Never use هؤلاء with nonhuman plural and use the singular feminine demonstrative pronoun هذا consistently in Standard Arabic.

(١٢) مدينة توسان فيها مكتبات عامة كبيرة، هم في كل مكان في المدينة.

(a) The pronoun هم refers to people and the sentence talks about the libraries.
(b) We do not use a pronoun such as هم before a preposition, so it should be deleted.
(c) In Standard Arabic, the pronoun هم is never used to refer to nonhuman plurals and it must be replaced with the pronoun هي (singular feminine).
(d) The sentence talks about the city of Tucson, which is feminine so the pronoun هي should be used instead of هم.

(١٣) أنا أسكن مع عمتي في القاهرة، أنا أسكن معه لأنني بعيدة عن والدي ووالدتي.

(a) The subject of the pronoun is "I" and the pronoun after مع should match that pronoun and takes ي. Therefore, معه should be replaced with معي.
(b) In Arabic, the preposition مع and the pronoun ـه should be separated.
(c) In Arabic, the preposition مع and the pronoun ها should be separated.
(d) The first clause sentence reads "I live with my aunt." Therefore, معه should be replaced with a feminine indirect pronoun معها.

(١٤) أخي يحب الأسماء العربية جدا، هي يقرأ عنهم كل يوم.

(a) Change the word عنهم to عن هم as two separate words. This is because they do not combine in Standard Arabic.
(b) The sentence is about a nonhuman plural noun, الأسماء العربية so it must take a singular feminine pronoun هي. So, the word عنهم should be replaced with the word عنها.
(c) Replace the word عنهم with the word عنه because the word أخي is masculine.
(d) We never use the preposition عن after a verb in Arabic.

(١٥) محمد: هل عندكم غرف كبيرة في البيت؟
أحمد: نعم، عندنا غرف كبيرة جدا فيهم طاولات جميلة.

(a) The sentence is about Ahmed, a masculine noun, and therefore هم should be replaced with هو.
(b) The sentence is about "the big rooms," a nonhuman plural noun, that takes the singular feminine pronoun ها. Therefore, فيهم should be replaced with فيها.
(c) Change the word فيهم to في هم as two separate words. This is because they do not combine in Standard Arabic.
(d) The sentence is about "we" and the verb عندنا agrees with that verb. Therefore, we should change فيهم to فينا to maintain this agreement/matching.

(١٦) أخي يحب قراءة الكتب الجديدة جدا. هو يقرأهم في نهاية الأسبوع.

(a) The word قراءة is feminine and so we need to use تقرأهم instead of يقرأهم.
(b) The sentence is about the new books, which is nonhuman plural. The pronoun that refers to a nonhuman plural has to be singular feminine in Arabic. So, يقرأهم must change to يقرأها.
(c) Delete هو because the ي at the beginning of the verb refers to "he."
(d) The sentence is about قراءة, singular feminine, and this should be referenced again. So, we need to replace يقرأهم with قراءتهم.

(١٧) الناس في الكورونا لا يخرجون كثيرا، هو دائما في البيت.

(a) The sentence is about a plural noun, which is الناس. The pronoun that refers to this plural noun should be هم instead of هو.
(b) The sentence is about الناس, which is singular feminine. The pronoun that refers to this noun should be هي instead of هو.
(c) The pronoun هو should not come before the pronoun; it should come after it. So, it should read دائما هو.
(d) The sentence is about الناس, which is singular feminine. The pronoun that refers to this noun should be هي and it should come after the word دائما to read دائما هي.

(١٨) أختي عندها صور جميلة جدا، هي رسمتهم عندما كانت في المدرسة الابتدائية.

(a) Replace the plural pronoun هم in the verb رسمتهم with the singular pronoun ها to read رسمتها because it refers back to a nonhuman plural that takes the singular feminine.
(b) The sentence is about a feminine singular أختي and therefore the verb has to agree with the subject. So, رسمتهم should be changed to ترسمهم.
(c) The word صور is singular masculine and therefore the pronoun attached to the verb should be ـه to read رسمته instead of رسمتهم.
(d) We never attach the pronoun هم to verbs. So, it should be رسمت هم as two words.

(١٩) مها: هل تدرسين الكلمات الجديدة كل يوم في صف اللغة العربية؟
سارة: نعم، أنا أدرسهم كل يوم في الصباح قبل الصف.

(a) We never attach the pronoun هم to verbs. So, it should be أدرس هم.
(b) The speaker is Sarah (singular feminine) and therefore, it should be تدرسهم instead of أدرسهم.
(c) A plural pronoun is never used to refer to the feminine plural in Arabic, and a masculine singular is used instead. So, أدرسهم should be أدرسه.
(d) The clause says "he studies them" in reference to the words. Since the word "words" الكلمات is nonhuman plural, a singular feminine pronoun should be used. Therefore, أدرسهم should be أدرسها.

(٢٠) في مدينة توسان شوارع جميلة جدا، أحب أن أسكن فيهم.

(a) Change فيهم to فيها because the context is about the streets and they are nonhuman plural. So, a singular feminine pronoun ها should be used instead.
(b) We never attach the pronoun هم to prepositions such as في. So, it should be في هم as two separate words.
(c) The word مدينة is feminine, so the verb must be تسكن instead of أسكن.
(d) The word شوارع is plural so the verb must be يسكنون to maintain agreement/matching.

Sample Instruments from Chapter 5

Instructed Second Language Acquisition of Subject–Verb Agreement Asymmetries

Sentence-Production Test

(١) أحيانا، ___________ الاولاد التلفزيون في المساء.
(٢) أصدقائي في المكتبة كثيرا ___________.
(٣) في رأيك ، هل_______الطلاب الأمريكيين الكثير من اللغات اليوم؟
(٤) كل أصدقائي الواجب في المكتبة كل يوم___________.
(٥) الأصدقاء بالسفر والسهر دائماً___________.
(٦) في برنامجنا، ___________ الاساتذة أسماء كل الطلاب
(٧) أصدقائي إلى الموسيقى العربية___________.
(٨) كل أصدقائي إلى كاليفورنيا في الصيف كل سنة___________.
(٩) كل أصدقائي في هذا المطعم كل يوم ___________.
(١٠) عادة، الشباب لا ___________ السياسة.
(١١) الى العمل كل صباح في الساعة الثامنة employees الموظفون ___________.
(١٢) الاولاد والدتهم في شغل البيت دائما ___________.
(١٣) أصحابي ___________أخي في الدراسة والعمل.
(١٤) أصحابي___________ التليفزيون في المساء كل يوم.

(١٥) أختي وزوجها وأولادها __________ معنا في نفس البيت.

(١٦) معظم أصدقائي __________ اللغة العربية.

(١٧) معظم أقاربي في ولاية كاليفورنيا __________.

(١٨) عادة، __________ المترجمون لساعات طويلة.

(١٩) الطلاب عائلاتهم كل عطلة صيف __________.

(٢٠) المترجمون عِدّة لغات __________

(٢١) كثير من الأساتذة __________ في جامعة أريزونا.

(٢٢) الطلاب لا __________ رقم تليفون الاستاذ.

Sentence-Interpretation Test

English Interpretation	*Arabic Sentence*
a. It is the male students who like the male teacher a lot. b. It is the male teacher who likes the male students a lot.	(١) الطلاب يحبون الأستاذ كثيرا.
a. It is the male students who like the male teacher a lot. b. It is the male teacher who likes the male students a lot.	(٢) يحب الطلاب الأستاذ كثيرا.
a. It is the male students who visit the male teacher every week. b. It is the male teacher who visit the male students every week.	(٣) الطلاب يزورون الأستاذ كل أسبوع.
a. It is the male students who visit the male teacher every week. b. It is the male teacher who visit the male students every week.	(٤) يزور الطلاب الأستاذ كل أسبوع.
a. It is the boys who help Mohamed every day. b. It is Mohamed who helps the boys every day.	(٥) يساعدون محمد كل يوم the boys الأولاد.
a. It is the boys who help Mohamed every day. b. It is Mohamed who helps the boys every day.	(٦) محمد كل يوم the boys يساعد الأولاد.

English Interpretation	*Arabic Sentence*
a. It is my male friends who watch/see my brother at the university every day. b. It is my brother who watches/sees my male friends at the university every day.	(٧) يشاهدون أخي في الجامعة كل يوم my friends أصحابي.
a. It is my male friends who watch/see my brother at the university every day. b. It is my brother who watches/sees my male friends at the university every day.	(٨) يشاهد أصحابي أخي في الجامعة كل يوم.
a. It is my male colleagues who know my male friend well. b. It is my male friend who knows my male colleagues well.	(٩) زملائي يعرفون صديقي جيدا.
a. It is my male colleagues who know my male friend well. b. It is my male friend who knows my male colleagues well.	(١٠) يعرف زملائي صديقي جيدا.
a. It is the male students who remember the male teacher well. b. It is the male teacher who remembers the students well.	(١١) الطلاب يتذكّرون الأستاذ جيدا.
a. It is the male students who remember the male teacher well. b. It is the male teacher who remembers the male teachers well.	(١٢) يتذكّر الطلاب الأستاذ جيدا.
a. It is the male students who understand the male teacher well. b. It is the male teacher who understands the male students well.	(١٣) الطلاب يفهمون الأستاذ جيدا.
a. It is the male students who understand the male teacher well. b. It is the male teacher who understands the male students well.	(١٤) يفهم الطلاب الأستاذ جيدا.

English Interpretation	*Arabic Sentence*
a. It is my male friends who wake up Mohamed in the morning. b. It is Mohamed who wakes up my male friends in the morning.	(١٥) محمد في wake up يوقظون my friends أصحابي الصباح .
a. It is my male friends who wake up Mohamed in the morning. b. It is Mohamed who wakes up my male friends in the morning.	(١٦) يوقظ أصحابي محمد في الصباح.
a. It is my male friends who are teaching Ahmed a new language. b. It is Ahmed who is teaching my male friends a new language.	(١٧) أحمد لغة جديدة teach أصدقائي يدرِّسون.
a. It is my male friends who are teaching Ahmed a new language. b. It is Ahmed who is teaching my male friends a new language.	(١٨) يدرِّس أصدقائي أحمد لغة جديدة.

Sample Instruments from Chapter 6

Instructed Second Language Acquisition of Numeral Agreement Asymmetries

Grammaticality Test

(١) هذه الشركة كبيرة جدا، United Airlines والدتي يعمل في شركة يونايتد ايرلينز.

Grammatical .... Ungrammatical ....

(٢) بيتي جميل جدا، هذا البيت فيه طاولات كبيرات في كل غرفة.

Grammatical .... Ungrammatical ....

(٣) مدينة توصان فيها جامعة واحدة فقط، هي جامعة أريزونا.

Grammatical .... Ungrammatical ....

(٤) عندي ثلاث واجبات هذ الأسبوع في صف اللغة العربية.

Grammatical .... Ungrammatical ....

(٥) هناك ثمانية أقلام على الطاولة

Grammatical .... Ungrammatical ....

(٦) أخي يأكل في مطعم واحد فقط في مدينة توسان، هو مطعم عربي.

Grammatical .... Ungrammatical ....

(٧) أمريكا بلد جميل جدا، فيه ولايات جميل في كل مكان.

Grammatical .... Ungrammatical ....

(٨) تاريخ مصر الحديث فيه خمسة رؤساء فقط بعد جمال عند الناصر.

Grammatical .... Ungrammatical ....

(٩) يا ساره، أنتِ لم تتكلمي معي بالأمس بالتيليفون. لماذا؟ هل كنتي مشغولة.

Grammatical .... Ungrammatical ....

(١٠) يا محمد، أنت لم حصلت على عمل جيد في هذه المدينة. فلماذا لا تنتقل إلى مدينة أخرى؟

Grammatical .... Ungrammatical ....

(١١) أختي تحب أنْ تقرا كثيرا لكن اليوم قرات قصة واحد فقط لأنها كانت مشغولة جدا.

Grammatical .... Ungrammatical ....

(١٢) في الحقيقة، أنا أحب مكان واحدة فقط في هذه المدينة، وهو الجامعة.

Grammatical .... Ungrammatical ....

(١٣) محمود: يا محمد، كم شارعا تعرف في مدينة توسان؟
محمد: أعرف عشر شوارع كبيرة في توسان.

Grammatical .... Ungrammatical ....

(١٤) في هذا الصف تعرفنا على ست ثقافات عربية في منطقة الشرق الأوسط.

Grammatical .... Ungrammatical ....

(١٥) أختي تحب أنْ تقرا عشرة كتب جديدة كل صيف، لكن الصيف الماضي لم تقرآ أي كتب، هي قرات قصص.

Grammatical .... Ungrammatical ....

(١٦) أنا عندي أربعة أخبار جيدة جدا قرأتها اليوم في الجريدة.

Grammatical .... Ungrammatical ....

(١٧) نحن نحب هذه المنطقة كثيرا لأنَّ فيها بيوت كبير وجميل.

Grammatical .... Ungrammatical ....

(١٨) منذ ٥ سنوات عملت في جامعة كبيرة جدا في الشرق الأوسط، لكن لم شعرت بالسعادة هناك، لذلك رجعت إلى أمريكا.

Grammatical .... Ungrammatical ....

(١٩) في الحقيقة، أنا عندي صفان طويلان هذ الفصل: صف الرياضة وصف الفيزياء.

Grammatical .... Ungrammatical ....

(٢٠) الثقافة العربية والثقافة الأمريكية هما ثقافتان مختلفان جدا جدا في أشياء كثيرة.

Grammatical .... Ungrammatical ....

(٢١) هناك كما نعرف جيشان قويتان في المنطقة العربية: الجيش المصري والجيش السوري.

Grammatical .... Ungrammatical ....

(٢٢) عندما كنت في المدرسة الثانوية لم عرفت الكثير عن التاريخ، ولذلك قررت أن أدرس التاريخ في الجامعة.

Grammatical .... Ungrammatical ....

(٢٣) صاحبيتي ساره طالبة ممتاز جدا، هي تتكلم لُغات كثيرة جدا.

Grammatical .... Ungrammatical ....

(٢٤) عندما كنا في القاهرة الصيف الماضي زرنا أربع مكتبات كبيرة هناك، منها مكتبة الإسكندرية.

Grammatical .... Ungrammatical ....

(٢٥) في المقابلة التي تمت العام الماضي كان هناك تسعة وزراء من العالم العربي لمناقشة مشكلة التلوث.

Grammatical .... Ungrammatical ....

(٢٦) تنتشر ثلاثة أديان هامة في الشرق الأوسط هي الاسلام والمسيحية واليهودية.

Grammatical .... Ungrammatical ....

(٢٧) لي صديق من مدينة القاهرة وهو يسافر إلى أمريكا كل سنة. العام الماضي زار مدينتين جميلتين في ولاية كاليفورنيا، هما لوس أنجلوس وسان دييجو.

Grammatical .... Ungrammatical ....

(٢٨) أنا لي صديق واحدة وصديقة واحد فقط.

Grammatical .... Ungrammatical ....

(٢٩) أيضا في هذا الصف تعرفنا على ثلاث لغات عربية في منطقة الشرق الأوسط: العربية والعبرية والأمازيغية.

Grammatical .... Ungrammatical ....

(٣٠) في صف اللغة العربية سبع كراسي صغيرة.

Grammatical .... Ungrammatical ....

(٣١) قرأت مقالة أمس عن أربعة حكومات عربية في منطقة الخليج العربي في السعودية والكويت والبحرين والإمارات.

Grammatical .... Ungrammatical ....

(٣٢) زميلي مايكل تدرس اللغة العربية، هو تعرف كلمات جديدة في كل درس.

Grammatical .... Ungrammatical ....

(٣٣) صاحبيتي ساره زارت ستة مناطق في المغرب ومصر والأردن العام الماضي.

Grammatical .... Ungrammatical ....

(٣٤) صديقي كان له ثلاثة علاقات عاطفية عندما كان في الجامعة.

Grammatical .... Ungrammatical ....

(٣٥) الصيف الماضي سافرنا إلى ولايتين في الصيف: ميشجن ونيويورك.

Grammatical .... Ungrammatical ....

(٣٦) قابلت العام الماضي ثماني مهاجرين من ليبيا وسوريا والأردن في مدينة توسان.

Grammatical .... Ungrammatical ....

(٣٧) في هذا الصف نحن نعمل في أربع مجموعات في الزووم مع الأستاذ محمود.

Grammatical .... Ungrammatical ....

(٣٨) عندما كنت في أمريكا العام الماضي زرت عشر ولايات هناك. كانت زيارة ممتعة للغاية

Grammatical .... Ungrammatical ....

(٣٩) ولاية أريزونا ليس فيها جامعات كبيرة، هي فيها ثلاث جامعات فقط.

Grammatical .... Ungrammatical ....

(٤٠) الصيف الماضي سافرنا إلى ثمان مدن عربية في الشرق الأوسط وشمال افريقيا.

Grammatical .... Ungrammatical ....

(٤١) لي صديق من مدينة نيويورك لكنه درس وتعلم في القاهرة. هو درس في أربع مدارس هناك في الابتدائية والإعدادية والثانوية.

Grammatical .... Ungrammatical ....

(٤٢) شركة أمازون لها ستة مكاتب في مدينة فينكس في ولاية أريزونا ولها مكتب واحد في مدينة توسان

Grammatical .... Ungrammatical ....

(٤٣) هناك ثلاثة أسماء عربية معروفة جدا في العالم العربي: أحمد ومحمد ومحمود.

Grammatical .... Ungrammatical ....

(٤٤) زميلة يحب ثلاثة كليات في جامعة أريزونا: كلية العلوم وكلية الطب وكلية الهندسة.

Grammatical .... Ungrammatical ....

Appendix 2

Sample Task

Task 1: City Task (Function: Create with Language)

Context: You have recently received two job offers, one from city A and another from city B.

السياق: أنت حصلت مؤخراً على عرضين للعمل، الأول من مدينة "أ "والثاني من مدينة " ب ".

Task: Engage in a conversation with your interlocutor (i.e., the teacher) to compare the set of pictures and decide which city you would like to live in. Give justification for your decision.

Note: Take five minutes to go over the suggested prompts to brainstorm some ideas.

Helpful structures		**Helpful vocabulary**			
Comparatives	مثال: أغلى، أرخص، أجمل	*safe*	آمِنة	*cheap*	رخيصة
It has . . .	فيها. . .	*dangerous*	خطيرة	*expensive*	غالية
It does not have	ليس فيها. . .	*quiet*	هادئة	*fairs*	ملاهي
Noun–adjective disagreement	مثال: شوارع جميلة وهادئة	*busy*	مزدحمة	*nature*	طبيعة
City A مدينة "أ" جديدة وكبيرة ممطرة مشهورة غالية مزدحمة خطيرة فيها ملاهي بها مرافق		City B مدينة "ب" قديمة وصغيرة مشمسة ليست مشهورة رخيصة ميست مزدحمة آمنة بها أماكن طبيعية جميلة فهيا مطاعم من ثقافات مختلفة			

Index

agreement 7; gender 77–78; noun-adjective 16–18, 55–58; numeric 25–26; referential 18–21; subject-verb 21–25, 97–98
Arabic: second language acquisition 1–2; subject-verb agreement research 77–78
asymmetries: agreement 1; noun-adjective agreement 54–55; numeral agreement 112–114; referential agreement 75–76; subject-verb agreement 95–97

case 13–16

definiteness 13
demonstratives 11

explicit knowledge 32, 36–37, 49–52, 118–119, 122–125, 133–135; instruction 14; instruction activities 117–118; relationship to implicit knowledge 135–136

feature mismatch 137; salience of 136
focus on form 48–49; incidental 82–83, 92–94; planned 80–82, 92–94; preemptive 84–85; reactive 84–85
focus on forms 48–49; conversational 137–139
form-focused instruction 48–49; integrated 49; isolated 49

gender 9–11, 12; reversal of 122–125
grammaticality judgment 64, 118–119, 122–125

implicit knowledge 49–52, 119–120, 132–135; instruction of 52, 141; instruction activities 116–117; learning 38–39; relationship to explicit knowledge 135–136
input-based incidental exposure 60–62
input-based instruction 39, 46–48; contextualized 140; enhanced 117–118; enriched 116–117
input: enhancement 40; enrichment 39; exposure 72–74
input processing 33–34; cognitive processes of 33–35; instruction 42–43
instructed second language acquisition 30–33
intake 34

knowledge: declarative 36; explicit 32, 36–37; implicit 49–52, 119–120, 132–135; L2 36; metalinguistic 85–86; procedural 36

meaning-focused activities 116–117

negotiation of form 139
noticing 35
number 8–9

oral narrative 86, 119–120, 125–127
output 43–45
output-based incidental exposure 62–63; instruction 43, 46–48

present –practice–produce 45–46, 72–74

salience 91; of grammatical features 76–77
sentence interpretation 103–105
sentence production test 105–106
structured-input instruction 100–102, 109–111
structured-output instruction 102–103, 109–111

test: elicitation 64; multiple choice 63

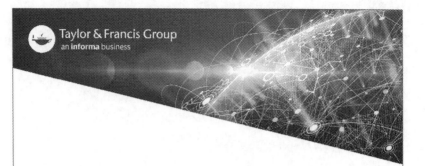

Printed in the United States
by Baker & Taylor Publisher Services